A Seneca Reader

Bc **LATIN** Readers

Series Editor:
Ronnie Ancona, Hunter College and CUNY Graduate Center

These readers provide well annotated Latin selections written by experts in the field, to be used as authoritative introductions to Latin authors, genres, topics, or themes for intermediate or advanced college Latin study. Their relatively small size (covering 500–600 lines) makes them ideal to use in combination. Each volume includes a comprehensive introduction, bibliography for further reading, Latin text with notes at the back, and complete vocabulary. Nineteen volumes are currently scheduled for publication; others are under consideration. Check our website for updates: www.BOLCHAZY.com.

A Seneca Reader
Selections from Prose and Tragedy

James Ker

Bolchazy-Carducci Publishers, Inc.
Mundelein, Illinois USA

Series Editor: Ronnie Ancona

Volume Editor: Laurie Haight Keenan

Cover Design & Typography: Adam Phillip Velez

Maps: Mapping Specialists, Ltd.

A Seneca Reader
Selections from Prose and Tragedy

James Ker

© 2011 Bolchazy-Carducci Publishers, Inc.

Bolchazy-Carducci Publishers, Inc.
1570 Baskin Road
Mundelein, Illinois 60060
www.bolchazy.com

Printed in the United States of America
2011
by United Graphics

ISBN 978-0-86516-758-2

Library of Congress Cataloging-in-Publication Data

Kerr, James.
  A Seneca reader : selections from prose and tragedy / James Kerr.
     p. cm. -- (BC Latin readers)
  ISBN 978-0-86516-758-2 (pbk. : alk. paper) 1. Latin language--Readers. 2. Latin
language--Grammar. 3. Seneca, Lucius Annaeus, ca. 4 B.C.-65 A.D. I. Title.
  PA2095.K47 2011
  878.01--dc23
                                                                          2011031459

Contents

List of Illustrations ix

Preface xi

Introduction xiii

Latin Text 1

Scenario 1: Seneca in Exile 1
   Consolatio ad Helviam 1
   Epistulae Morales 85.40 6
   Consolatio ad Polybium 13.3–4 6

Scenario 2: Seneca and Nero .7
   De Clementia (book 1) 7
   Apocolocyntosis 10.1–3 12
   De Ira 1.2.1–3 12

Scenario 3: The Drama of Revenge 13
   Medea 13

Scenario 4: Letters to a Friend 21
   Epistulae Morales 2 21
   Epistulae Morales 40.1 22
   Epistulae Morales 49.1–3 23
   Epistulae Morales 55 24
   De Amicitia (fragment 59.5–6 Vottero) 26

Commentary. 27

Scenario 1: Seneca in Exile 27

Consolatio ad Helviam 30

  1.1–4: The exile writes home 30

  2.1–3: Justifying an aggressive consolation 32

  2.4–5: The mother's many wounds 34

  3.1–2: A veteran of suffering 37

  17.3–5: The consolations of philosophy 38

  18.1–3: Comfort in Seneca's brothers. 41

  20.1–2: Seneca's happy life on Corsica 42

Epistulae Morales 85.40: Insights on exile
  as artistic "material" 45

Consolatio ad Polybium 13.3–4: A plea for clemency 46

Scenario 2: Seneca and Nero. 48

De Clementia (book 1) 50

  1.1: A mirror for the prince 50

  1.2: The emperor recognizes his power 52

  1.3–4: Young Nero's boast 53

  1.5–6: You are your own best model 55

  9.1–3: Augustus and the conspirator 57

  9.4–6: The emperor's exasperation and Livia's
   remedy 60

  9.7–10: Interview with the would-be assassin 62

  9.11–12: I forgive you 64

  10.1–3: Augustus lives on 65

Apocolocyntosis 10.1–3: The deified Augustus
  ashamed of his successors 66

De Ira 1.2.1–3: The costs of anger 69

Scenario 3: The Drama of Revenge 71

Medea 75

   1–18: Calling all gods 75

   40–50: I'm not a girl anymore 78

   155–76: Rejecting sensible advice 80

   301–8: Blame the boat 82

   361–79: The Argo's price 83

   537–50: Finding Jason's weak spot 85

   670–93: She's planning something evil 87

   849–69: Her rage is visible 90

   904–15: You ain't seen nothin' yet 91

   926–36: A brief return of maternal affection 93

   1008–13: Double infanticide 94

   1018–27: Kill me instead 95

Scenario 4: Letters to a Friend 96

Epistulae Morales 2 97

   1–2: About your reading habits 97

   3–4: Watch your "diet" 99

   5–6: Be happy with little 101

Epistulae Morales 40.1: Our letters unite us 103

Epistulae Morales 49.1–3: Memories triggered by
   a visit to Pompeii 104

Epistulae Morales 55 107

   1–2: A "stroll" along the seashore 108

   3–5: But was it *life*? 110

   8–11: You're right here, Lucilius! 112

De Amicitia (fragment 59.5–6 Vottero):
   A technique for keeping an absent friend in mind . . . 114

Illustration Credits 117

Appendix A
Timeline 119

Appendix B
Map of Seneca's World, Together with the
World of the *Medea* 121

Appendix C
Meter and Rhythm 124

Vocabulary 133

List of Illustrations

1. Family Tree of the Annaei xviii
2. Double Herm of Seneca and Socrates 1
3. Medieval Ruin in the Mountains of Corsica 28
4. Bronze Sculpture of Seneca and Nero 48
5. Medea Contemplates Killing Her Children 72
6. The Villa of Servilius Vatia 109
7. (Appendix B) Map of Seneca's World, Together with the
   World of the *Medea* 123

Preface

In Seneca's writing a drama takes place before our eyes: the human mind taken to extremes, at its worst and at its best. It is a pleasure to introduce new readers to Seneca as he stages this drama in all its forms, sometimes disturbing, sometimes inspiring, always arresting.

This volume has the goal of sampling Seneca's writings in all his major genres. Here the reader can get to know Seneca the consoler alongside Seneca the strategic advisor, the tragedian, and the epistolographer—Senecas that have more often been presented in isolation from one another. The volume can serve as a gateway to further, deeper reading in a chosen genre. But it makes good sense, at least initially, to read these writings together, since each adds something distinctive to the mosaic that is Seneca.

Taken together, the works collected here also help to clarify Seneca's broader significance in the Roman imagination. What happened to prose after the age of Cicero? What happened to poetry after the age of Virgil? What stories or dilemmas did elite Romans of Seneca's age find it useful to see played out in literature? How might they have sought to navigate their volatile world of Rome under the emperors? The fact that one and the same writer, Seneca, helps us to answer these and other questions about Latin literature and Roman history makes it essential, not just pleasurable, to read him in all his breadth.

This volume could not have been produced without the inexhaustible advice and encouragement of Ronnie Ancona, the series editor, or without the high standards that she and Bolchazy-Carducci have established for the series. Two anonymous readers for the press gave generously of their time, going far beyond the call of duty, and their many corrections and suggestions were hugely helpful. Laurie Haight Keenan, the volume editor, has given wonderful guidance throughout the process. I would also like to thank Victoria Pagán for sharing with me the benefits of her experience from the *Sallust Reader*, and my colleague Ann Kuttner for bringing to my attention the image reproduced here as Fig. 4. Colleagues and students at Penn have been very supportive; in particular, I have been assisted in seeing Seneca through fresh eyes by the insightful readings of Carrie Mowbray, a Ph.D. student working on Senecan tragedy, and also the members of an undergraduate course on "Seneca: Prose and Poetry" in spring of 2010, where some of these materials were first piloted. And for her day-to-day support and willingness to discuss the project, I thank Jo Park.

I dedicate the book to my mother, Barbara Ker-Mann, whose creativity and commitment to education I have found more inspiring than all the wisdom of the sages.

Introduction

ᏆᏤ *Seneca's scenarios*

The historian Tacitus, describing a speech given by Nero at the beginning of his reign in 54 CE, observes that Seneca, who had written the speech, had "a rhetorical style that was pleasing and fitted to the ears of his age" (*Annales* 13.3.1). Certainly Seneca took the language he knew—the language of Cicero, the language of Virgil, and the language of everyday life—and retooled it to fit the challenging scenarios that he and his contemporaries faced in Rome under the emperors of his time, from Caligula to Nero. In the process, he wrote not only speeches, but also dialogues, tragedies, letters, satire, and various other literary works, fitting each one to suit the ears of his age.

What was Seneca's goal in all these writings? To engage not only the reader's ears, or eyes, but also his or her mind. To convey moral predicaments. To transform the reader's sense of what is important in life. And the important thing in life, according to Seneca, a Stoic, is the mind's own power—its power to face the provocations of the world with rationality and tranquillity, resisting the emotions that lead us to unhappiness and violence.

But if Seneca was so focused on catering to his own age, you may find yourself wondering whether Seneca can be comprehensible to the modern reader. Seneca himself, in one of his *Epistulae Morales* ("Moral Letters"), confesses to his friend Lucilius: "The profound depths of time will sweep over us"—a metaphor that portrays time's passage with one of Seneca's favorite images of a great flood or inundation. But then he adds: "A few minds (*pauca ingenia*) will keep their head above the surface and, even if they too will eventually disappear into the same silence, they will take a stand against being forgotten (*obliuioni resistent*)" (*Ep.* 21.5).

The book you are holding is intended to show how Seneca himself has kept his head above time's deep waters, and to show how clear his thoughts about the mind can be for you as you read, even if you may not be the one for whom Seneca originally wrote. Or perhaps you are. For Seneca also explains to Lucilius: "I am working for posterity (*posterorum negotium ago*). . . . I am entrusting to writing some healthy advice, like concoctions of useful medicine, having found them to be effective on my own sores" (*Ep.* 8.2). It seems that although Seneca sent his letters to Lucilius, he was aware, and he even hoped, that they would fall into your hands, and that they might be therapeutic for you.

This volume presents four separate scenarios where Seneca's writing is at its most compelling. In the first scenario (the *Consolatio ad Helviam*, "Consolation to Helvia") Seneca writes to his mother from exile, seeking to counteract her feelings of grief at his banishment to the island of Corsica. In the second (the *De Clementia*, "On Mercy") he advises the young emperor Nero on how to govern the world without putting people to death (a lesson that Nero appears not entirely to have mastered . . .). The third scenario comes from Seneca's tragedy *Medea*, in which the recently divorced wife of Jason the Argonaut rejects all moral advice and devises the most evil revenge she can think of: killing the children that she and Jason have had together. In the fourth and final scenario Seneca, in retirement and estranged from Nero, writes letters to Lucilius far away in Sicily (the *Epistulae Morales*), with advice on the best methods for taking a philosophical path through life and keeping absent friends alive in our minds.

These four scenarios are united by the fact that in each a person receives advice (even if Medea rejects hers). The advice concerns how to overcome moral predicaments, and centers upon the capacity of the mind (*animus*) to give us everything we need for happiness—advice drawn both from Seneca's deep learning in Stoic philosophy and from his reservoir of worldly experience.

There is also much variety. In writing to his mother, Seneca tries his hand at the specialized form of ancient grief counseling known as "consolation." For Nero he writes a form of advice that came to be known as the "mirror for the prince." The vengeful Medea stars in Seneca's own reinvention of classical Greek drama. The letters to Lucilius are an experiment in the writing of "moral letters," interweaving everyday life with exercises in self-transformation.

And whereas the *Medea* is entirely fictional, the three other scenarios are more "documentary." Each of them builds upon a separate section of Seneca's career, first as an outsider banished to Corsica, then as a wealthy and powerful insider of Nero's court, and finally as an outsider again, pursuing a life of solitude and study and getting ready for death.

∾ *Meet the Senecas*

Our Seneca is sometimes called Seneca the Younger, to distinguish him from his less famous father. **Seneca the Elder** was born around 50 BCE to a wealthy family in Cordoba, Spain. (To track events in time and space, see the TIMELINE in Appendix A and the MAP in Appendix B). Sometime after the death of Cicero (43 BCE) he was brought to Rome to begin his education in grammar and rhetoric, and he pursued an equestrian career, perhaps in business, together with literary studies. Although we have lost his major work, a history of Rome from the Republican period down to the end of his own life (he died around 38 or 39 CE), we possess his memoir about rhetorical exercises known as "declamations" (*declamationes*), mock speeches devised for imaginary court cases (*controuersiae*) or advice for famous decision-making scenarios from myth or history (*suasoriae*).

Declamation was especially popular in the generations following Cicero's death, when the public oratory of the Republican period had become obsolete. Indeed, a favorite *suasoria* topic was to revisit the days before Cicero's death, seeking to persuade or dissuade Cicero on whether he should burn his *Philippics*, the speeches he had composed against Mark Antony, in exchange for his life. In a great feat of memory Seneca the Elder reproduces, supposedly verbatim, some of the more accomplished performances by declaimers in the reigns of Augustus (31 BCE–14 CE) and Tiberius (14–37 CE).

The Elder's memoir was dedicated to his three sons, two of whom, **Marcus Novatus** and **Lucius Annaeus Seneca** (Seneca the Younger), were embarking on political careers, whereas the youngest, **Marcus Annaeus Mela**, was avoiding political office to live an equestrian lifestyle much like their father's (*Controversiae* 2.pref.3–4). Seneca the Elder explains that the purpose of his memoir is to teach his sons about orators whom they were too young to have witnessed, and he analyzes for them the "complexions" (*colores*), "maxims" (*sententiae*), and other techniques that were employed by the declaimers. It is easy to see how the father's very public advertisement of his sons' education was calculated to further their careers at Rome, whether they followed in their father's footsteps or sought to become members of the senatorial aristocracy during the perilous reign of Tiberius.

Seneca the Younger received something more than the expected Roman education in grammar, rhetoric, and literature. An important model for him was a certain Papirius Fabianus, who is one of the most prominent declaimers mentioned by Seneca the Elder. Fabianus had not been content to apply his rhetoric to the imaginary scenarios of declamatory exercises, but became a moral philosopher. As Seneca himself admiringly writes in the *Epistulae Morales*, Fabianus "composed not words but moral character, and wrote what he wrote not for the ears, but for minds (*animis . . . non auribus*)" (*Ep.* 100.3). Seneca was also exposed to other philosophers, such as Attalus, a Stoic, and Sotion, whose teachings overlapped with those of the Pythagoreans.

This philosophical education was not necessarily in keeping with the public career Seneca the Elder had envisaged for his son: Seneca the Younger recalls how, as a young man, he had taken up vegetarianism for philosophical reasons, but then explains: "At the request of my father, who was not afraid of scandal but hated philosophy, I returned to my former habit" (*Ep.* 108.22). In another letter he mentions that, during a period of protracted illness, he contemplated suicide but then resolved to continue living, again out of consideration for his father (*Ep.* 78.1–2). These anecdotes illustrate the tension between Seneca's philosophical education and his father's plans for the advancement of his family at Rome. Our Seneca would in fact break all sorts of molds in a career that took him to differing extremes.

Before we turn to consider Seneca's life in its own right, however, let us complete our introductions to his family members. Together they make up one of the most interesting households preserved in ancient literature. And their fates were intimately connected with Seneca's own. When Seneca was banished by the emperor Claudius, we find him anxious about the impact that it might have on his kin and wishing that his exile might serve as an "atonement" (*piamentum*) on behalf of his whole household—a prevention of any further grief for the others, like a lightning rod or a scapegoat (*Helv.* 18.6).

Much of our information about the Annaean family comes from the *Consolatio ad Helviam* (see Fig. 1), and this work throws light on the relationship, whether real or idealized, that Roman women had to their various family members. Seneca's mother **Helvia**, to whom he addresses his consolation from exile, appears to have remained in Spain for much of her life. Seneca mentions that just a few days before his banishment to Corsica (41 CE), Helvia, by now a widow, had concluded a visit with him and was en route back to Spain. Seneca also reveals that he himself was born in Spain, because he recalls how he was first brought to Rome by his **aunt;** in Fig. 1 this aunt has been represented as Helvia's sister, though she probably had a different father and was her stepsister. This aunt was, Seneca says, something of a second mother to him: not only did she introduce him to Rome as a child, but during the 30s CE Seneca spent some years with her and her husband **C. Galerius** in Egypt, and she was instrumental in his returning to Rome to take up a quaestorship during the reign of Gaius/Caligula (37–41).

In the same consolation we also learn of the earlier losses Helvia has endured in life, and of her surviving family members who can serve as comforts for her now. She has lost **three grandchildren**, including Seneca's own **young son**; from this we can also surmise that Seneca was married before the time of his exile, though we know nothing further about his **first wife**. We also learn that, in

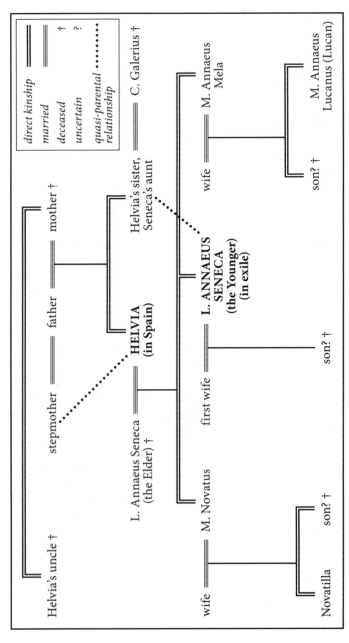

Fig. 1. The Annaei at the Time of the *Consolatio ad Helviam* (42 CE).

addition to Helvia's stepsister and her two other sons, Novatus and Mela, each of the sons has produced at least one child in whom Helvia can find comfort. One of these is Novatus' daughter, **Novatilla**, and the other is Mela's son **Marcus**, described as "a most endearing child" (*blandissimum puerum, Helv.* 18.4). This is in all likelihood the poet Lucan (Marcus Annaeus Lucanus, 39–65), Seneca's nephew. Lucan would go on to write the epic poem *Bellum Civile* ("The Civil War"), and he participated in an intense rivalry with his sometime friend and fellow poet, Nero. When the poet Martial later writes of Cordoba's "two Senecas and the one and only Lucan" (*duosque Senecas unicumque Lucanum, Epigrams* 1.61.7–8), he is referring to the three famous writers of the Annaean family: our Seneca, his father, and his nephew.

The only other family member we hear about after the *Ad Helviam* is Seneca's second(?) wife **Pompeia Paulina**, a woman of aristocratic background, much younger than him, whom he appears to have married at some time during the 50s CE. Paulina is mentioned by Seneca himself in a fascinating letter (*Ep.* 104) that identifies an exception to the philosophical arguments that would normally encourage an old or sick man to contemplate making his own "exit" from life—that is, suicide. This exception concerns situations in which we have concerns for the loved ones we would leave behind. In a passage echoing his anecdote about his father quoted above, Seneca writes of Paulina: "She causes my well-being to be a concern for me. For recognizing that her spirit turns upon mine, I begin to take care of myself in order to take care of her" (*incipio, ut illi consulam, mihi consulere, Ep.* 104.2). As an interesting sequel to this, we also hear about Paulina in historians' accounts of Seneca's death scene, discussed below.

As for Novatus and Mela, like their brother they enjoyed prominent careers. Novatus, for example, who was later known as Gallio after being adopted by L. Iunius Gallio, is mentioned in the Acts of the Apostles as the proconsul of Achaea who passed judgment on the apostle Paul (Acts 18.12–17). But it seems that they were all *too* prominent. Soon after the deaths of Seneca and Lucan in the wake of the Pisonian conspiracy (discussed below), Mela and Gallio were unable to escape being condemned by Nero, in part because of their illustrious and controversial brother. In the end, then, Seneca was unable to be an effective scapegoat for the Annaean family.

ᦈ *Seneca's life*

About Seneca's early years we know little more than what was stated above: that he was brought to Rome as a child by his aunt, evidently during the reign of Augustus, that he received a rhetorical and philosophical education, and that he did not fully commence his public career until becoming quaestor during the reign of Caligula (37–41 CE). From this time forward we are able to construct a sporadic narrative of his life through the *Annales* ("Annals") of Tacitus (c. 55–117) and the *Roman History* of Cassius Dio (c. 150–235) written in Greek. Neither of these historians gives an objective account of Seneca's career (Dio in particular is extremely hostile to Seneca), but both throw much light on the strong impressions he made. Seneca's violent fluctuations between the heights and the depths frequently serve to illustrate the opportunities and the risks in pursuing a public career under the Julio-Claudian emperors.

Dio mentions that, already during the reign of Caligula, Seneca enjoyed the reputation of being "the one preeminent in learning (Greek *sophia*) beyond all the Romans of his time as well as many others" (D.C. 59.19.7). But this visibility also explains two major calamities for Seneca mentioned by Dio. First, a speech of Seneca's aroused the jealousy of Caligula, who came close to putting Seneca to death. Second, Seneca incurred the hostility of Messalina, the first wife of the emperor Claudius, who had him banished into exile on Corsica in the year 41 on a charge of committing adultery with Julia Livilla, one of Caligula's sisters (D.C. 59.19, 60.8). We cannot be certain how credible this charge was, but Seneca's supposed adultery could be mentioned for many years to come by anyone who sought to tarnish his image.

At the other extreme, however, Tacitus explains how, in 49, Agrippina, Claudius' second wife and the mother of the young Nero,

> *so as not to be known solely for bad deeds, secured a*
> *pardon for exile on behalf of Annaeus Seneca, and at*
> *the same time a praetorship, judging that it would be a*
> *cause for public celebration on account of his renown*
> *for his studies. [She did this also] so that the boyhood of*
> *Domitius [i.e., Nero] would mature with such a teacher*
> *[i.e., Seneca] and that they might use the same man's*
> *advice toward their hope for domination, because Seneca*
> *was believed to be loyal to Agrippina due to memory of*
> *her good service, and hostile to Claudius from grief over*
> *the injury. (Ann. 12.8.2)*

The historian's reference to Seneca's "renown for his studies" (*claritudo studiorum*) is tantalizing, because we do not know exactly what literary accomplishments Seneca had completed by this time, except for three consolations (one written prior to his exile, two during) and a major work of moral philosophy, *De Ira* ("On Anger"), which included many direct criticisms of the deceased emperor Caligula. We cannot determine, for example, whether Seneca began writing tragedies during his exile or only later. But clearly his writings, whether due solely to their rhetorical and literary excellence or due also to their philosophical learning and political acumen, had brought him to the notice of the ruling household as a useful consultant.

Suetonius, however, the biographer of the Caesars, relates an anecdote that Seneca dreamt he had been given not Nero, but Caligula (!), to educate (*Nero* 7.1). He also mentions that Agrippina had forbidden Seneca to instruct Nero in philosophy, requiring him to focus only on rhetoric (*Nero* 52). These tales belong to a set of contradictory accounts concerning Nero's unteachable nature and the Seneca's failings as an educator. Although the first five of Nero's fourteen years as emperor (54–68 CE) would later be celebrated as the best five years of *any* emperor's reign (the *quinquennium Neronis*), later events, particularly Nero's killing of his mother Agrippina in 59, his divorce and execution of his wife Octavia in 62, and his possible involvement in setting the Great Fire at Rome in 64 (for which the Christians received the blame), raised questions about Seneca's possibly bad influence, or at least his failure to influence Nero for the better.

One of the most extreme indictments against Seneca comes in the form of Dio's labeling of Seneca as "tyrant teacher" (Greek *turannodidaskalos*, D.C. 61.10.2). The historian also mentions that at the height of his influence Seneca was accused of adultery with Agrippina and other scandalous behavior (D.C. 61.10). Dio's criticisms are connected with an episode that Tacitus also tells us about, from the year 58, when one of Seneca's detractors, named P. Suillius Rufus, sought to paint Seneca as a hypocrite, asking sarcastically: "By what wisdom, what precepts of the philosophers (*qua sapientia, quibus philosophorum praeceptis*), had [Seneca] acquired three hundred million sesterces in four years of friendship with the emperor?" (*Ann.* 13.42.4). At least one of Seneca's philosophical dialogues, the *De Vita Beata* ("On the Happy Life"), appears to be a response to these charges: Seneca justifies his wealth by pointing out that "no one condemns wisdom to poverty," and he emphasizes the wise person's activities as a generous donor (*VB* 23).

There is no ignoring the problematic accounts of Seneca's involvement in Nero's reign. Tacitus reports that Seneca helped Nero to write the letter to the senate that justified the killing of Agrippina, and that he thereby earned an adverse reputation (*Ann.* 14.11.3). Clearly, Seneca's rivals found it easy to exploit apparent contradictions between his philosophical writings on the one hand and his conduct as a political operator and celebrity on the other. These contradictions appear to have made Seneca a problematic and fascinating figure in the eyes of the Roman public—"good to think with," as Thomas Habinek has observed (2000, 265).

Yet if we compare the historians' accounts with works that can be reliably dated, we find Seneca publicizing his role, at the beginning of Nero's reign, in guiding the emperor toward a policy of shedding as little blood as possible. His satire entitled *Apocolocyntosis* ("Pumpkinification") belongs to the year 54 CE and mocks the Roman senate for having deified the recently deceased emperor Claudius, bitterly recalling the ineptness and cruelty of Claudius' reign; the work also celebrates the Golden Age that is about to return under the new young emperor Nero. In conjunction with the *Apocolocyntosis*, the more serious work *De Clementia*, written in the first year of Nero's reign, shows Seneca offering praise to Nero on the bloodless beginning of his reign and presenting him with a strategy for ruling that builds upon the better parts of the reign of Augustus. These works are in accord with what Tacitus reports about this period: Seneca, working as Nero's speechwriter, composed a funeral speech for the deceased Claudius that provoked laughter when it was delivered in the senate, and also composed several speeches in which Nero committed himself to exercising clemency and to governing in accord with the model of Augustus (*Ann.* 13.3.1, 13.11.1–2). The only apparent exception in this picture is Nero's poisoning, in 55, of his stepbrother Britannicus, the son of Claudius and thus Nero's rival. Whether Seneca overlooked this murder as an acceptable piece of realpolitik, or simply sought to capture Nero's goodwill and appeal to his better nature, remains uncertain.

In the year 62, by contrast, Tacitus mentions the various events that conspired to undermine Seneca's influence, explaining that Seneca withdrew from Nero's circle so as to avoid being associated with the excesses of his now "tyrannical" rule. The death of the praetorian prefect Burrus, who had long been Seneca's partner in guiding Nero, opened the way to new attacks from Seneca's rivals. The rivals charged that Seneca "was diverting the people's enthusiasm toward himself, and with his beautiful gardens and splendid villas was overtaking the emperor," and they urged Nero "to remove his teacher" (*Ann.* 14.52.2, 4).

Tacitus presents in detail a final showdown interview consisting of paired speeches by Seneca and Nero. First, Seneca pleads with Nero to be allowed to retire, giving back to the emperor the wealth, houses, and gardens he has received from him. Nero then responds by showing off what he has learnt from his rhetoric teacher (that is, Seneca!), arguing the exact opposite point: his reign is just beginning, he needs Seneca's help more than ever, and to let Seneca go would be to appear cruel (*Ann.* 14.53–56). But Tacitus sums up the real outcome of the meeting: "Seneca (was) struck down" (*perculso Seneca*, *Ann.* 14.57.1). The historian describes how Seneca then appeared "seldom in the city (*rarus per urbem*), as if detained at home by poor health or philosophical studies" (*Ann.* 14.56.3). During this period, beginning with the rupture in 62 and concluding in Seneca's final "exit" in 65, Seneca appears to have written his *Naturales Quaestiones* ("Investigations of Nature") and his *Epistulae Morales*. In both these works Seneca repeatedly mentions to Lucilius the increasing signs of his own old age, and in the *Epistulae* he urges his friend to retire from his official position in Sicily. They serve as a portrait of Seneca's own final years, on the outside of politics once again.

∾ *Seneca's death*

One of the recurring themes in Seneca's writings, from his first published consolations to the letters of his final years, is the challenge to face death—to cope with the deaths of those we love, to accept the approach of our own death, and even, if circumstances require it, to take death into our own hands. Seneca's philosophical heroes included Socrates (469–399 BCE), who had patiently waited in the public prison of Athens until the time came for him to drink the hemlock. He also celebrates Cato the Younger (95–46 BCE) as a kind of "Roman Socrates." Cato's violent suicide, attempted first with a sword and completed by tearing open the stitched-up wound with his bare hands, had ensured that he would not outlive the Roman *res publica*, which the victory of Julius Caesar in the Civil War had effectively killed off. Examples such as these serve as useful comparisons and models during the executions and suicides (some voluntary, some forced) of many members of the Roman elite during the bloodiest part of Nero's reign in the years 65–66. Tacitus mentions a rumor that already in 64 Seneca, by confining himself to a diet of spring water and fresh fruit, had narrowly evaded an attempt by Nero to poison him (*Ann.* 15.45).

Seneca died in 65, in the aftermath of the failed conspiracy against Nero led by C. Calpurnius Piso. Seneca, Lucan, and ultimately both of Seneca's brothers, were implicated in the conspiracy—in Seneca's case, on the basis of somewhat slender evidence. Tacitus describes in detail the night in April of 65 when Nero sent soldiers to Seneca's villa on the outskirts of Rome to deliver a death warrant, on the understanding that Seneca would take matters into his own hands. Over the course of several hours, Seneca first opened his veins, and then, as the blood flowed too slowly from his aged body, took hemlock just as Socrates did, again without success. Finally he resorted to a bath of hot water followed by a steam bath, in which he expired. The scene evoked by Tacitus is in many ways a solemn spectacle that belongs within the tradition of "exits of illustrious men" (*exitus illustrium uirorum*), which owed much to Plato's account of Socrates' death in the *Phaedo* and was influential on the Christian tradition of describing martyrs' deaths in gruesome and yet glorious detail. The historian describes how Seneca consoled his friends who had gathered for the deathwatch: "He called their tears back to resoluteness, now conversing with them, now more intently and in a forceful manner, asking them what had happened to their philosophical precepts and their rationality rehearsed for so many years against impending misfortunes" (*Ann.* 15.62.2).

A striking element of Seneca's death scene is the involvement of his wife Paulina. Like some of the heroines of Seneca's work on marriage, *De Matrimonio* ("On Marriage"), of which only a few fragments survive, Paulina volunteered to die with her husband, and she too opened her veins—with Seneca's consent or even, as Dio tells it, at Seneca's insistence. There is an element of the theatrical, and perhaps of the farcical, in the slow and protracted scene, and already in antiquity it provoked some hostile reactions. Tacitus mentions that while Seneca dictated his last words to his scribes (words published in a posthumous work now lost), and while he used his blood and bathwater to make a libation to "Jupiter the Liberator" (*Ioui liberatori*), in a separate room Paulina was being bandaged up by Nero's men so as to be saved from death. Paulina's revival exposed some weaknesses in her resolve: "Since the mob is ready to assume what is more disreputable, there were those who believed that for as long as she feared that Nero was implacable, she had sought the fame of sharing death with her husband, but that after she was given reason to hope for a milder outcome, she was won over by the enticements of life" (*Ann.* 15.64.2).

Tacitus also describes, some chapters later, how Petronius, known to modern audiences as the author of the brilliant and scandalous novel entitled *Satyrica* (or *Satyricon*), undertook his own forced suicide in a manner evidently critical of Seneca's: "he listened to (readers) reciting nothing about the immortality of the soul or the doctrines of the philosophers, but light poems and easy verses," and he even had his wounds temporarily bandaged up again, like Paulina (*Ann.* 16.19.2). Clearly, Seneca's death had made an impression in the Roman public imagination, but not a uniquely positive one. Much like the death of Socrates, it provoked contrasting responses from different audiences. This mixed picture parallels the controversies of his political career and people's different reactions to his writings.

∾ *Writings*

In his work entitled *Institutio Oratoria* ("Oratorical Education"), written in the generation after Seneca's death, the rhetorical theorist Quintilian devotes a whole chapter to Seneca. He describes him as having been extremely popular in his day, being "virtually the only [author] in the hands of the young men" (*Inst.* 10.1.126). One of the things Quintilian emphasizes is the range of Seneca's writings: "He pursued almost every type of literary activity: we have speeches (*orationes*) by him, poems (*poemata*), letters (*epistulae*), and dialogues (*dialogi*)" (*Inst.* 10.1.129). Not all of Quintilian's terms correspond to Seneca's surviving writings: for example, Seneca's speeches have been lost, and it is far from certain that the "poems" mentioned by Quintilian are to be identified with the tragedies that survive. But Quintilian's sketch leaves no doubt that, as a writer, Seneca was distinguished by his versatility—like Cicero before him, who wrote poetry as well as speeches and dialogues.

The extent of Seneca's versatility, however, has sometimes appeared puzzling. Why, for example, would an author so committed to writing philosophical advice also be interested in writing tragedies that dramatize extreme emotions and unthinkable acts? Some of the recent answers to this question are sketched out below in section 3, "The tragedies," but you may want to develop your own solution as you read Seneca's tragic and philosophical writings side by side. Further puzzles concern the fact that we cannot always be sure when in Seneca's career various works were written, and in the case of the tragedies, whether they were performed or were simply recited or read.

With these provisos made, let us look more closely at the distinct areas of Seneca's writings that are illustrated by the four scenarios in this volume.

1. Consolations and "Dialogues"

The focus of our first scenario, the *Consolatio ad Helviam*, is one of three consolations that survive from Seneca's hand. The earlier *Consolatio ad Marciam*, written in the late 30s CE, had sought to end the grief of Marcia, an aristocratic woman still mourning for her adult son some three years after his death. The other two consolations were written during Seneca's exile (41–49), and they present the exile in contrasting ways. In the *Ad Helviam* Seneca seeks to end his mother's grief over his exile by arguing that exile has done him no harm. But in the *Consolatio ad Polybium*, while ostensibly comforting Polybius, one of Claudius' secretaries, on the death of his brother, Seneca indirectly begs the emperor to allow him to return to Rome, enlisting Polybius as a kind of petitioner on his behalf. This was in many ways an understandable request for Seneca to make, and it had a fine literary precedent in the exile letters of Cicero and the exile poetry of Ovid, though some readers have regarded Seneca as a hypocrite in contradicting what he had previously written to his mother. A passage from the *Ad Polybium* has been included in this volume as a follow-up and contrast to the more extensive readings from the *Ad Helviam*.

The three consolations belong to the well-established tradition in Greek and Roman philosophy of advising someone who has suffered any kind of calamity, ranging from death to exile to blindness. As Cicero points out, the consoler's task is understood variously by different philosophical schools as "to remove the feeling of pain altogether, or settle it, or dislodge it as much as possible, or suppress it and not let it overflow too far or spill into other things" (*Tusculanae Disputationes* 3.75). Seneca's consolations follow in this tradition. In each work he intervenes in the addressee's grief concerning a loved one's misfortune and presents a sequence of arguments (*praecepta*), examples (*exempla*), and comforts (*solacia*). These are tailored to help the addressee put an end to his or her grief sooner rather than later, without having to rely on the slow therapy of "time the healer." The tailoring can be quite detailed, as we will see in the case of Seneca's highly personal appeal to his mother in the *Ad Helviam*.

Seneca's consolations are contained in a group of ten works by him that survive under the title *Dialogi* ("Dialogues"). The *Dialogi* deal with distinct moral topics and problems, and each is addressed to a family member or friend, being written at different points in Seneca's career, from the 30s to the 60s. They are "dialogues" only in a loose sense, because they do not depict conversations in the manner of the philosophical dialogues by Plato or, more recently, Cicero. Scholars have often referred to them as "Moral Essays," because they are almost exclusively in the voice of Seneca, who lets himself be interrupted only occcasionally by other imaginary speakers who make a brief objection or deliver a monologue (Latin *sermocinatio*, Greek *prosōpopoeia*). One of the dialogues, *De Providentia* ("On Providence"), seeks to answer Lucilius' question about why bad things happen to good men, explaining that the gods think there is no more worthy spectacle to behold than a good man face-to-face with a supposed "misfortune" and overcoming it. This work features a monologue by Cato the Younger bravely tearing open his wound, and another by God urging human beings: "Scorn pain (*contemnite dolorem*): it will either be dissolved or it will dissolve you. . . . Scorn Fortune (*contemnite Fortunam*): I did not give her any weapon by which she might injure your mind (*animum*)" (*Prov.* 6.6–7). Another dialogue, the *De Brevitate Vitae* ("On the Brevity of Life"), is addressed to Seneca's father-in-law, Pompeius Paulinus, and offers advice on turning away from his public duties as a grain commissioner and toward his moral duty to pursue philosophy, which can transform even our short existence into a long and happy life.

The most extensive dialogue is the *De Ira*, which dates from the beginning of Claudius' reign in 41. Addressed to Seneca's brother Novatus, the work proceeds from a basic definition of anger to advice on how to remedy anger in ourselves and others, presenting both positive and negative examples extending from Greek history right down to recent times in the reign of Caligula. The advice offered in the work is evidently not only for Novatus, but also for other members of the Roman elite *and* for the new emperor Claudius himself, because it is frequently concerned with how to maintain a placid existence amid the tense and often violent conditions of an imperial court. Given the *De Ira*'s importance, and its obvious political relevance, a sample is given in this volume as a follow-up to the readings from the *De Clementia* in the second scenario.

Beyond the *Dialogi*, several other philosophical works by Seneca have been preserved in separate manuscript traditions. One of these gives theoretical and practical advice on gift giving (the *De Beneficiis*, "On Benefits"). Another conducts a philosophical inquiry into nature, focusing on such topics as earthquakes, winds, celestial fires, waters, and the source(s) of the Nile (*Naturales Quaestiones*). A number of other scientific and moral works have been lost, or survive only in fragments, including *De Situ Indiae* ("On the Geography of India"), *De Matrimonio* ("On Marriage"), and *Quomodo Amicitia Continenda Sit* ("How To Maintain Friendship," often referred to by the shorter title *De Amicitia*). A fragment of the latter has been included in this volume as a follow-up to the *Epistulae Morales* below.

2. Political works

Our second scenario concerns the *De Clementia*, a work not fundamentally different from the *Dialogi* except that its purpose is openly political. It is comparable in form and topic to the *De Ira*, but Seneca now addresses the young emperor Nero directly and deals with a virtue rather than a vice. He draws upon the Greek tradition of defining ideal kingship, combining this with clemency's history as a catchphrase exploited by Nero's imperial predecessors as far back as Julius Caesar. The work offers Nero a blueprint for safety and security into the future, not only for the empire but for the emperor himself.

Few of Seneca's works were as explicitly political as the *De Clementia*, though our view of this might have been different had any of the speeches that he wrote for Nero survived. Quintilian preserves a tantalizing line of Seneca's controversial letter written for Nero to send to the senate after Agrippina's death: "That I am safe I so far neither believe nor rejoice" (*saluum me esse adhuc nec credo nec gaudeo*, *Inst.* 8.5.18). The line is deviously ambiguous, allowing Nero to seem both justified and regretful about eliminating his mother after she supposedly plotted against him.

We also possess the *Apocolocyntosis*, the satirical work that mocks the deification of Claudius and parodies the art of history writing. With its scandalous humor and its alternations between colloquial prose and verse, the work is utterly unique in Seneca's writings, and its closest parallels as a "prosimetric" satire are Petronius' *Satyrica* and the surviving fragments of "Menippean" satire. The work was apparently published in the period immediately following Claudius' death, and serves in part to prepare for the superior reign of Nero. One section of the *Apocolocyntosis* in which the deified Augustus speaks up against Claudius in a council of the gods is included in this volume as a follow-up to the *De Clementia*.

3. The tragedies

Our third scenario concerns Medea's tragic predicament and her monstrous act of revenge. Although in some ways the *Medea* play stands apart from the prose works, in other ways it complements them well, dramatizing the same grief, anger, and hostility that Seneca in the other three scenarios is so concerned to banish. And although there is nothing quite like Seneca's Medea character, the play is also a good introduction to the workings of Senecan tragedy.

Like most of Seneca's tragedies, the *Medea*'s plot has a model in the Greek tradition, in this case in the *Medea* of Euripides, which may have been the first version of the myth in which Medea herself killed her children. The Medea plot had already had been adapted in Roman versions before Seneca, including a version by Ennius and, most recently, a much praised (but now lost) *Medea* by Ovid. Seneca appears to borrow some elements from Ovid, such as Medea's ambition to improve upon the crimes of her youth by doing something *maius* ("greater"). But Seneca's Medea seems even more self-conscious about her literary predecessors, announcing at one point that she has lived up to herself ("Now I am Medea," *Medea nunc sum*, line 910), and she seems determined to outdo previous Medeas when she kills the children not behind the scenes but actually on stage. This last touch was something that Horace in his *Ars Poetica* had once flagged as a dramatic extreme to be avoided (*Ars Poetica* 185), but it nicely captures the vivid and transgressive aspect of Senecan drama, whether or not the plays were actually staged.

Apart from the *Medea*, the surviving tragedies firmly ascribed to Seneca are the *Hercules Furens* (the hero returns from the underworld only to go mad and kill his children), *Troades* ("Trojan Women"; after the Trojan war the Greeks need to sacrifice two Trojan children before they can return home), *Phaedra* (the heroine, her amorous advances rejected by her stepson Hippolytus, tricks her husband into causing Hippolytus' death), *Oedipus* (the king of Thebes discovers he has killed his father and married his mother, and blinds himself), *Phoenissae* ("Phoenician Women"; Oedipus wanders blind in the wilderness, while his two sons, Eteocles and Polynices, prepare for civil war against one another), *Agamemnon* (the king of Argos, returning from the Trojan War, is killed by his wife Clytemnestra), and *Thyestes* (an earlier king of Argos, Atreus, entices his brother and rival, Thyestes, into returning home, and tricks him into eating his own sons). In addition, two other ancient plays, probably not by Seneca but written in a Senecan style, are preserved in the manuscripts: *Hercules Oetaeus* ("Hercules on Mount Oeta"; Hercules, being poisoned, is cremated on a funeral pyre and transformed into a god); and *Octavia*, a fascinating historical drama in which Seneca himself appears as a character, discussed below in the section "Early impact."

A recent book on Senecan tragedy by Alessandro Schiesaro is entitled *Passions in Play: Thyestes and the Dynamics of Senecan Drama* (Cambridge 2003). This title is a useful encapsulation of the way in which Seneca in these plays focuses much less on any kind of social drama unfolding before the eyes of a citizen Chorus (as in Greek tragedy), and zooms in on the central characters' emotional experience. This experience is dominated by anger (*ira*), desire (*amor*), madness (*furor*), or grief (*dolor*), and in most cases it leads the hero or heroine to pursue revenge through some unspeakable act (*nefas*) or crime (*scelus*). These experiences and actions are played out in the vivid monologues of the protagonists, in their rhetorical duels against the other characters who seek to advise them or challenge them in dialogue, and in the voice of the Chorus, which amplifies the moral resonances of the main action. The world of Senecan tragedy is dominated by the interior moral landscape of the characters as they make misguided judgments about what is most valuable. It is equally defined, however, by the cosmic sympathy of the whole universe, as internal passions and crimes unleash the infernal forces of the underworld, such as the monstrous and vengeful Furies, or provoke unusual events such as omens or eclipses at the level of nature writ large. All of this is conveyed in poetic language that echoes the Augustan poets, especially Virgil and Ovid. Virgil's portrait of Dido as a passionate and suicidal heroine, for example, is highly influential on Seneca's portrait of Phaedra, and to some extent also of Medea. But Seneca pushes far beyond his models and amplifies their darker sides, producing a new tragic vision that appeals to post-Augustan sensibilities.

We cannot pinpoint exactly when these plays were written, or in what order. But Seneca had apparently begun writing them by the early 50s, because the *Apocolocyntosis* (written in 54) includes some clear echoes of Seneca's own *Hercules Furens*. At the other end of his career, the *Thyestes* has convincingly been identified as a mature and crowning achievement, while the unfinished *Phoenissae* may have been his last dramatic work.

We can also say little about the plays' exact purpose. Perhaps Seneca sought to transform the audience's inner moral lives by holding up an image of the human mind at its most irrational. Perhaps he sought to undermine the philosophical works with a dark and pessimistic (but more accurate?) vision of the world—a world that included the likes of Caligula. Perhaps the plays simply offered a form of sophisticated literary entertainment, with aesthetic goals entirely separate from those of the philosophical writings, yet in their own way equally, or more, compelling. Whichever explanation satisfies you the best, the tragedies' existence alongside the prose works makes reading Seneca a unique and exciting challenge.

4. The *Epistulae Morales*

Our fourth and final scenario focuses on a few of the letters Seneca addressed to Lucilius. As mentioned above, the *Epistulae Morales* were written in Seneca's final years (62–65) and therefore belong to the period of his withdrawal from the court of Nero.

Lucilius Iunior was a slightly younger friend who, for a significant portion of the correspondence, was serving as an imperial administrator (*procurator*) on the island of Sicily. In the course of their correspondence Seneca often urges his friend to retire—a seeming reflection of Seneca's own situation that has led some to see in *Lucilius* a diminutive model of *Lucius* Annaeus Seneca himself. And certainly, to some extent, it is Seneca's show: although each letter begins with a greeting to Lucilius (*SENECA LVCILIO SVO SALVTEM*, "Seneca [sends] greetings to his Lucilius") and most of the letters respond to questions about various moral problems raised by Lucilius, Lucilius' own letters, if there were any, are not preserved.

Yet much of our pleasure in reading the letters comes from seeing the drama Seneca creates around his friend, and how he draws Lucilius—and us, too—into the correspondence. In letter 21, for example, it emerges that Lucilius has been distracted by the demands of his public career. So Seneca reminds Lucilius that Idomeneus, the correspondent of Epicurus, and Atticus, the correspondent of Cicero, did not become famous for anything they did in their public lives but because of their involvement with famous letter writers. Reminding Lucilius of the dangers of oblivion—of being submerged beneath the "profound depths of time," as mentioned above—he then proposes an epistolary partnership, in which Lucilius will focus on becoming famous through his devotion to Seneca's letters and the philosophical studies they involve. "I promise you this, Lucilius: I will enjoy favor with posterity, I can bring names with me and give them permanence" (*hoc tibi promitto, Lucili: habebo apud posteros gratiam, possum mecum duratura nomina educere*, 21.5). Seneca caps this off by doing something he does a lot in the letters—he takes lines from Virgil's *Aeneid* and turns them to his own ends, here adapting the poet's promise to the two friends Nisus and Euryalus, who died in a daring night raid to help the Trojans:

> *Fortunati ambo! si quid mea carmina possunt,*
> *nulla dies umquam memori uos eximet aeuo.*
>
> (Virgil *Aen.* 9.446–47)

> *Fortunate pair! If my poetry has any sway,*
> *no day will ever remove you from the memory of*
>   *eternity.*

This is more than just a flourish: in an important sense the *Epistulae Morales* are as ambitious, and poetic, as Virgil's epic, just as the parallels Seneca draws with Epicurus and Cicero reveal the famous epistolary models to which he aspires.

The *Epistulae Morales* may indeed have been Seneca's attempt to rival Cicero's famous correspondence with his friend T. Pomponius Atticus, in which Atticus' letters are likewise omitted. But the differences from Cicero's correspondence are also revealing. Although Cicero really did correspond with Atticus, we cannot be sure that Seneca sent his letters to Lucilius at all. For Seneca's letters are so polished that they either belong to the world of epistolary fiction, or at least were carefully revised after being sent. In this respect a better comparison may be the *Epistulae* of Horace, which are elaborate poetic experiments in the letter form. As Seneca plays upon the conventions of letter writing that were habitual for all elite Romans, he makes a point of emphasizing that his letters lack the everyday gossip of Cicero's letters, such as who is running for office or who is the best money-lender, and instead focus their attention on moral "self-scrutiny" (*se excutere, Ep.* 118.1–3).

The title *Epistulae Morales* in all likelihood dates back to Seneca himself, and was intended to capture the letters' repeated movements from everyday life to philosophical instruction. In the 124 letters that survive, we are witnesses to one side of an energetic conversation. In this conversation Seneca advises Lucilius on whatever topic Lucilius has raised or what seems most urgent for Lucilius' (and/or Seneca's own) progression toward wisdom: how to use his time, how to use books, how to be a good friend, how to prepare for death, and so forth. On one occasion, early in the correspondence, Seneca writes with exciting news: "I realize, Lucilius, that I am not simply mending my faults but actually being transfigured (*non emendari me tantum sed transfigurari*," *Ep.* 6.1). As Seneca and Lucilius both "transfigure" themselves and make halting progress toward greater moral consistency, the topics become more technical and the discussions more in-depth. The two friends scrutinize together some fundamental questions of Stoic moral philosophy, especially the central tenet that "virtue" (*uirtus*) is the "highest good" (*summum bonum*)—i.e., that virtue alone is sufficient for the happy life. And Seneca repeatedly turns Lucilius' attention back upon himself, exhorting him to trust in the mind's invulnerability against any external threat.

The letters included in the final scenario of this volume take us from one of Seneca's earliest letters, which discusses our practices of reading as a form of "travel" (*Ep.* 2), to letters in which he meditates on his distance from Lucilius and describes his own travels in the region of Campania (*Ep.* 40, 49, 55). A passage from letter 85 has also been included as a follow-up to the first scenario on Seneca's response to his exile.

Some famous letters have had to be omitted in our selection. One warns Lucilius to avoid the amphitheater (*Ep.* 7), another describes Seneca's crumbling villa, which reminds him to give thought to his own old age and mortality (*Ep.* 12), and another portrays in fine detail the distractions of living above a bathhouse (*Ep.* 56). A fuller selection can be found in A. L. Motto's *Seneca's Moral Epistles* (Wauconda, Ill., 2001).

❧ *Misfortune, grief, and the power of the mind*

The predicaments faced by Seneca's characters, and the remedies he offers, are all molded around one consistent system of ideas. So, although each predicament and each remedy is worked out in its own unique context, it may be helpful here to trace out the underlying pattern.

First, we learn that the person who is central to the scenario faces an actual or potential misfortune of some kind: loss, injury, separation, or some such. Seneca does not in the end believe that our state of fortune (*fortuna*), whether it is good, bad, or neutral, should have any power over us. But he goes to great lengths to depict calamities in the most vivid terms possible, partly to gain the trust of the person who feels vulnerable or emotional, and partly perhaps to make his own efforts to vanquish the threat seem all the more impressive. In his detailed portrayal of extreme misfortune he frequently personifies Fortune as a sadistic oppressor. Even in instances where the Latin word *fortuna* is printed in lower case by modern editors, there often lurks behind this the traditional deity *Fortuna*, a powerful Roman goddess with her own temples and her own cult.

Seneca also typically acknowledges that the person's most likely response to this misfortune will be pain, grief, or grievance—feelings often grouped together under the term *dolor*. Seneca does not in the end think that even the slightest amount of grief is acceptable, even if some initial flinching is quite natural for anyone, including the wise person. Yet, as with fortune, he often goes out of his way to depict grief's finer effects, revealing an intimate familiarity with the darker shades of psychological disturbance and with the literary devices by which they can be writ large. Occasionally he will personify a person's *dolor* as if it were a powerful and irresistible agent inside the mind, reacting to the perceived misfortune and seeking to glut itself on melancholy or revenge. Sometimes this grief feeds into, or out of, more specific passions such as anger or desire. Sometimes, especially in the tragedies, it assumes the form of an avenging Fury—one of the creatures in the underworld who exact vengeance of their own, or fuel human insanity. In one of the tragedies (the *Hercules Furens*), this takes the form of the goddess Juno, who is exported from Virgil's *Aeneid* to help stage Hercules' sudden descent into madness.

But at this point the advisor seeks to intervene. If we succumb to grief, we are making our happiness dependent on the agency of Fortune. We become Fortune's slaves. For the wise person or sage (Latin *sapiens*, Greek *sophos*) in Stoic philosophy, or even for the imperfect student, this development is unnecessary and indeed wrong. Grief can and must be resisted, and our happiness can and must be immunized against the variations in our external circumstances that are attributed to Fortune. The answer lies in the mind (*animus*). With the help of philosophy, the mind can be made invulnerable to all external circumstances. Our mind can be made free, and can make *us* free.

∽ *The Stoics: Life according to nature*

Seneca's ideas about the mind's invulnerabilty are grounded in Stoic doctrine, which dates from the fourth century BCE, at the beginning of the Hellenistic period. Cicero recounts for us vividly in his dialogues on Greek philosophy how, in addition to philosophers who identified most closely with the teaching of Plato (427–348 BCE; the Academics) and with that of his pupil Aristotle (384–322; the Peripatetics), several new philosophical schools had offered their own accounts of the nature of the world and their own advice on how to live a happy human life or (which is the same thing) how to be wise. The followers of Epicurus (341–270; the Epicureans) believed in a universe composed of atoms and void, in which the gods exist but do not have a care for human affairs, and the highest good for human beings is pleasure (in the sense of freedom from pain and distress). At Rome Epicureanism found its most eloquent expression in the magnificent hexameter poem *De Rerum Natura* ("On the Nature of the Universe") by Lucretius (c. 99–c. 55). Some of the poetry of Horace (65–8 BCE) also adopts an Epicurean perspective on Roman life.

Stoicism, with its emphasis on public duty, was equally or even more popular at Rome. The Stoics (so-called Stoics because they gathered in the *Stoa Poikilē*, or "Painted Colonnade," in Athens) developed a doctrine begun by Zeno of Citium (fl. c. 300 BCE). His central advice was, simply, to "live according to nature" (translated into Latin as *secundum naturam vivere*). Nothing else is required for obtaining "wisdom" (Latin *sapientia*, Greek *sophia*) and living the "happy life"

(Latin *vita beata*, Greek *eudaimonia*). But Zeno and his successors understood this advice in a highly specific sense informed by Stoic tenets not only about "nature" (Latin *natura*, Greek *phusis*), but also about the mind and about morality.

Living according to nature means primarily perfecting our distinctive human nature, namely our "reason" or "rationality" (Latin *ratio*; Greek *logos*). Doing so is equivalent to the perfection of virtue (Latin *uirtus*, Greek *aretē*), because for the Stoics virtue *is* a fully logical and rational disposition of the mind, and being rational inherently involves the application of virtue to all the duties that are specific to us as social persons. Furthermore, virtue is the highest good and is sufficient on its own for happiness. All other things in the world, such as wealth, or even the health of the body, even if they are to be preferred if circumstances allow, have no intrinsic value. The Stoics' term for such things is "indifferents" (Latin *indifferentia*, Greek *adiaphora*). A life in accordance with nature also involves living in harmony with Nature, because the whole universe is also rational, being permeated by a "breath" (Latin *spiritus*, Greek *pneuma*) that is both rational and divine—a monotheistic but impersonal conception of God. The world's events are all predetermined and are guided by Providence. If we are unhappy with our circumstances, it is only because we have allowed our state of happiness to be influenced by indifferents, being distracted from our goal of living rationally and virtuously—that is, of living in accordance with nature.

It is clear why Seneca goes to such great efforts to attack both Fortune and grief. To accept that any state of fortune is relevant to our state of happiness is mistakenly to ascribe value to indifferents. To succumb to grief is nothing other than allowing this erroneous sense of value to lead us into an irrational reaction to our external circumstances, inconsistent with a rational understanding of the providential universe. These mistakes can be counteracted by training the mind.

∾ *Techniques of philosophical training*

In Seneca we encounter a highly practical form of philosophical training that is less concerned with teaching fine-grained philosophical doctrines than with introducing us to an "art of living."

Seneca frequently compares this training to military exercises, athletic training, medical regimen, or rehearsal for life's drama. As one might expect, Seneca exploits the power of rhetoric to "move" or "affect" (*mouere*) the audience, treating his addressees as if they were judges in the law courts and adapting his speech to persuade them that Fortune has done nothing that can harm us and can therefore be "acquitted." But he also draws on literary methods and spiritual exercises—Michel Foucault called them "technologies of the self"— that had a long tradition both in Stoicism and in ancient philosophy more generally for transfiguring people's lives. Techniques include the genres on display in our four scenarios (consolation, mirror of the prince, tragic drama, and epistolography), but they also include smaller-scale exercises, such as preparing ourselves to say "Thank you" when Fortune reclaims what is hers, or practising the so-called "premeditation of future evils" (*praemeditatio futurorum malorum*).

It is worth pausing to consider the practice of premeditation, by which we can practice for the arrival of supposed misfortunes and can rehearse our response. In one of the letters to Lucilius, Seneca models the exercise, repeating formulas to establish habits of thought that can help when the needs arises:

> *Pauper fiam: inter plures ero. Exul fiam: ibi me natum putabo quo mittar. Alligabor: quid enim? nunc solutus sum? . . . Moriar: hoc dicis, desinam aegrotare posse, desinam alligari posse, desinam mori posse. (Ep. 24.17)*

> *I will become poor? I will be in company. I will become an exile? I will imagine that I was born in the place to which I am sent. I will be put in chains? So what? Am I free of chains now? . . . I will die? What you're saying is, I will cease to be able to be sick, I will cease to run the risk of being put in chains, I will cease to be able to die.*

Each supposed misfortune is answered not by succumbing to grief but with a staunch response that scorns the given event as an "indifferent." Note, by the way, the rather paradoxical view we are asked to embrace in the final sentence: even death is not to be feared as the end of our living but rather to be welcomed as the end of our vulnerability to further misfortune, including death! In a fragment of a lost work, Seneca echoes this thought in a concise and cogent formula: "After death all things are ended—even death" (*post mortem omnia finiuntur, etiam ipsa*; *De Inmatura Morte*, "On Premature Death," fragment 63 Vottero). Premeditation thus sketches a path to freedom (*libertas*), a total escape from our subservience to Fortune. Not that we *need* to die in order to liberate ourselves: freedom is ultimately just a state of our mind, of which being ready for death is simply the clearest demonstration.

✎ *Seneca's style*

As mentioned above, Tacitus writes that Seneca had "a rhetorical style that was pleasing and fitted to the ears of his age" (*ingenium amoenum et temporis eius auribus accommodatum, Ann.* 13.3.1). With these words the historian signals that Seneca kept pace with, and perhaps helped to influence, the changing tastes of first-century CE audiences and readers.

It has become customary for commentators to characterize Seneca as a writer of "Silver Latin," an inferior successor to the "Golden Age" styles of Cicero or Virgil. Indeed, Seneca did not please the ears of *all* his contemporaries, and not all audiences liked the way the rhetorical fashions were changing. Early in Seneca's career Caligula criticized Seneca's style as "sand without lime" (*harena sine calce*, Suetonius *Caligula* 53.2), as if Seneca's concise maxims had nothing to hold them together. And Quintilian himself, who much prefers the style of Cicero, recalls having openly criticized Seneca's "corrupt style of speaking, broken by every kind of fault" (*corruptum et omnibus uitiis fractum dicendi genus*). He wishes that Seneca's occasional "outstanding maxims" (*clarae sententiae*) had not been undone by "enticing flaws" (*dulcibus uitiis*) and that "he had not broken up weighty topics into the tiniest sentences" (*rerum pondera minutissimis sententiis non fregisset, Inst.* 10.1.125, 129–30).

Modern scholars, too, have often seen Seneca, together with his contemporaries, such as Lucan, and authors of the Flavian period that followed, such as the poet Statius, as yielding to the pressures of the Imperial age. Imperial literature is sometimes caricatured as artificial or mannerist: writers shifted from public oratory toward the sensationalism of declamation; turned their attention toward depicting violence, emotions, and the spectacular; wrote prose that sounds more like poetry and poetry that sounds more like rhetoric; or cultivated brevity of expression because this catered best to the shrinking attention spans of audiences. Sometimes Ovid is blamed: his poetry was to a significant extent shaped by a training in declamation (Seneca the Elder tells us that Ovid favored *suasoriae*; see *Controversiae* 2.2.8–12). Ovid introduced new layers of irony and poetic self-consciousness, and he is often seen as the pivotal figure who ended the Augustan age and ushered in an era of Latin "baroque," indulging in excessive ornamentation and playfulness and diluting the literary power of the Golden Age.

If we put aside the moralizing aspects of this account, there is certainly some truth to the claim that the changing times brought changes in style. And in Seneca's case the changes are part of a decisive, "modernizing" shift away from Ciceronian style toward his own distinctive approach to moral advising, whether to depict moral experience more vividly or to engage more actively with the minds of his readers. The changes are also part of a shift away from the poetic narratives of Virgil, which, on the surface at least, reaffirm the stability of the Augustan political world, toward the bleaker vision of the tragedies in which chaotic moral and political forces prevail.

Seneca himself has a lot to say about style, at least as he deploys it in his prose writings. When seeking to justify the informal style of his letters, for example, he puts it like this:

> *I want my letters to be just like my speech* (sermo)
> *would be if we were inquiring together or walking
> together: effortless and easy* (inlaboratus et facilis). *The
> letters have no contrivance or fashioning. If I could, I*

> *would prefer to show what I feel rather than to say it*
> (quid sentiam ostendere quam loqui mallem). . . . *Let*
> *our whole purpose be this: to say what we feel and feel*
> *what we say* (quod sentimus loquamur, quod loquimur
> sentiamus). *Let our speech be in harmony with our way*
> *of living* (concordet sermo cum uita). . . . *Let our words*
> *not delight but do good. . . . The other arts are concerned*
> *with style, but here [i.e., in the philosophical letters] it is*
> *the mind's work that is being done* (hic animi negotium
> agitur)" (*Ep.* 75.1–2, 4–5).

This does not mean that Seneca's style is artless, but that its art lies in
its ability to appeal to the mind simply and directly.

It will be useful here to survey a number of distinctive features
of the style preferred by Seneca (and, in many instances, by other
first-century writers). The following list is not meant to be exhaus-
tive, but illustrates the sorts of things you can expect. Other features
are signaled in the Commentary whenever they arise. On METER and
PROSE RHYTHM in Seneca's writings, see Appendix C.

Three stylistic tendencies

1. Brevity

Seneca often compresses an idea into a concise, "pointed" or "epigrammatic" form. E.g., *Nusquam est qui ubique est* ("He who is everywhere is nowhere," *Ep.* 2.2); and *Fortuna fortes metuit, ignauos
premit*, "Fortune fears the brave, crushes the cowardly" (*Med.* 159).
Both these examples are *sententiae*, i.e., concise formulations of proverbial knowledge, or "maxims."

This kind of expression belongs within Seneca's more general
aesthetic tendency toward encapsulation, which has close ties to
his philosophical ideal of curtailed desire. In one of his letters he
persuades Lucilius not to seek godlike immortality but to accept the
finitude of human existence by reminding him that "it is the hall-
mark of a great artisan to encapsulate everything in a brief space"
(*magni artificis est clusisse totum in exiguo, Ep.* 53.11). In another

letter he asserts that "whether you draw a larger or a smaller circle is relevant to its size, not its shape," and he indicates that virtue, too, is not increased if we have vast possessions and extensive power, because happiness "is located in one place: the mind itself" (*beatum . . . illud uno loco positum est, in ipsa mente, Ep.* 74.27–29). The image of a tighter circle thus acquires great moral power.

2. Visual effects
Seneca frequently appeals to the reader's eyes, as if he or she were being invited to watch a spectacle. E.g., *si effectus eius damnaque intueri uelis, . . . uidebis caedes ac uenena . . . . Aspice . . .* , "If you are willing to examine (anger's) effects, you will see murders and poisonings . . . . Behold . . . !" (*Ira* 1.2.1). This example is followed by Seneca's description of anger's effects in a sequence of vivid images. This is what the rhetorical theorists refer to as *euidentia* or *subiectio sub oculis* ("placing before the eyes").

This has close ties to Seneca's preference for the concrete over the conceptual. As he points out in one of his letters, "The way is long through precepts, but brief and effective through examples" (*longum iter est per praecepta, breue et efficax per exempla, Ep.* 6.5).

3. Comparison
Seneca likes to explain one thing through another. This means his writings are full of analogies and illustrative examples (pl. *exempla*; sing. *exemplum*). E.g., Seneca appeals to Helvia's courage by writing, *quemadmodum . . . ueterani . . . ita tu nunc . . .* , "just as veteran soldiers [do], . . . so too you now [should do] . . ." (*Helv.* 3.1).

Seneca's comparisons take numerous linguistic forms, ranging from explicit similes to more subtle uses of metaphor. Often they are simply an instructional device, but sometimes they are connected to the idea of self-transformation—of changing oneself through imitating someone else. As a negative contrast to this, however, the Chorus in the *Medea* liken Medea's irrational behavior to that of a wild beast (e.g., *Med.* 863–65).

Three recurring structures

1. Anaphoric repetition

Seneca frequently begins successive clauses with the same word or words, in the figure of speech known as anaphora (Greek *epanaphora*, Latin *repetitio*). E.g., <u>*Illae*</u> *(bonae artes) consolabuntur,* <u>*illae*</u> *delectabunt,* <u>*illae*</u> *si . . . in animum tuum intrauerint,* <u>*numquam*</u> *amplius intrabit dolor,* <u>*numquam*</u> *sollicitudo,* <u>*numquam*</u> *. . . uexatio,* "Those good morals will console (you), they will delight you, (and) if they enter your mind, never will grief enter further, never will anxiety, never will vexation" (*Helv.* 17.5).

This allows Seneca to draw up lists, catalogues, and comparisons. Often also it has a strong impact on the reader, as a learning tool or an emotional trigger, especially when the third item is longest (the "rising tricolon").

2. Anticipatory *hoc* or *illud*

The neuter singular of the demonstrative pronoun frequently introduces a following clause. E.g., <u>*hoc*</u> *adhuc defuerat tibi,* <u>*lugere uiuos*</u>, "<u>This</u> had been lacking to you up till now: <u>namely, to mourn living persons</u>" (*Helv.* 2.5). This helps to focus the listener's attention on what the speaker is about to say—a simple and effective device ensuring clarity and concentration. See Bennett 246.2.

3. Asyndeton (omission of coordinating conjunction)

Seneca often omits a conjunction such as "and" or "but," leaving it for the reader to supply it mentally. E.g., *non summam cutem rupit, pectus et uiscera ipsa diuisit,* "it did not only break the surface of the skin, <u>(but also)</u> split open your breast and your insides" (*Helv.* 3.1). See Bennett 346.

Three favorite syntactic constructions

1. Objective genitive

Seneca frequently employs the genitive to give a richer syntactic structure to a noun phrase, and the objective genitive is particularly frequent. E.g., *animum . . . uix* <u>*unius (aerumnae) patientem*</u>, "a mind scarcely <u>enduring a single misfortune</u>"; *animum tot <u>miseriarum uic-</u>* <u>*torem*</u>, "a mind (that has been) <u>conqueror of</u> so many <u>miseries</u>" (*Helv.* 2.2). See Bennett 200.

2. Relative clauses with subjunctive
Seneca uses relative clauses with subjunctive verbs particularly often. E.g., *adminiculis <u>quibus innitaris</u> opus est*, "There is a need for supports for you to lean on (of the sort that you can lean on)" (*Helv.* 18.1). Such clauses can always be categorized as relative clauses of characteristic, although they often have a sense of purpose as well, whether explicit or implicit. See Bennett 282–83.

3. *Ex* + ablative
Where other writers might use the genitive of the whole, Seneca equally often uses *ex* + ablative E.g., *nec quemquam . . . <u>ex liberis</u>* <u>*tuis*</u>, "nor any <u>of your children</u>" (*Helv.* 20.1). This is different from the more conventional use of *ex* in the sense "from." See Bennett 201.1a.

Three words to watch
1. *In* + accusative
Seneca often uses *in* + accusative in a sense that cannot be translated with English "in," such as purpose or opposition. E.g., *liberos tuos et <u>in auxilium</u> et <u>in oblectamentum</u> Fortuna disposuit*, "Fortune arranged your children <u>to serve</u> both <u>as help</u> and <u>as entertainment</u>" (*Helv.* 18.3); *caput, <u>in quod</u> mucrones acuant*, "a head for them to sharpen their swordpoints <u>against</u>" (*Clem.* 1.9.5).

2. *Quoque*
This word is always doing important work in Seneca. Most usually it means "also" or "even" and modifies the preceding word. E.g., Medea says, *istud facinus . . . / <u>a me quoque</u> absit*, "Let that deed be far <u>even from me</u>" (*Med.* 932), emphasizing that even Medea, despite her record of violent deeds, finds it abhorrent.

3. Any future participle

Seneca puts the future participle to stronger use than most earlier authors. E.g., *domituram freta . . . nouam . . . ratem*, "the new ship that would master the seas" (*Med.* 2).

Two things that *happen* to words

1. Compound verbs

Seneca is innovative in his use of verbs with prefixes, which can give special emphases to verbs. This also results in more verbs taking the dative rather than the accusative. E.g., *non prodest cibus nec corpori accedit . . .* , "food is not beneficial and makes no addition to the body" (*Ep.* 2.3); and *adiciamus illi quae . . . pertinent*, "let us add to it things which are relevant" (*Amic.* 59.6). On compound verbs taking the dative, see Bennett 187, III.

This tendency of Seneca's also means that the Vocabulary at the back of this volume contains many combinations of prefixes and verbs whose meaning you could predict quite easily. Consider, for example, all the compounds formed with the prefix *e(x)-*: you should be able to find at least 45, and while not all their meanings are predictable on the basis of the underlying verb, most of them are. Then consider compounds formed from the verb *fundo*, "to pour": in this volume we find Seneca using *circumfundo*, "pour around"; *effundo*, "pour out"; and *profundo*, "pour forth." In general such meanings will be transparent.

2. Syncopation of perfects

Seneca regularly shortens verbs in the perfect, pluperfect, or future perfect tenses—in other words, any verb formed in the perfect system. E.g., at *Helv.* 17.3 he uses *adsuesses* (from pluperfect subjunctive *adsueuisses*) and at *Clem.* 1.9.7, *arcessît* (from perfect indicative *arcessiuit*). (Note that the *î* in *arcessît* is the standard editorial convention for indicating that an otherwise ambiguous form [*arcessit*] is not pres. but pf. tense, i.e., that the *i* is a contraction from *i(u)i*; see also the pf. forms *transît* [*Ep.* 49.3] and *desîmus* [55.1].)

❧ *Early impact*

Seneca made a splash. Already in his own lifetime, and in the generation after his death, his life and writings were taken up as topics for literary *imitatio*, or "emulation." Two particular cases are worth noting here because of the perspective they can offer on several of our scenarios.

A set of up to seventy-two epigrams is ascribed somewhat uncertainly to Seneca in the collection known as the *Latin Anthology*. It is possible that some of these were written by Seneca himself, but it is also likely that some were written by others, either during his lifetime or after his death, to capitalize upon his reputation, or to criticize him. One of these epigrams, for example, is in the voice of an exile who has been banished to Corsica and laments:

> *Barbarous Corsica is enclosed by precipitous rocks,*
> *   horrible and desolate in every direction.*
> *Autumn brings no fruit, summer produces no harvest,*
> *   its frosty winter is devoid of olive oil.*
> *5 The rainy spring is utterly infertile*
> *   and in its luckless ground no greenery takes root.*
> *No bread, no draught of water, no fire with which to*
> *   cremate.*
> *   These two things are here: the exile and his exile.*
> > (*Epigram* 3 Prato)

In its description of the bleak landscape, and especially in the final line expressing the exile's loneliness, *hic sola haec duo sunt: exul et exilium*, the poem would seem to contradict the image of contentment that Seneca projects in the *Ad Helviam*. If anything, it resembles the *Ad Polybium*, where Seneca had admitted to finding exile difficult.

The second early reception is the historical drama entitled *Octavia*. Sometime in the years after Nero's death, this play's anonymous author took up Senecan tragedy as a useful framework within which to dramatize events of Nero's reign, in particular the

emperor's divorce of Octavia and his marriage to Poppaea in the
year 62 (the inspiration for one of the earliest operas, Claudio Mon-
teverdi's *L'Incoronazione di Poppea*, in 1643). In addition to its Senecan style and meter, the play has some resemblances to the *Medea*
in particular, since it represents the replacement of one wife with
another—even if Octavia does not seek revenge but is sent into exile.
It also draws on Seneca's prose works. A character named "Seneca"
appears, assailing Fortune and echoing the *Ad Helviam* in talking
nostalgically about his own exile:

> *It would have been better for me to remain hidden far*
>   *from the evils of resentment,*
> *remote among the rocks of the Corsican sea,*
> *where my mind was free and had its own authority*
> *and was always available for me as I renewed my*
>   *studies.*
> *What joy it was—unsurpassed by anything created by*
> *mother Nature, the architect of this immense work—*
> *to contemplate the heavens . . . (Oct. 381–90)*

"Seneca" also enters into a debate with the Nero character, repeating the advice of the *De Clementia*. Describing the beauty of re-
fraining from anger and of "giving calm to the world, peace to one's
own age" (*Oct.* 475), he remarks:

> *This is the greatest virtue, this the path to the heavens.*
> *This is how it is that Augustus, the first parent of the*
>   *nation,*
> *reached the stars, and is worshipped in temples as a god.*
>   (*Oct.* 477–79)

But Nero talks back, and draws instead on other parts of Seneca's
account of Augustus from the *De Clementia*, describing Augustus'
more violent early years:

> He who earned the heavens
> through his parental virtue, the deified Augustus,
> how many noble men he killed, young and old
> scattered around the world . . . !
> I too can expect the stars, if first with lethal sword
> I cut off whatever is hostile to me . . .

(*Oct.* 504–7, 530–31)

Nero, then, charts his own bloody path to deification, using Seneca's writings against him. In such complex rereadings of Seneca's works, the *Octavia* shows that Seneca's near contemporaries were willing to combine Seneca's different authorial identities, and to interpret the story of his life in a tragic light.

These two anonymous examples belong to a more general pattern that extends to some of the best-known Latin authors of the first and second centuries. Within Seneca's own lifetime, we find significant overlaps between Senecan tragedy and the aesthetics and language of Lucan's *Bellum Civile*, and in Petronius' *Satyrica* there are several thinly veiled parodies of Seneca both as a tragedian and as a moralist. Scholars looking at the generations after Seneca's death have traced clear lines of Senecan reception in the poetry of Statius and Valerius Flaccus (the latter especially in his depiction of Medea in his *Argonautica*) and in the letters of Pliny the Younger and the prose style of the historian Tacitus—including in those very passages in which Tacitus relates the events of Seneca's life and death.

∾ *Afterlives*

For most of the last two thousand years, Seneca has been just as influential and controversial as he was in the first century. The survival of a third-century double herm of Seneca and Socrates joined at the head (Fig. 2) shows that Seneca's self-fashioning as a Roman Socrates had been partly successful. But this did not prevent Boethius (480–524 CE), in his *Consolatio Philosophiae* ("Consolation of Philosophy"), from criticizing Seneca for having joined himself so closely to Nero (*Cons.* 3.5.25–26).

Fig. 2. Double Herm of Seneca and Socrates, third century.

Although Seneca's writings faded into the background somewhat in later pagan classical culture, they were successively rediscovered. He was an important author for St. Jerome (347–420) and other Christians into the Middle Ages, and for over a thousand years a forged correspondence in Latin between Seneca and St. Paul was believed to be genuine. Seneca was a major stylistic and literary model for Petrarch (1304–1374) and other humanists in the Italian Renaissance—so much so, that when Petrarch visited Campania, he borrowed from Seneca's *Epistulae Morales* 55 (in this volume), although in another letter he also criticized Seneca for not standing up to Nero. Seneca was also an influence on the Flemish scholar Justus Lipsius (1547–1606), who developed his neo-Stoic philosophy from Seneca's writings and also inspired the master painter Peter Paul Rubens to develop the most familiar modern image of Seneca, in his *Death of Seneca* (1614). Although Rubens' painting has not been reproduced here, it is easy to locate it by an image search on the internet, and you may find it interesting to compare it with portrayals of Seneca's death scene by Gerrit van Honthorst, Luca Giordano, Jörg Syrlin the Elder, and other early modern artists.

During much of this period, several misunderstandings prevailed in the tradition on Seneca. One of them, mentioned above, was the supposed Christianization of Seneca fueled by the forged correspondence between Seneca and St. Paul. This was not fully debunked until the sixteenth century. Another misunderstanding involved the distinction between the two Senecas whom we know as the Elder and the Younger. Although the mention of "two Senecas" (*duos Senecas*) by the poet Martial (*Epigrams* 1.61.7–8), mentioned above, was well known in the Renaissance, already in the fifth century the writer Sidonius Apollinaris had misidentified the two by referring to (1) a prose-writing stateseman and (2) a tragedian. Partly as a result of Sidonius' influence, the Elder's declamations were lumped together with the Younger's prose writings as the work of one and the same statesman, while all (or at least some) of the tragedies, together with the *Octavia*, were ascribed to the tragedian, whom some humanists speculated was a son of the prose writer. This confusion was solved by the seventeenth century, with the declamations being properly ascribed to the Elder, and all the rest of the prose works *and* the tragedies to the Younger. Still, even today a handful of scholars remain quietly skeptical (unnecessarily, in my view) about whether the tragedian and the writer of the philosophical works were indeed the same person.

When Shakespeare (1564–1616) and other tragedians of the English Renaissance looked for classical dramatic models, they looked not to Greek tragedy but to Seneca. Modern tragedy's five-act structure and thematic elements such as ghosts and revenge plots became popular largely due to Seneca's influence. During the seventeenth century, Senecan prose style also became one of the major competing models, privileging brevity, asymmetry, and coordinated ("paratactic") structures, in contrast to the long periods, symmetries, and subordinate ("hypotactic") structures of Ciceronian style. Lipsius writes, in his own conspicuously Senecan style:

> [Seneca's] words are well chosen, specific, and significant.
> Indeed, they always say more than they say (plus aliquid
> semper dicunt quam dicunt). His characteristic genius
> seems to be that in his economic use of words there is a
> wonderful energy and efficacy, and in his brevity there
> is distinction and splendor. There are frequent allusions,
> similes, and metaphors, virtually without interruption.
> These delight at the same time as they teach (quae delec-
> tant simul et docent), and focus the mind upon the topic,
> and beyond the topic (et in rem animum atque extra
> rem mittunt). (Manductio ad Stoicam Philosophiam,
> "Handbook to Stoic Philosophy")

Lipsius' praise helped to fuel the *imitatio* of Senecan style not only in Latin, but across the modern languages of Europe, including English. By the nineteenth century, however, Seneca's style came to be devalued, together with increasing distaste for his moralizing voice and impatience with the "bombast" and excess of his tragedies.

Only since the middle of the twentieth century have Seneca's writings been read in a more positive light once again. Readers have been less concerned with the supposed contradictions and excesses of Seneca's life and writing; and less interested, also, in upholding Seneca as an authoritative moral guide for life. They have been more interested in his systems of thought and the techniques—literary, philosophical, cultural—by which he engaged with his first readers. Seneca was an innovator in, and is our best witness for, the Latin literature of philosophical advising as well as the reshaping of Greek myth in tragic drama. This realization has been among the most exciting recent developments in Latin literary studies.

So read on, and enjoy the eavesdropping. You may not agree with the work that Seneca claims to have done for you and the rest of posterity. But as you read, you will be playing an intimate role in helping this author to keep his head above "the deep waters of time" (*altitudo temporis*) for a little longer.

❧ *How to use this volume*

Each of the four scenarios below focuses on getting to know a single work, although scenarios 1, 2, and 4 conclude with brief follow-up passages from other works. The four scenarios are arranged chronologically (except for the *Medea*, of unknown date), and so you are likely to acquire the most coherent sense of Seneca's life and works through reading them in this order. The scenarios may, however, be read in any order, or they can be selected from, to suit the reader's interests and time available.

In the Commentary, each scenario and each passage has its own brief introduction (including recommendations for further reading), followed by running notes. Specialized meanings of individual words are occasionally discussed in the Commentary, but these are often identified only in the Vocabulary at the back. Grammatical references are for the most part self-contained, except for one or two references to C. E. Bennett, *New Latin Grammar* (Wauconda, Ill., 1998).

For TIMELINE, MAP, and explanations of METER and PROSE RHYTHM, see the three Appendices.

❧ *Suggested reading*

Introductory

Conte, G. B. "Seneca," in *Latin Literature. A History*, trans. J. B. Solodow (Baltimore, 1994) 408–25

Duff, A. M., and J. D. Duff, "Seneca the Philosopher" and "Senecan Satire and Poetry," in *A Literary History of Rome in the Silver Age* (London, 1964) 159–90, 191–223

Essay collections

Bartsch, S. and D. Wray, eds. *Seneca and the Self* (Cambridge, 2009)

Costa, C. D. N., ed. *Seneca* (London, 1974)

Fitch, J. G., ed. *Oxford Readings in Seneca* (Oxford, 2008)

Harrison, G. W. M., ed. *Seneca in Performance* (London, 2000)

Volk, K., and G. Williams, eds. *Seeing Seneca Whole*: *Perspectives on Philosophy, Poetry, and Politics* (Boston, 2006)

Life, career, death

Griffin, M. *Seneca*: *A Philosopher in Politics*, 2nd ed. (Oxford, 1992)

———. "Imago Vitae Suae," in Fitch (2008) 23–58

Habinek, T. N. "Seneca's Renown," in *Classical Antiquity* 19 (2000) 264–303

Ker, J. *The Deaths of Seneca* (Oxford, 2009)

Style

Fantham, E. *Seneca's Troades*: *A Literary Intoduction with Text, Translation, and Commentary* (Princeton, 1982) 92–103

Summers, W. C. "The Language and Style of Seneca's Prose," in *Select Letters of Seneca* (London, 1910) xlii–xcv

Williams, G. D. "Style and Language," in *Seneca*: *De Otio, De Brevitate Vitae* (Cambridge, 2003) 25–32

Philosophy and prose works

Armisen-Marchetti, M. "Imagination and Meditation in Seneca: The Example of the *Praemeditatio*," in Fitch (2008) 102–113

Asmis, E. "Seneca on Fortune and the Kingdom of God," in Bartsch and Wray (2009) 115–38

Edwards, C. "Self-Scrutiny and Self-Transformation in Seneca's Letters," in Fitch (2008) 84–101

Foucault, M. "The Cultivation of the Self," in *The Care of the Self*: *The History of Sexuality*, vol. 3, trans. R. Hurley (New York, 1988) 37–68

Henderson, J. *Morals and Villas in Seneca's Letters*: *Places to Dwell* (Cambridge, 2004)

Inwood, B. *Reading Seneca*: *Stoic Philosophy at Rome* (Oxford, 2005)

Leach, E. W. "The Implied Reader and the Politicial Argument in Seneca's *Apocolocyntosis* and *De Clementia*," in Fitch (2008) 268–98

Wilcox, A. "Exemplary Grief: Gender and Virtue in Seneca's Consolations to Women," *Helios* 33 (2006) 73–100

Williams, G. D. "States of Exile. States of Mind: Paradox and Reversal in Seneca's *Consolatio ad Helviam Matrem*," in Volk and Williams (2006) 147–73

Wilson, M. "Seneca's Epistles to Lucilius: A Revaluation," in Fitch (2008) 59–84

Wright, J. R. G. "Form and Content in the *Moral Essays*," in Costa (1974) 39–69

The tragedies

Boyle, A. J. *Tragic Seneca: An Essay in the Tragic Tradition* (New York, 1997)

———. *Octavia, Attributed to Seneca* (Oxford, 2008)

Fitch, J. G., and S. McElduff, "Construction of the Self in Senecan Drama," in Fitch (2008) 157–80

Guastella, G. "Virgo, Coniunx, Mater: The Wrath of Seneca's Medea," *Classical Antiquity* 20 (2001) 197–219

Herington, C. J. "Senecan Tragedy," *Arion* 5 (1966) 422–71

Littlewood, C. *Self-Representation and Illusion in Senecan Tragedy* (Oxford, 2004)

Nussbaum, M. "Serpents in the Soul: A Reading of Seneca's *Medea*," in J. J. Clauss and S. I. Johnston, eds. *Medea in Myth, Literature, Philosophy, and Art* (Princeton, 1997) 219–47

Schiesaro, A. *The Passions in Play: Thyestes and the Dynamics of Senecan Drama* (Cambridge, 2003)

Star, C. "Commanding *Constantia* in Senecan Tragedy," *Transactions of the American Philological Association* 126 (2006) 207–44

Tarrant, R. J. "Senecan Drama and Its Antecedents," *Harvard Studies in Classical Philology* 82 (1978) 213–63

Reception

Braden, G. *Renaissance Tragedy and the Senecan Tradition* (New Haven, 1985)

Ross, G. M. "Seneca's Philosophical Influence," in Costa (1974) 116–65

Latin editions with commentary

Braund, S. M. *Seneca: De Clementia* (Oxford, 2008)

Duff, J. D. *L. Annaei Senecae Dialogorum libri x, xi, xii / Three Dialogues of Seneca* (Cambridge, 1915) [includes *Consolatio ad Helviam*]

Eden, P. T. *Seneca, Apocolocyntosis* (Cambridge, 1984)

Hine, H. M. *Seneca, Medea* (London, 2000)

Motto, A. L. *Seneca's Moral Epistles* (Wauconda, Ill., 2001)

Summers, W. C. *Select Letters of Seneca* (London, 1910)

Tarrant, R. J. *Seneca's Thyestes* (Atlanta, 1985)

Usher, M. D. *A Student's Seneca: Ten Letters and Selections from De Providentia and De Vita Beata* (Norman, 2006)

Williams, G. D. *Seneca: De Otio, De Brevitate Vitae* (Cambridge, 2003)

Seneca in English

Lucius Annaeus Seneca, Anger, Mercy, Revenge [= *De Ira, De Clementia, Apocolocyntosis*], trans. R. Kaster and M. Nussbaum (Chicago, 2010)

Lucius Annaeus Seneca, Natural Questions, trans. H. Hine (Chicago, 2010)

Lucius Annaeus Seneca, On Benefits, trans. M. Griffin and B. Inwood (Chicago, 2010)

Seneca, Dialogues and Essays, trans. J. Davie (Oxford, 2007)

Seneca, Selected Letters, trans. E. Fantham (Oxford, 2010)

Seneca, Six Tragedies, trans. E. Wilson (Oxford, 2010)

Seneca, Tragedies, 2 vols., trans. J. G. Fitch, Loeb Classical Library, (Cambridge, MA, 2002–2004)

Latin Text

NOTE: I have used the Oxford Classical Text throughout, with the following exceptions: for the *De Clementia* I have used Braund (2008), for the *Apocolocyntosis*, Eden (1984), and for the *De Amicitia*, D. Vottero, *Lucio Anneo Seneca, I frammenti* (Bologna, 1998).

No changes have been made to the text except for the following: at *Helv.* 20.1 I have inserted parentheses followed by a comma, and I have capitalized *Fortuna* at *Helv.* 2.4 (twice), 18.2, and 18.3, to emphasize the personification.

Scenario 1: Seneca in Exile

❧ *CONSOLATIO AD HELVIAM*

1.1–4: The exile writes home

1.1 Saepe iam, mater optima, impetum cepi consolandi te, saepe continui. . . . **2** Cum omnia clarissimorum ingeniorum monumenta ad compescendos moderandosque luctus composita euoluerem, non inueniebam exemplum eius qui consolatus suos
5   esset, cum ipse ab illis comploraretur; ita in re noua haesitabam uerebarque ne haec non consolatio esset sed exulceratio. . . .
4 Vtcumque conitar, non fiducia ingenii, sed quia possum instar efficacissimae consolationis esse ipse consolator.

2.1–3: Justifying an aggressive consolation

2.1 Vide quantum de indulgentia tua promiserim mihi:
potentiorem me futurum apud te non dubito quam dolorem
tuum, quo nihil est apud miseros potentius. Itaque ne statim
cum eo concurram, adero prius illi et quibus excitetur
5 ingeram; omnia proferam et rescindam quae iam obducta
sunt. **2** Dicet aliquis: "quod hoc genus est consolandi, obliterata
mala reuocare et animum in omnium aerumnarum suarum
conspectu conlocare uix unius patientem?" . . . Quid consequar?
ut pudeat animum tot miseriarum uictorem aegre ferre unum
10 uulnus in corpore tam cicatricoso. **3** Fleant itaque diutius et
gemant, quorum delicatas mentes eneruauit longa felicitas, et ad
leuissimarum iniuriarum motus conlabantur: at quorum omnes
anni per calamitates transierunt, grauissima quoque forti et
inmobili constantia perferant. Vnum habet adsidua infelicitas
15 bonum, quod quos semper uexat nouissime indurat.

2.4–5: The mother's many wounds

2.4 Nullam tibi Fortuna uacationem dedit a grauissimis
luctibus, ne natalem quidem tuum excepit: amisisti matrem
statim nata, immo dum nasceris, et ad uitam quodam modo
exposita es. Creuisti sub nouerca, quam tu quidem omni
5 obsequio et pietate, quanta uel in filia conspici potest, matrem
fieri coegisti. . . . Auunculum indulgentissimum, optimum ac
fortissimum uirum, cum aduentum eius expectares, amisisti;
et ne saeuitiam suam Fortuna leuiorem diducendo faceret,
intra tricesimum diem carissimum uirum, ex quo mater trium
10 liberorum eras, extulisti. **5** Lugenti tibi luctus nuntiatus est

omnibus quidem absentibus liberis, quasi de industria in id
tempus coniectis malis tuis ut nihil esset ubi se dolor tuus
reclinaret. Transeo tot pericula, tot metus, quos sine interuallo
in te incursantis pertulisti: modo modo in eundem sinum ex
15 quo tres nepotes emiseras ossa trium nepotum recepisti; intra
uicesimum diem quam filium meum in manibus et in osculis
tuis mortuum funeraueras, raptum me audisti: hoc adhuc
defuerat tibi, lugere uiuos.

3.1–2: A veteran of suffering

3.1 Grauissimum est ex omnibus quae umquam in corpus
tuum descenderunt recens uulnus, fateor; non summam cutem
rupit, pectus et uiscera ipsa diuisit. Sed quemadmodum tirones
leuiter saucii tamen uociferantur et manus medicorum magis
5 quam ferrum horrent, at ueterani quamuis confossi patienter ac
sine gemitu uelut aliena corpora exsaniari patiuntur, ita tu nunc
debes fortiter praebere te curationi. **2** Lamentationes quidem
et eiulatus et alia per quae fere muliebris dolor tumultuatur
amoue; perdidisti enim tot mala, si nondum misera esse
10 didicisti. Ecquid uideor non timide tecum egisse? nihil tibi
subduxi ex malis tuis, sed omnia coaceruata ante te posui.

17.3–5: The consolations of philosophy

17.3 Itaque illo te duco quo omnibus qui fortunam fugiunt
confugiendum est, ad liberalia studia: illa sanabunt uulnus
tuum, illa omnem tristitiam tibi euellent. His etiam si
numquam adsuesses, nunc utendum erat; sed quantum tibi
5 patris mei antiquus rigor permisit, omnes bonas artes non

quidem comprendisti, attigisti tamen. **4** Vtinam quidem
uirorum optimus, pater meus, minus maiorum consuetudini
deditus uoluisset te praeceptis sapientiae erudiri potius quam
inbui! non parandum tibi nunc esset auxilium contra fortunam
10 sed proferendum. Propter istas quae litteris non ad sapientiam
utuntur sed ad luxuriam instruuntur minus te indulgere
studiis passus est. Beneficio tamen rapacis ingenii plus quam
pro tempore hausisti; iacta sunt disciplinarum omnium
fundamenta: nunc ad illas reuertere; tutam te praestabunt.
15 **5** Illae consolabuntur, illae delectabunt, illae si bona fide
in animum tuum intrauerint, numquam amplius intrabit
dolor, numquam sollicitudo, numquam adflictationis inritae
superuacua uexatio. Nulli horum patebit pectus tuum; nam
ceteris uitiis iam pridem clusum est. Haec quidem certissima
20 praesidia sunt et quae sola te fortunae eripere possint.

18.1–3: Comfort in Seneca's brothers

18.1 Sed quia, dum in illum portum quem tibi studia
promittunt peruenis, adminiculis quibus innitaris opus est, uolo
interim solacia tibi tua ostendere. **2** Respice fratres meos, quibus
saluis fas tibi non est accusare Fortunam. In utroque habes quod
5 te diuersa uirtute delectet: alter honores industria consecutus
est, alter sapienter contempsit. Adquiesce alterius fili dignitate,
alterius quiete, utriusque pietate. Noui fratrum meorum intimos
adfectus: alter in hoc dignitatem excolit ut tibi ornamento sit,
alter in hoc se ad tranquillam quietamque uitam recepit ut tibi

10 uacet. **3** Bene liberos tuos et in auxilium et in oblectamentum
Fortuna disposuit: potes alterius dignitate defendi, alterius otio
frui. Certabunt in te officiis et unius desiderium duorum pietate
supplebitur. Audacter possum promittere: nihil tibi deerit
praeter numerum.

20.1–2: Seneca's happy life on Corsica

20.1 Ceterum quia necesse est, cum omnia feceris, cogitationes
tamen tuas subinde ad me recurrere nec quemquam nunc
ex liberis tuis frequentius tibi obuersari (non quia illi minus
cari sunt sed quia naturale est manum saepius ad id referre
5 quod dolet), qualem me cogites accipe: laetum et alacrem
uelut optimis rebus. Sunt enim optimae, quoniam animus
omnis occupationis expers operibus suis uacat et modo se
leuioribus studiis oblectat, modo ad considerandam suam
uniuersique naturam ueri auidus insurgit. **2** Terras primum
10 situmque earum quaerit, deinde condicionem circumfusi
maris cursusque eius alternos et recursus; tunc quidquid inter
caelum terrasque plenum formidinis interiacet perspicit et hoc
tonitribus fulminibus uentorum flatibus ac nimborum niuisque
et grandinis iactu tumultuosum spatium; tum peragratis
15 humilioribus ad summa perrumpit et pulcherrimo diuinorum
spectaculo fruitur, aeternitatis suae memor in omne quod fuit
futurumque est uadit omnibus saeculis.

❧ *Follow-ups to the* CONSOLATIO AD HELVIAM

Epistulae Morales 85.40: Insights on exile as artistic "material"

40 Non ex ebore tantum Phidias sciebat facere simulacra; faciebat ex aere. Si marmor illi, si adhuc uiliorem materiam obtulisses, fecisset quale ex illa fieri optimum posset. Sic sapiens uirtutem, si licebit, in diuitiis explicabit, si minus, in paupertate;

5 si poterit, in patria, si minus, in exilio; si poterit, imperator, si minus, miles; si poterit, integer, si minus, debilis. Quamcumque fortunam acceperit, aliquid ex illa memorabile efficiet.

Consolatio ad Polybium 13.3–4: A plea for clemency

13.3 Interim magnum miseriarum mearum solacium est uidere misericordiam eius totum orbem peruagantem: quae cum ex hoc ipso angulo, in quo ego defixus sum, complures multorum iam annorum ruina obrutos effoderit et in lucem

5 reduxerit, non uereor ne me unum transeat. Ipse autem optime nouit tempus quo cuique debeat succurrere; ego omnem operam dabo ne peruenire ad me erubescat. **4** O felicem clementiam tuam, Caesar, quae efficit ut quietiorem sub te agant uitam exsules quam nuper sub Gaio egere principes!

Scenario 2: Seneca and Nero

∾ *DE CLEMENTIA* (book 1)

1.1: A mirror for the prince

1.1 Scribere de clementia, Nero Caesar, institui, ut quodam
modo speculi uice fungerer et te tibi ostenderem peruenturum
ad uoluptatem maximam omnium. Quamuis enim recte
factorum uerus fructus sit fecisse nec ullum uirtutum pretium
5 dignum illis extra ipsas sit, iuuat inspicere et circumire bonam
conscientiam, tum immittere oculos in hanc immensam
multitudinem discordem, seditiosam, impotentem, in perniciem
alienam suamque pariter exultaturam, si hoc iugum fregerit ***,
et ita loqui secum: . . .

1.2: The emperor recognizes his power

1.2 "Egone ex omnibus mortalibus placui electusque sum, qui
in terris deorum uice fungerer? Ego uitae necisque gentibus
arbiter; qualem quisque sortem statumque habeat, in mea manu
positum est; quid cuique mortalium Fortuna datum uelit,
5 meo ore pronuntiat; ex nostro responso laetitiae causas populi
urbesque concipiunt; nulla pars usquam nisi uolente propitioque
me floret; haec tot milia gladiorum, quae pax mea comprimit,
ad nutum meum stringentur; quas nationes funditus excidi,
quas transportari, quibus libertatem dari, quibus eripi, quos
10 reges mancipia fieri quorumque capiti regium circumdari decus
oporteat, quae ruant urbes, quae oriantur, mea iuris dictio est.

1.3–4: Young Nero's boast

1.3 "In hac tanta facultate rerum non ira me ad iniqua
supplicia compulit, non iuuenilis impetus, non temeritas
hominum et contumacia, quae saepe tranquillissimis quoque
pectoribus patientiam extorsit, non ipsa ostentandae per terrores

5 potentiae dira, sed frequens magnis imperiis, gloria. Conditum,
immo constrictum apud me ferrum est, summa parsimonia
etiam uilissimi sanguinis; nemo non, cui alia desunt, hominis
nomine apud me gratiosus est. **4** Seueritatem abditam, at
clementiam in procinctu habeo; sic me custodio, tamquam

10 legibus, quas ex situ ac tenebris in lucem euocaui, rationem
redditurus sim. Alterius aetate prima motus sum, alterius
ultima; alium dignitati donaui, alium humilitati; quotiens
nullam inueneram misericordiae causam, mihi peperci. Hodie
dis immortalibus, si a me rationem repetant, adnumerare genus

15 humanum paratus sum."

1.5–6: You are your own best model

1.5 Potes hoc, Caesar, audacter praedicare: omnia, quae in
fidem tutelamque tuam uenerunt, tuta haberi, nihil per te
neque ui neque clam adimi rei publicae. Rarissimam laudem
et nulli adhuc principum concessam concupisti, innocentiam.

5 Non perdis operam nec bonitas ista tua singularis ingratos
aut malignos aestimatores nancta est. Refertur tibi gratia;
nemo unus homo uni homini tam carus umquam fuit, quam
tu populo Romano, magnum longumque eius bonum. **6** Sed
ingens tibi onus imposuisti; nemo iam diuum Augustum nec

10 Ti. Caesaris prima tempora loquitur nec quod te imitari uelit

exemplar extra te quaerit; principatus tuus ad gustum exigitur.
Difficile hoc fuisset, si non naturalis tibi ista bonitas esset, sed
ad tempus sumpta. Nemo enim potest personam diu ferre, ficta
cito in naturam suam recidunt; quibus ueritas subest quaeque,
15 ut ita dicam, ex solido enascuntur, tempore ipso in maius
meliusque procedunt.

9.1–3: Augustus and the conspirator

9.1 Hoc quam uerum sit, admonere te exemplo domestico
uolo. Diuus Augustus fuit mitis princeps, si quis illum a
principatu suo aestimare incipiat; in communi quidem
republica gladium mouit. Cum hoc aetatis esset, quod tu nunc
5 es, duodeuicensimum egressus annum, iam pugiones in sinum
amicorum absconderat, iam insidiis M. Antonii consulis latus
petierat, iam fuerat collega proscriptionis. **2** Sed cum annum
quadragensimum transisset et in Gallia moraretur, delatum est
ad eum indicium L. Cinnam, stolidi ingenii uirum, insidias ei
10 struere; dictum est et ubi et quando et quemadmodum adgredi
uellet; unus ex consciis deferebat. **3** Constituit se ab eo uindicare
et consilium amicorum aduocari iussit. Nox illi inquieta erat,
cum cogitaret adulescentem nobilem, hoc detracto integrum,
Cn. Pompei nepotem, damnandum . . .

9.4–6: The emperor's exasperation and Livia's remedy

9.4 Gemens subinde uoces uarias emittebat et inter se
contrarias: "Quid ergo? Ego percussorem meum securum
ambulare patiar me sollicito? . . ." **5** Rursus silentio interposito
maiore multo uoce sibi quam Cinnae irascebatur: "Quid uiuis,

5   si perire te tam multorum interest? Quis finis erit suppliciorum?
    Quis sanguinis? Ego sum nobilibus adulescentulis expositum
    caput, in quod mucrones acuant; non est tanti uita, si, ut ego
    non peream, tam multa perdenda sunt." **6** Interpellauit tandem
    illum Liuia uxor et: "Admittis" inquit "muliebre consilium? Fac,
10 quod medici solent, qui, ubi usitata remedia non procedunt,
    temptant contraria. Seueritate nihil adhuc profecisti . . . Nunc
    tempta, quomodo tibi cedat clementia; ignosce L. Cinnae.
    Deprensus est; iam nocere tibi non potest, prodesse famae tuae
    potest."

9.7–10: Interview with the would-be assassin

    9.7 Gauisus, sibi quod aduocatum inuenerat, uxori quidem
    gratias egit, renuntiari autem extemplo amicis, quos in
    consilium rogauerat, imperauit et Cinnam unum ad se arcessît
    dimissisque omnibus e cubiculo, cum alteram Cinnae poni
5   cathedram iussisset, "Hoc" inquit "primum a te peto, ne me
    loquentem interpelles, ne medio sermone meo proclames;
    dabitur tibi loquendi liberum tempus. **8** Ego te, Cinna, cum in
    hostium castris inuenissem, non factum tantum mihi inimicum
    sed natum, seruaui, patrimonium tibi omne concessi. . . . Cum
10 sic de te meruerim, occidere me constituisti." **9** Cum ad hanc
    uocem exclamasset procul hanc ab se abesse dementiam: "Non
    praestas" inquit "fidem, Cinna; conuenerat ne interloquereris.
    Occidere, inquam, me paras"; adiecit locum, socios, diem,
    ordinem insidiarum, cui commissum esset ferrum. **10** Et cum
15 defixum uideret nec ex conuentione iam, sed ex conscientia

tacentem: "Quo" inquit "hoc animo facis? ut ipse sis princeps?
male mehercules cum populo Romano agitur, si tibi ad
imperandum nihil praeter me obstat. Domum tueri tuam non
potes, nuper libertini hominis gratia in priuato iudicio
20 superatus es . . ."

9.11–12: I forgive you

9.11 Ne totam eius orationem repetendo magnam partem
uoluminis occupem (diutius enim quam duabus horis locutum
esse constat . . .), "Vitam" inquit "tibi, Cinna, iterum do, prius
hosti, nunc insidiatori ac parricidae. Ex hodierno die inter
5 nos amicitia incipiat; contendamus, utrum ego meliore fide
tibi uitam dederim an tu debeas." **12** Post hoc detulit ultro
consulatum questus quod non auderet petere. Amicissimum
fidelissimumque habuit, heres solus illi fuit. Nullis amplius
insidiis ab ullo petitus est.

10.1–3: Augustus lives on

10.1 Ignouit abauus tuus uictis; nam si non ignouisset,
quibus imperasset? . . . **2** Haec eum clementia ad salutem
securitatemque perduxit; haec gratum ac fauorabilem reddidit,
quamuis nondum subactis populi Romani ceruicibus manum
5 imposuisset; haec hodieque praestat illi famam, quae uix uiuis
principibus seruit. **3** Deum esse non tamquam iussi credimus;
bonum fuisse principem Augustum, bene illi parentis nomen
conuenisse fatemur . . .

✧ Follow-ups to the *DE CLEMENTIA*

Apocolocyntosis 10.1–3: The deified Augustus ashamed of his successors

10.1 Tunc diuus Augustus surrexit sententiae suae loco
dicendae, et summa facundia disseruit: "Ego" inquit "p. c.,
uos testes habeo, ex quo deus factus sum, nullum me
uerbum fecisse: semper meum negotium ago. Et non possum
5   amplius dissimulare, et dolorem, quem grauiorem pudor facit,
continere. **2** In hoc terra marique pacem peperi? Ideo ciuilia
bella compescui? Ideo legibus urbem fundaui, operibus ornaui,
ut—quid dicam, p. c., non inuenio: omnia infra indignationem
uerba sunt. Confugiendum est itaque ad Messalae Coruini,
10 disertissimi uiri, illam sententiam "pudet imperii." **3** Hic,
p. c., qui uobis non posse uidetur muscam excitare, tam facile
homines occidebat, quam canis adsidit. . . . **4** . . . Dic mihi,
diue Claudi, quare quemquam ex his, quos quasque occidisti,
antequam de causa cognosceres, antequam audires, damnasti?
15 Hoc ubi fieri solet? In caelo non fit. . . ."

De Ira 1.2.1–3: The costs of anger

2.1 Iam uero si effectus eius damnaque intueri uelis, nulla
pestis humano generi pluris stetit. Videbis caedes ac uenena et
reorum mutuas sordes et urbium clades et totarum exitia
gentium et principum sub ciuili hasta capita uenalia et subiectas
5   tectis faces nec intra moenia coercitos ignes sed ingentia spatia
regionum hostili flamma relucentia. **2** Aspice nobilissimarum
ciuitatum fundamenta uix notabilia: has ira deiecit. Aspice
solitudines per multa milia sine habitatore desertas: has ira

exhausit. Aspice tot memoriae proditos duces mali exempla fati:

10   alium ira in cubili suo confodit, alium intra sacra mensae iura

percussit, alium intra leges celebrisque spectaculum fori

lancinauit, alium filii parricidio dare sanguinem iussit, alium

seruili manu regalem aperire iugulum, alium in cruce membra

diffindere. 3 Et adhuc singulorum supplicia narro: quid si tibi

15   libuerit, relictis in quos ira uiritim exarsit, aspicere caesas gladio

contiones et plebem inmisso milite contrucidatam et in

perniciem promiscuam totos populos capitis damnatos *** ?

Scenario 3: The Drama of Revenge

∾ *MEDEA*

1–18: Calling all gods

MEDEA. Di coniugales tuque genialis tori,

Lucina, custos quaeque domituram freta

Tiphyn nouam frenare docuisti ratem,

et tu, profundi saeue dominator maris,

5   clarumque Titan diuidens orbi diem,   5

tacitisque praebens conscium sacris iubar

Hecate triformis, quosque iurauit mihi

deos Iason, quosque Medeae magis

fas est precari: noctis aeternae chaos,

10   auersa superis regna manesque impios   10

dominumque regni tristis et dominam fide

meliore raptam, uoce non fausta precor.

nunc, nunc adeste sceleris ultrices deae,

crinem solutis squalidae serpentibus,

15 atram cruentis manibus amplexae facem, 15
adeste, thalamis horridae quondam meis
quales stetistis: coniugi letum nouae
letumque socero et regiae stirpi date.

40–50: I'm not a girl anymore

Per uiscera ipsa quaere supplicio uiam, 40
si uiuis, anime, si quid antiqui tibi
remanet uigoris; pelle femineos metus
et inhospitalem Caucasum mente indue.
5 quodcumque uidit Phasis aut Pontus nefas,
uidebit Isthmos. effera ignota horrida, 45
tremenda caelo pariter ac terris mala
mens intus agitat: uulnera et caedem et uagum
funus per artus—leuia memoraui nimis:
10 haec uirgo feci; grauior exurgat dolor:
maiora iam me scelera post partus decent. 50

155–76: Rejecting sensible advice

MEDEA. Leuis est dolor, qui capere consilium potest 155
et clepere sese: magna non latitant mala.
libet ire contra. NVTRIX. Siste furialem impetum,
alumna: uix te tacita defendit quies.
5 MED. Fortuna fortes metuit, ignauos premit.
NVT. Tunc est probanda, si locum uirtus habet. 160
MED. Numquam potest non esse uirtuti locus.
NVT. Spes nulla rebus monstrat adflictis uiam.

MED. Qui nil potest sperare, desperet nihil.

10 NVT. Abiere Colchi, coniugis nulla est fides

nihilque superest opibus e tantis tibi.   165

MED. Medea superest: hic mare et terras uides

ferrumque et ignes et deos et fulmina.

NVT. Rex est timendus. MED. Rex meus fuerat pater.

15 NVT. Non metuis arma? MED. Sint licet terra edita.

NVT. Moriere. MED. Cupio. NVT. Profuge. MED.
    Paenituit fugae.   170

NVT. Medea— MED. Fiam. NVT. Mater es. MED.
    Cui sim uide.

NVT. Profugere dubitas? MED. Fugiam, at ulciscar prius.

NVT. Vindex sequetur. MED. Forsan inueniam moras.

20 NVT. Compesce uerba, parce iam, demens, minis

animosque minue: tempori aptari decet.   175

MED. Fortuna opes auferre, non animum potest.

301–8: Blame the boat

CHORVS. Audax nimium qui freta primus

rate tam fragili perfida rupit

terrasque suas posterga uidens

animam leuibus credidit auris,

5 dubioque secans aequora cursu   305

potuit tenui fidere ligno

inter uitae mortisque uices

nimium gracili limite ducto.

361–79: The Argo's price

Quod fuit huius pretium cursus?	361a
aurea pellis	361b
maiusque mari Medea malum,	
merces prima digna carina.	
5 Nunc iam cessit pontus et omnes	
patitur leges:	365a
non Palladia compacta manu	365b
regum referens inclita remos	
quaeritur Argo—	
10 quaelibet altum cumba pererrat.	
Terminus omnis motus et urbes	
muros terra posuere noua,	370
nil qua fuerat sede reliquit	
peruius orbis:	
15 Indus gelidum potat Araxen,	
Albin Persae Rhenumque bibunt—	
uenient annis saecula seris,	375
quibus Oceanus uincula rerum	
laxet et ingens pateat tellus	
20 Tethysque nouos detegat orbes	
nec sit terris ultima Thule.	

537–50: Finding Jason's weak spot

IASON. . . . Sana meditari incipe	
et placida fare. si quod ex soceri domo	
potest fugam leuare solamen, pete.	
MEDEA. Contemnere animus regias, ut scis, opes	540

5   potest soletque; liberos tantum fugae
    habere comites liceat, in quorum sinu
    lacrimas profundam. te noui gnati manent.
    IAS. Parere precibus cupere me fateor tuis;
    pietas uetat: namque istud ut possim pati,   545
10 non ipse memet cogat et rex et socer.
    haec causa uitae est, hoc perusti pectoris
    curis leuamen. spiritu citius queam
    carere, membris, luce. MED. (*aside*) Sic natos amat?
    bene est, tenetur, uulneri patuit locus.   550

670–93: She's planning something evil

    NVTRIX   Pauet animus, horret: magna pernicies adest.   670
    immane quantum augescit et semet dolor
    accendit ipse uimque praeteritam integrat.
    uidi furentem saepe et aggressam deos,
5   caelum trahentem: maius his, maius parat
    Medea monstrum. namque ut attonito gradu   675
    euasit et penetrale funestum attigit,
    totas opes effundit et quidquid diu
    etiam ipsa timuit promit atque omnem explicat
10 turbam malorum, arcana secreta abdita,
    et triste laeua comparans sacrum manu   680
    pestes uocat quascumque feruentis creat
    harena Libyae quasque perpetua niue
    Taurus coercet frigore Arctoo rigens,
15 et omne monstrum. tracta magicis cantibus
    squamifera latebris turba desertis adest.   685

    hic saeua serpens corpus immensum trahit

    trifidamque linguam exertat et quaerit quibus

    mortifera ueniat: carmine audito stupet

20 tumidumque nodis corpus aggestis plicat

    cogitque in orbes. "Parua sunt" inquit "mala   690

    et uile telum est, ima quod tellus creat:

    caelo petam uenena. iam iam tempus est

    aliquid mouere fraude uulgari altius. . . ."

849–69: Her rage is visible

    CHORVS. Quonam cruenta maenas

    praeceps amore saeuo   850

    rapitur? quod impotenti

    facinus parat furore?

5 uultus citatus ira

    riget et caput feroci

    quatiens superba motu   855

    regi minatur ultro.

      quis credat exulem?

10 Flagrant genae rubentes,

    pallor fugat ruborem.

    nullum uagante forma   860

    seruat diu colorem.

    huc fert pedes et illuc,

15 ut tigris orba natis

    cursu furente lustrat

      Gangeticum nemus.   865

Frenare nescit iras

Medea, non amores;

20   nunc ira amorque causam

iunxere: quid sequetur?

904–15: You ain't seen nothin' yet

MEDEA. . . . quidquid admissum est adhuc,

pietas uocetur. hoc age! en faxo sciant   905

quam leuia fuerint quamque uulgaris notae

quae commodaui scelera. prolusit dolor

5   per ista noster: quid manus poterant rudes

audere magnum, quid puellaris furor?

Medea nunc sum; creuit ingenium malis: 910

iuuat, iuuat rapuisse fraternum caput,

artus iuuat secuisse et arcano patrem

10   spoliasse sacro, iuuat in exitium senis

armasse natas. quaere materiam, dolor:

ad omne facinus non rudem dextram afferes.   915

926–36: A brief return of maternal affection

Cor pepulit horror, membra torpescunt gelu

pectusque tremuit. ira discessit loco

materque tota coniuge expulsa redit.

egone ut meorum liberum ac prolis meae

5   fundam cruorem? melius, a, demens furor!   930

incognitum istud facinus ac dirum nefas

a me quoque absit; quod scelus miseri luent?

scelus est Iason genitor et maius scelus

Medea mater—occidant, non sunt mei;

10 pereant, mei sunt. crimine et culpa carent,   935

sunt innocentes, fateor: et frater fuit.

1008–13: Double infanticide

. . .   IASON. Vnus est poenae satis.

MEDEA. Si posset una caede satiari manus,

nullam petisset. ut duos perimam, tamen   1010

nimium est dolori numerus angustus meo.

5   in matre si quod pignus etiamnunc latet,

scrutabor ense uiscera et ferro extraham.

1018–27: Kill me instead

IASON. Infesta, memet perime. MEDEA. Misereri iubes.—

bene est, peractum est. plura non habui, dolor,

quae tibi litarem. lumina huc tumida alleua,   1020

ingrate Iason. coniugem agnoscis tuam?

5   sic fugere soleo. patuit in caelum uia:

squamosa gemini colla serpentes iugo

summissa praebent. recipe iam gnatos, parens;

ego inter auras aliti curru uehar.   1025

IAS. Per alta uade spatia sublime aetheris,

10 testare nullos esse, qua ueheris, deos.

Scenario 4: Letters to a Friend

❧ *EPISTULAE MORALES 2*

1–2: About your reading habits . . .

SENECA LVCILIO SVO SALVTEM.

1 Ex iis quae mihi scribis et ex iis quae audio bonam spem de te concipio: non discurris nec locorum mutationibus inquietaris. Aegri animi ista iactatio est: primum argumentum
5 compositae mentis existimo posse consistere et secum morari. **2** Illud autem uide, ne ista lectio auctorum multorum et omnis generis uoluminum habeat aliquid uagum et instabile. Certis ingeniis inmorari et innutriri oportet, si uelis aliquid trahere quod in animo fideliter sedeat. Nusquam est qui ubique est.
10 Vitam in peregrinatione exigentibus hoc euenit, ut multa hospitia habeant, nullas amicitias; idem accidat necesse est iis qui nullius se ingenio familiariter applicant sed omnia cursim et properantes transmittunt.

3–4: Watch your "diet"

3 Non prodest cibus nec corpori accedit qui statim sumptus emittitur; nihil aeque sanitatem impedit quam remediorum crebra mutatio; non uenit uulnus ad cicatricem in quo medicamenta temptantur; non conualescit planta quae saepe
5 transfertur; nihil tam utile est ut in transitu prosit. Distringit librorum multitudo; itaque cum legere non possis quantum habueris, satis est habere quantum legas. **4** "Sed modo" inquis "hunc librum euoluere uolo, modo illum." Fastidientis stomachi

est multa degustare; quae ubi uaria sunt et diuersa, inquinant
10   non alunt. Probatos itaque semper lege, et si quando ad alios
deuerti libuerit, ad priores redi. Aliquid cotidie aduersus
paupertatem, aliquid aduersus mortem auxili compara, nec
minus aduersus ceteras pestes; et cum multa percurreris, unum
excerpe quod illo die concoquas.

5–6: Be happy with little

5 Hoc ipse quoque facio; ex pluribus quae legi aliquid
apprehendo. Hodiernum hoc est quod apud Epicurum nanctus
sum (soleo enim et in aliena castra transire, non tamquam
transfuga, sed tamquam explorator): "honesta" inquit "res
5   est laeta paupertas." **6** Illa uero non est paupertas, si laeta est;
non qui parum habet, sed qui plus cupit, pauper est. Quid
enim refert quantum illi in arca, quantum in horreis iaceat,
quantum pascat aut feneret, si alieno imminet, si non acquisita
sed acquirenda computat? Quis sit diuitiarum modus quaeris?
10   primus habere quod necesse est, proximus quod sat est. Vale.

❧ *Epistulae Morales* 40.1: Our letters unite us

SENECA LVCILIO SVO SALVTEM.

1 Quod frequenter mihi scribis gratias ago; nam quo uno
modo potes te mihi ostendis. Numquam epistulam tuam
accipio ut non protinus una simus. Si imagines nobis amicorum
5   absentium iucundae sunt, quae memoriam renouant et

desiderium falso atque inani solacio leuant, quanto iucundiores
sunt litterae, quae uera amici absentis uestigia, ueras notas
adferunt? Nam quod in conspectu dulcissimum est, id amici
manus epistulae inpressa praestat, agnoscere.

❧ *EPISTULAE MORALES* 49.1–3: Memories triggered by a visit to Pompeii

SENECA LVCILIO SVO SALVTEM.

1 Est quidem, mi Lucili, supinus et neglegens qui in amici
memoriam ab aliqua regione admonitus reducitur; tamen
repositum in animo nostro desiderium loca interdum familiaria
5 euocant, nec exstinctam memoriam reddunt sed quiescentem
irritant, sicut dolorem lugentium, etiam si mitigatus est
tempore, aut seruulus familiaris amisso aut uestis aut domus
renouat. Ecce Campania et maxime Neapolis ac Pompeiorum
tuorum conspectus incredibile est quam recens desiderium
10 tui fecerint: totus mihi in oculis es. Cum maxime a te discedo;
uideo lacrimas conbibentem et affectibus tuis inter ipsam
coercitionem exeuntibus non satis resistentem. **2** Modo amisisse
te uideor; quid enim non "modo" est, si recorderis? Modo apud
Sotionem philosophum puer sedi, modo causas agere coepi,
15 modo desii uelle agere, modo desii posse. Infinita est uelocitas
temporis, quae magis apparet respicientibus. Nam ad praesentia
intentos fallit; adeo praecipitis fugae transitus lenis est. **3**
Causam huius rei quaeris? quidquid temporis transît eodem
loco est; pariter aspicitur, una iacet; omnia in idem profundum
20 cadunt. . . .

✣ *EPISTULAE MORALES* 55

1–2: A "stroll" along the seashore

SENECA LVCILIO SVO SALVTEM.

1 A gestatione cum maxime uenio, non minus fatigatus quam si tantum ambulassem quantum sedi; labor est enim et diu ferri, ac nescio an eo maior quia contra naturam est, quae pedes
5 dedit ut per nos ambularemus, oculos ut per nos uideremus. Debilitatem nobis indixere deliciae, et quod diu noluimus posse desîmus. **2** Mihi tamen necessarium erat concutere corpus, ut, siue bilis insederat faucibus, discuteretur, siue ipse ex aliqua causa spiritus densior erat, extenuaret illum iactatio, quam
10 profuisse mihi sensi. Ideo diutius uehi perseueraui inuitante ipso litore, quod inter Cumas et Seruili Vatiae uillam curuatur et hinc mari, illinc lacu uelut angustum iter cluditur. . . .

3–5: But was it *life*?

3 Ex consuetudine tamen mea circumspicere coepi an aliquid illic inuenirem quod mihi posset bono esse, et derexi oculos in uillam quae aliquando Vatiae fuit. In hac ille praetorius diues, nulla alia re quam otio notus, consenuit, et ob hoc unum
5 felix habebatur. . . . exclamabant homines, "o Vatia, solus scis uiuere." **4** At ille latere sciebat, non uiuere; multum autem interest utrum uita tua otiosa sit an ignaua. Numquam aliter hanc uillam Vatia uiuo praeteribam quam ut dicerem, "Vatia hic situs est." Sed adeo, mi Lucili, philosophia sacrum quiddam est
10 et uenerabile ut etiam si quid illi simile est mendacio placeat.

Otiosum enim hominem seductum existimat uulgus et securum
et se contentum, sibi uiuentem, quorum nihil ulli contingere
nisi sapienti potest. Ille solus scit sibi uiuere; ille enim, quod
est primum, scit uiuere. **5** Nam qui res et homines fugit, quem
15 cupiditatum suarum infelicitas relegauit, qui alios feliciores
uidere non potuit, qui uelut timidum atque iners animal metu
oblituit, ille sibi non uiuit, sed, quod est turpissimum, uentri,
somno, libidini; non continuo sibi uiuit qui nemini. Adeo tamen
magna res est constantia et in proposito suo perseuerantia ut
20 habeat auctoritatem inertia quoque pertinax.

8–11: You're right here, Lucilius!

8 Sed non multum ad tranquillitatem locus confert: animus
est qui sibi commendet omnia. Vidi ego in uilla hilari et amoena
maestos, uidi in media solitudine occupatis similes. Quare non
est quod existimes ideo parum bene compositum esse te quod in
5 Campania non es. Quare autem non es? huc usque cogitationes
tuas mitte. **9** Conuersari cum amicis absentibus licet, et quidem
quotiens uelis, quamdiu uelis. . . . **11** Amicus animo possidendus
est; hic autem numquam abest; quemcumque uult cotidie uidet.
Itaque mecum stude, mecum cena, mecum ambula: in angusto
10 uiuebamus, si quicquam esset cogitationibus clusum. Video te,
mi Lucili; cum maxime audio; adeo tecum sum ut dubitem an
incipiam non epistulas sed codicellos tibi scribere. Vale.

～ *Follow-up to the* EPISTULAE MORALES

De Amicitia (fragment 59.5–6 Vottero): A technique for keeping an absent friend in mind

    5 . . . Vna peregrinatio eradit animo ius omne; si uero longior

haec est et longinquior, excidit notitia quoque, non tantum

amicitia. Quod ne possit accidere, omni ope resistamus, et

fugientem memoriam reducamus . . . **6** . . . Imago effingatur

5   animo notabilis et e uiuo petita, non euanida et muta. "Sic

ille manus, sic ora ferebat": adiciamus illi quae magis ad rem

pertinent: sic loquebatur, sic hortabatur, sic deterrebat, sic erat

in dando consilio expeditus, in accipiendo facilis, in mutando

non pertinax; sic solebat beneficia libenter dare, patienter

10 perdere, sic properabat benignitas eius; sic irascebatur, eo

uultu ab amico uincebatur, quo solent uincere: ceteras uirtutes

pererremus, in harum usu tractatuque uersemur.

Commentary

Scenario 1: Seneca in Exile

Seneca was banished to Corsica in 41 and was not pardoned until 49. He appears to have written the *Consolatio ad Helviam* around 42. At this stage in his exile Seneca sought to portray himself as happy, in contrast with later works such as the *Consolatio ad Polybium*, written in 43, in which he pleads for his return, and a certain "book" (now lost), which Dio tells us that Seneca supposedly sent to the empress Messalina and some of Claudius' freedmen, flattering them and seeking his recall (D.C. 60.8).

Seneca doesn't tell us much about the material conditions of his life on Corsica, though it is possible that he was permitted to take his wife with him as well as one or more friends. Corsica itself is a large island, not so very far from Italy (see MAP in Appendix B), and it was not in itself an utterly barren place: as Seneca himself points out in the *Ad Helviam*, the present inhabitants had settled there by choice. A bleak ruin from the Middle Ages, poised atop one of Corsica's highest peaks, has fancifully been identified as the "Tower of Seneca," and clearly some imagination is needed to envisage what his isolation there would have looked like (see Fig. 3).

In the Greek and Roman tradition exile was a virtual death, an annihilation of the person's social identity that might be irreversible. This made for a good literary topic, and Seneca had a number of models to consider, or to allude to, for traditional conceptions of exile and its deprivations. The exile writings of Cicero (in his letters) and of Ovid (in his *Tristia*, "Sorrows," and *Epistulae ex Ponto*, "Letters from the Black Sea") are melancholy dramatizations of the experience of becoming a nobody while trying to remain "somebody," at least through one's lingering reputation back home. Seneca

Fig. 3. Medieval Ruin in the Mountains of Corsica, the So-called "Tower of Seneca" (Torre di Seneca).

occasionally echoes Ovid's melancholy experience of exile directly, such as in the mournful final paragraph of the *Ad Polybium*, where he suggests that life among barbarians has begun to damage his fluency in Latin.

But there were forceful philosophical responses to exile, especially in the form of consolations seeking to counteract the impression that exile was somehow bad, and upholding the ideal of being a "citizen of the world" (Greek *kosmopolitēs*). Such an argument was particularly useful for Greek philosophers in the early Imperial period, when philosophers were intermittently banished from Rome en masse or individually. They had the means to present themselves as quietly powerful in the face of the emperor's dictates. In Seneca's case, the consolation on exile served as an opportunity to advertise his own household as an independent moral and literary institution in its own right. At the heart of Seneca's household is the figure of the enduring mother, Helvia, a symbol of the family's resilience.

The selections from the *Ad Helviam* below come from the preface and the final part of the work. The overall structure of the *Ad Helviam* is very clearly mapped out by Seneca himself. In the preface (*Helv.* 1–4), he explains to his mother that he expects her to overcome her grief just as she has overcome past griefs, even if hearing directly from Seneca may exacerbate her pain. He devotes most of the work (5–13) to outlining the arguments that have convinced him that he himself is not suffering anything bad in exile. For example, he defangs exile by describing it simply as "a change of place" (*loci commutatio*, 6.1). Furthermore, the exile who must change one place for another shares something in common with the divine celestial bodies—the sun, moon, and planets, which are perpetually in motion. Seneca also deploys encouraging examples, such as the travels of Aeneas, whose very foundation of Rome came at the end of a protracted wandering away from his homeland (7.7). Then, having shown Helvia that she need not worry about him, Seneca devotes the final part of the work (14–19) to explaining why she has no grounds for complaint. As we will see, he reminds her of the consolations that can be offered by studying philosophy, and he also encourages her to find comfort in his brothers and the other members of her family who remain unscathed. In the final chapter of the work (20) Seneca turns back to himself, offering Helvia an image of her exiled son luxuriating in contemplation of the skies.

Following the selections below from the *Ad Helviam* are two follow-up passages, one from the *Ad Polybium* that serves as a contrast, and one from the *Epistulae Morales* concerning the wise person as an "artist" who can make something even out of the poor material offered by exile.

For further background on Seneca's exile and on the consolatory tradition, see "Meet the Senecas," "Seneca's life," and "1. Consolations and 'Dialogues'" in the Introduction. Full commentary on the *Ad Helviam* and *Ad Polybium* is given in Duff (1915). For discussion of Seneca's consolations and exile, useful starting points are Williams (2006); Wilcox (2006); and Ker (2009) 87–112.

❧ *CONSOLATIO AD HELVIAM*

1.1–4: The exile writes home

As is usual in a preface, Seneca explains how he came to write the present work, and in this instance he begins by admitting that he has been slow to write. The main reason for this, he explains, is that there is no precedent for a consolation written by the very person whose loss is being mourned. But he also suggests that this aspect of his work may in the end make it especially persuasive.

1 **mater optima** i.e., Helvia. Strictly speaking, Seneca is writing to Helvia in Spain: she had been visiting Seneca in Rome, but had returned to Spain shortly before his banishment.

   impetum . . . consolandi te with *consolandi* gen. gerund governed by *impetum* ("the impulse to console") and taking *te* as direct object

   cepi, continui Both verbs have *impetum* as direct object.

2 **Cum . . . euoluerem** the *cum* clause is either circumstantial ("when") or concessive ("although"). The image is of Seneca going through his library opening one consolation after another in search of a precedent for his present situation. As Duff notes, this suggests that Seneca "in his exile had access to books" (1915, 227).

   monumenta a striking metaphor, referring to great works of literature as if they were carved in stone; in addition, however, given its etymological connection to the verb *monere*, the term *monumenta* may hint at the works' dispensing of "advice."

ad compescendos moderandosque luctus *ad* + acc. gerundive expressing purpose. The two verbs allude to slight differences in traditional consolatory theories: some philosophers thought that grief could be entirely suppressed, whereas others thought it best to aim simply to alleviate it (cf. Cicero, *Tusculanae Disputationes* 3.75–79).

non inueniebam exemplum Seneca emphasizes the unprecedented nature of the present work. Analogous claims to uniqueness had been made by Cicero, who claimed that his own *Consolatio*, which he wrote for himself after the death of his daughter Tullia, was the first ever self-addressed consolation (*Ad Atticum* 12.14.3).

consolatus suos esset The direct object *suos* is embedded within the verb *consolatus est*, in an "iconic" mirroring of the consoler's embrace; *suos* refers loosely to all those close to the person, but especially to his or her family members.

cum ipse . . . comploraretur emphasizes the paradox of the "departed" person who is a consoler, which is possible in Seneca's case because he is only in exile.

in re noua "in such a novel situation"

ne haec non consolatio esset a negated fear clause following *uerebar*: "I was afraid that this would not be a consolation . . ."

exulceratio The term suggests a violent reopening of wounds, a metaphor that will continue in following sections as Seneca in fact adopts an aggressive approach to Helvia's grief. In the following lines (here omitted), Seneca acknowledges the dangers of premature therapy; he also compares himself to a dead man rising up from the funeral pyre and struggling to find appropriate words for addressing his own mourners.

4   **Vtcumque** "in any event"

conitar fut. indicative

fiducia ingenii "because I have faith in my rhetorical ability"; *fiducia* is abl. of cause; *ingenii* is objective gen.

instar efficacissimae consolationis "equal to the most effective consolation." In the work as a whole, Seneca will console Helvia above all through showing that he himself experiences no grief over his exile.

ipse consolator "being the consoler myself"

2.1–3: Justifying an aggressive consolation

Seneca warns Helvia that he will be adopting a harsh method, exacerbating her feelings of pain and reopening old wounds, and he knows that some observers will question this tactic. But someone who has endured as much as Helvia has in her lifetime should be embarrassed to yield now.

1   **quantum . . . promiserim mihi** an indirect question introduced by *Vide*, with *promiserim* pf. subjunctive: "what a great gift I have promised myself from your indulgence" (trans. Davie). In this economic image, Seneca presents himself as freely drawing on the coffers of maternal affection that he can presuppose in Helvia.

me futurum . . . non dubito "I have no doubt that I will be . . . ," introducing a future indirect statement with *me* the acc. subject and *futurum (esse)* the infinitive

apud te "over you"

dolorem tuum almost personifies Helvia's *dolor* as a rival with whom Seneca will enter into a contest.

quo abl. of comparison with *potentius*; the antecedent of *quo* is *dolor* in general.

ne statim . . . concurram, adero prius illi Seneca wants to add to Helvia's *dolor* further before going into combat against it.

eo . . . illi The antecedent for both words is *dolorem tuum*.

quibus excitetur rel. clause of characteristic; the antecedent of *quibus* is the implied object of *ingeram,* as if Seneca had written *ea ingeram quibus excitetur.*

obducta sunt "have scarred over"

2   **Dicet aliquis** Seneca introduces an imaginary speaker who
         objects to his method.

         hoc genus . . . consolandi "this method of consolation, name-
         ly . . . ." The speaker then goes on to define the method in the
         following long clause.

         animum direct object of *conlocare*

         omnium aerumnarum suarum objective gen. governed by *in
         . . . conspectu* ("in sight of . . .")

         unius objective gen. with *animum . . . uix . . . patientem* ("the
         mind . . . scarcely enduring . . ."); *unius* refers to "a single (mis-
         fortune)"

         ut pudeat animum . . . a substantive clause governed by *con-
         sequar* in the preceding rhetorical question. Seneca responds
         to the objector, and to Helvia, by emphasizing the shame in
         breaking down now, when she has endured so much so well
         before.

         tot miseriarum objective gen. with *uictorem*: "conqueror of
         so many tragedies"

         uulnus . . . cicatricoso Seneca exploits the vivid language of
         bodily wounds and scars to characterize the emotional expe-
         rience of loss, grief, and endurance.

3   **Fleant . . . et gemant** The subject is the implied antecedent
         of *quorum*: "Let those ones weep . . . and groan, whose . . . ";
         Fleant is first in a series of jussive subjunctives. For an analysis
         of the sound and sense of this passage, see on PROSE RHYTHM
         in Appendix C.

         ad . . . motus "in response to the tremors"

         inmobili a clear contrast to *motus*

         constantia "consistency"; an important ideal of Seneca's mor-
         al writings, by which someone is reminded of their bravery in
         the past, and the need to continue it in the present and future.
         See also *Clem.* 1.1.6 and *Ep.* 55.5 below.

         perferant The subject is the implied antecedent of *quorum*:
         "those whose . . . , let them endure."

Vnum . . . bonum acc. sing. "one good thing"; *bonum* (or *bona*) is frequently substantive in Seneca. Here *bonum* introduces the *quod* clause: "namely, the fact that . . . ."

indurat The image is suggestive of calluses created by toil.

2.4–5: The mother's many wounds

Seneca intensifies his appeal to Helvia by cataloguing the many deaths of family members she has endured. The climax of her sufferings (and of the passage) is Seneca's banishment, even though it does not involve death at all.

4 **Fortuna** here depicted as a sadistic agent, seeking out the most painful combination of injuries for Helvia

grauissimis the first of several superlatives that will add to the emotional intensity of Seneca's account

luctibus a key term for the passage (along with *lugere*), encompassing both the initial causes of grief (i.e., death, exile) and the grieving process that ensues in each case

ne natalem quidem "not even the day of your birth." Helvia's dates are uncertain, but she was probably born sometime before 25 BCE, making her over 65 at the time of writing.

amisisti . . . Creuisti . . . coegisti the repetition of the same verb ending *-isti* (*homeoteleuton*) emphasizes the incessant suffering and Helvia's consistent endurance. The repetition continues through 2.4–5, where it is intensified both by the sentence-final position of the verbs and by the recurrence of compounds of *mitto* (*amisisti, amisisti, emiseras*) and *fero* (*extulisti, pertulisti*).

statim nata "as soon as you were born"; *nata* is nom. sing. f.

immo introduces a correction to *statim nata*: the mother's death took place *during* Helvia's birth.

dum nasceris regular construction of *dum* + pres. with past sense

quodam modo "in a certain sense," qualifying the stark image of *ad uitam . . . exposita es*, which evokes an unwanted infant being abandoned to the elements

sub nouerca "under the tutelage of a stepmother." In literary contexts stepmothers were typically viewed as unsympathetic parents, and often regarded with suspicion.

quam direct object of *coegisti*

omni obsequio et pietate, quanta . . . potest The antecedent of *quanta* is *omni obsequio et pietate*, but *quanta* has been attracted into the gender of the closest noun, *pietate*.

uel in filia "even in a daughter," i.e., far beyond her obligations as a stepdaughter

Auunculum . . . amisisti Nothing further is known about Helvia's uncle or his death; his failure to arrive (cf. *aduentum*) may suggest death at sea.

ne . . . Fortuna . . . faceret negative purpose clause. Seneca comments further on Fortune's seemingly deliberate cruelty.

diducendo abl. gerund: "by spacing out"

carissimum uirum i.e., Seneca the Elder, who died around 38–40 CE. On the Elder's relationship to Helvia, see 17.3–5 below.

trium liberorum i.e., Novatus, Seneca the Younger, and Mela. Seneca writes further about his brothers at 18.1–3 below.

5   **Lugenti tibi luctus . . .** refers to the quick succession of grief over her uncle followed by grief over her husband.

nuntiatus est Her husband was probably in Italy when he died, whereas Helvia would have been in Spain.

omnibus . . . absentibus liberis abl. absolute, referring to Seneca and his brothers, who were probably all in Italy at the time of their father's death

quasi . . . coniectis malis tuis "as if all your woes were made to coincide . . ."; an abl. absolute introducing its own purpose clause in *ut nihil esset*

de industria an idiom: "deliberately," here reinforcing the emphasis of *quidem*

in id tempus "into that moment," referring to the brief period of time within which her uncle and her husband died

ubi . . . reclinaret rel. clause of characteristic or purpose. Seneca's choice of the verb *reclinaret* suggests a personification of Helvia's *dolor*, as if it were looking in vain for somewhere to hide from further exacerbation.

in te "against you," with *te* acc.

incursantis acc. pl. m. agreeing with *quos*

modo modo The repetition intensifies the meaning and emotion of *modo*: "just recently."

in eundem sinum "into the very same lap"; Seneca presents a vivid and emotional image of Helvia's bodily actions first as nurturer, then as mourner.

tres nepotes includes Seneca's son mentioned in the following sentence, and two other unknown grandchildren.

emiseras i.e., she had finished caring for them as infants

ossa . . . recepisti The bones of the deceased were collected from the funeral pyre after cremation (*ossilegium*), in preparation for burial (cf. Duff 1915, 231).

intra uicesimum diem quam "less than twenty days after the time when"

raptum infinitive with *esse* implied; a violent image for Seneca's banishment, evoking again the familiar idea of exile as death

audisti syncopated from *audiuisti*. Helvia had been visiting Italy until three days before Seneca's banishment, and so she only heard about it after leaving for Spain (cf. *Helv.* 15.2).

hoc "this . . . , namely"; *hoc* nom. is the subject of *defuerat* and anticipates the clause *lugere uiuos* that follows.

lugere uiuos captures the paradoxical idea of exiles as alive but also "dead" to their community.

3.1–2: A veteran of suffering

Long practice has given Helvia the stamina to endure now. By encouraging Helvia to think of herself as like an older soldier toughened by experience, Seneca pushes her away from stereotypes of feminine emotional weakness.

1   **ex omnibus** "of all (those wounds)," equivalent to gen. of the whole. Seneca's exceptional emphasis on Helvia's present challenge incidentally glorifies *him* in two ways: his sufferings cause her the greatest pain and his consolation will conquer the greatest adversary.

recens uulnus i.e., the news of Seneca's banishment. The image of the wound is developed in vivid detail over the following lines, somewhat beyond the traditional image of a mourning woman mutilating her body.

quemadmodum . . . ita a simile: "just as . . . so too . . . ." The simile focuses on the differences between young and old soldiers, not on the battlefield but when undergoing surgery in the military hospital.

tamen goes closely with *uociferantur*, drawing a contrast with *leuiter*.

manus acc. pl., in a comparison with *ferrum*

at "whereas," drawing the contrast between *tirones* and *ueterani*

quamuis goes closely with *confossi*.

uelut aliena corpora exsaniari patiuntur "allow their bodies to be drained as if they were someone else's"; the verb *patiuntur* echoes the adv. *patienter*.

fortiter makes explicit Helvia's need for a kind of soldierly "courage."

curationi Seneca's most explicit characterization of his work as a form of quasi-medical care—though attending not to Helvia's literal body, but to the "wounds" in her mind

2   **Lamentationes ... eiulatus ... alia** all direct objects of *amoue*

quidem "at the very least"

fere This adv. couches the statement about *muliebris dolor* as a generalization.

perdidisti ... didicisti The idea is that Helvia's earlier griefs were valuable lessons in endurance, which she should not squander.

misera esse lit. "to be wretched," but really "to endure suffering"

non goes closely with *timide*: "without holding back."

ex malis tuis "of your woes," equivalent to gen. of the whole

omnia i.e., *omnia mala tua*

coaceruata The image recalls his promise above that he would "heap up" (*ingeram*) memories to provoke her grief (*Helv.* 2.1).

17.3–5: The consolations of philosophy

In the intervening chapters omitted here, Seneca had already explained that philosophy prevented him from being harmed by his exile: indeed, he is perfectly happy. He then began encouraging Helvia herself by pointing out the uselessness of certain distractions that people sometimes turn to, such as watching gladiators in the amphitheater or going on an overseas journey (17.1–2). Now he recommends that she return to the philosophical studies she had dabbled in earlier in her life, because they will provide the best remedy to her grief.

3   **illo ... quo** "to that place ... to which," anticipating *ad liberalia studia*

omnibus "by everyone"; dat. of agent with gerundive

confugiendum est impers. pass. periphrastic gerundive: "a retreat must be made (to)" or "refuge must be taken (in)"

liberalia studia in this context Seneca means philosophy, though the term *studia liberalia* was also applied to the broader set of studies that included grammar, geometry, music, etc.

illa . . . illa anaphoric repetition, emphasizing the wonderful benefits of *studia*

His again referring to *studia*; either dat. with *adsuesses* or abl. with *utendum erat*

adsuesses syncopated form of *adsueuisses*

utendum erat impers. pass. periphrastic gerundive, "it would have been necessary to use them"; here *erat* is strictly speaking indicative, but indicative is quite typical in a periphrastic in the apodosis of a contrafactual conditional (cf. Bennett 304.3b).

quantum "as much as"

patris mei antiquus rigor Seneca gently portrays his deceased father, Seneca the Elder, as old fashioned in his suspicion both of women's learning and of philosophy. Seneca mentions elsewhere that as a young man he took up vegetarianism for philosophical reasons, but then gave it up *patre . . . meo rogante, qui . . . philosophiam oderat* ("at the request of my father, who hated philosophy," *Ep.* 108.22). On this and other aspects of Seneca's relationship with his father, see "Meet the Senecas" in the Introduction.

4   **Vtinam** introduces the optative subjunctive *uoluisset*: "If only he had wanted."

minus modifies *deditus*: "less devoted." Seneca also creates wordplay by juxtaposing *minus* with *maiorum*.

praeceptis abl. of means

parandum . . . proferendum two pass. periphrastic gerundives, both taken with *esset* and both with *auxilium* as subject. The contrast is between the present situation, in which Helvia in fact has to acquire (*parare*) philosophy to begin with, and the imagined ideal situation, in which she would already have had it and would only need to apply it (*proferre*).

istas "those women," referring harshly to women who had given learning a bad name by their abuse of it

ad sapientiam with *ad* expressing purpose

passus est The implicit subject is Seneca's father.

Beneficio lit. "on account of the benefit (of)" + gen., by extension here "thanks to . . ."

plus quam pro tempore lit. "more than was proportionate to the time," i.e., quickly in a short time

hausisti the implicit object is *studia*.

illas i.e., *disciplinas* (or, more generally, *bonas artes*)

reuertere pres. second person sing. imperative of deponent verb

5   **Illae . . . illae . . . illae** echoes the anaphoric repetition at the beginning of the passage, but now in a rising tricolon, followed by another tricolon in *numquam . . . numquam . . . numquam*, itself culminating in the extravagant noun phrase *adflictationis . . . uexatio*. See further on "Anaphoric repetition" in the Introduction.

illae si Strictly *illae* belongs within the protasis, as if Seneca had written *si illae*.

intrabit The verb is shared by all three nominatives: *dolor, sollicitudo, uexatio*.

horum i.e., the three problems just mentioned: *dolor, sollicitudo, uexatio*

iam pridem Seneca appeals to Helvia's longstanding record of good morality.

ceteris uitiis . . . clusum est "is closed off to the other vices" (dat. of disadvantage)

clusum est The subject is *pectus tuum*.

Haec i.e., philosophical studies; although Seneca had been referring to these with f. pl. (*illae* above), now the subject is assimilated to the n. gender of the predicate noun *praesidia*.

et quae sola . . . possint here *sola* is drawn into the rel. clause, but treat as if it were written *et sola quae . . . possint*: "and the only ones which can . . . ."

18.1–3: Comfort in Seneca's brothers

Seneca now turns to reminding Helvia of the "comforts" (*solacia*) that still remain to her, and he begins by pointing out that his two brothers are still safe. He exploits the contrast between the lifestyles of Novatus and Mela to offer Helvia a dual remedy that can help her even while he himself is absent. On Seneca's brothers, see "Meet the Senecas" in the Introduction.

1   **dum . . . peruenis** "until you arrive"; i.e., the path of philosophy will provide total relief, but it will take some time

     adminiculis abl. with *opus est*

     quibus abl. with *innitaris*

     solacia "comforts," one of the three major components of consolation, along with *praecepta* ("arguments") and *exempla* ("examples"). Here *solacia* effectively refers to the persons themselves who can serve as comforts or as substitutes for the one who has been lost.

     ostendere strongly visual language, continued in the next sentence with *Respice*

2   **fratres meos** i.e., Novatus and Mela

     quibus saluis abl. absolute

     fas . . . non est a stern reminder on the wrongness of being ungrateful for the sons she still has. To be ungrateful would be a violation of maternal *pietas*.

     accusare fortunam i.e., to assert that Fortune has been unfair to her, when in fact she enjoys good fortune also

     in utroque "in both my brothers"

     habes quod i.e., "you have something that . . . ," introducing rel. clause of characteristic

     alter . . . alter "the one . . . the other," referring to Novatus and Mela respectively

     honores i.e., political honors such as magistracies

sapienter suggests a philosophical motivation behind Mela's avoidance of politics.

Adquiesce "take comfort (in)," governing abl. in *dignitate, quiete, pietate*

in hoc "for this purpose, namely . . . ," anticipating *ut . . .* ; *hoc* is acc.

tibi ornamento double dat.: "a source of pride for you"

3   **in auxilium** with *in* expressing purpose

dignitate defendi i.e., since Novatus' political standing would make him a powerful protector of her interests

Certabunt The subject is the two brothers.

in te probably goes closely with *officiis* ("by their duties toward you"), with *te* acc.

unius desiderium objective gen.: "your longing for one" (i.e., for me)

duorum pietate subjective gen.: "by the dutifulness of two"

nihil . . . praeter numerum i.e., Seneca's banishment reduces the number of Helvia's family members, but not the family's overall composition

20.1–2: Seneca's happy life on Corsica

In some omitted chapters Seneca mentioned other family members who can serve as comforts. Now, however, he concludes the whole work by explaining to Helvia how she should picture his life on Corsica. His closing image of a mind liberated from all limitations and investigating the natural world foreshadows Seneca's own writing in the *Naturales Quaestiones*.

1   **Ceterum** "but"

necesse est introduces acc. and infinitive clauses, beginning with *cogitationes . . . recurrere.*

cum . . . feceris concessive, as signaled by *tamen*; *feceris* is pf. subjunctive. The idea is that, no matter what else Helvia does (such as spending time with his brothers), she will inevitably return to thinking about Seneca.

nec quemquam "and that no one"

ex liberis tuis "of your children," equivalent to gen. of the whole

illi i.e., her other sons

naturale est introduces infinitive *referre*; the implicit subject of *referre* is either Helvia or a generalized "one." The image of hand and wound recalls Seneca's earlier wound metaphors and medical comparisons, beginning from *Helv.* 1.2 above.

qualem . . . cogites indirect question, corresponding to an implied original question with jussive or deliberative subjunctive. Translate: "how you should imagine me."

accipe "hear"

optimis rebus abl. absolute referring to attendant circumstances

Sunt enim emphatic word order: "For they *are* . . . ." The implied subject is *res.*

omnis occupationis gen. governed by *expers*

modo . . . modo "now . . . now," i.e., "at one moment . . . at another"

operibus suis i.e., the activities specific to the mind, such as contemplation

leuioribus studiis perhaps refers to poetry or other pursuits that help to pass the time. Elsewhere Seneca alludes to the fact that Socrates in prison converted Aesopic fables into verse (*Polyb.* 8.3). Some scholars have suspected (though there is no way to verify) that the studies mentioned here may have included some of the tragedies, written in exile.

suam universique naturam "one's own and the universe's nature," i.e., one's own rational nature as a human being and the system of nature writ large

ueri objective gen. with *auidus*: "greedy for truth"

insurgit The image of rising informs the following sketch of mental elevation.

2   **primum . . . deinde . . . tunc . . . tum** Seneca sketches a rising sequence of mental (and strongly visual) activities, beginning from the earth and ending in the heavens.

eius i.e., of the sea

quidquid subject of *interiacet* and modified by *plenum*

formidinis gen. with *plenum*, lit. "full of fear," i.e., "inspiring much fear." The region between earth and sky is the source of many terrifying meteorological phenomena, which Seneca will now list.

hoc acc. sing. n. agreeing with *spatium*, bracketing a remarkable clause consisting entirely of nouns and adjs.

tonitribus fulminibus . . . flatibus . . . ac . . . iactu all abl. going with *tumultuosum*, "tempestuous with . . . ." The first three nouns, *tonitribus*, *fulminibus*, and *flatibus*, are in asyndeton.

nimborum niuisque et grandinis three forms of precipitation (rain, snow, hail), all to be taken closely with *iactu*

humilioribus and **summa** refer to the "lowest regions" and "highest regions" of the universe.

aeternitatis suae memor The spectacle of the divine regions of the universe reminds the mind of its own divinity and longevity, its kinship with the divine breath that permeates all things; here *memor* agrees with the implicit subject, *animus*.

in omne . . . uadit "ventures confidently into everything"

omnibus saeculis "over all the ages," using abl. of time (or space) throughout which—a common use in Seneca and his contemporaries (cf. Bennett 231.1)

∾ *Follow-ups to the* CONSOLATIO AD HELVIAM

Epistulae Morales 85.40: Insights on exile as artistic "material"

In this passage from his letters, Seneca explains how the wise person can "sculpt" something from any misfortune, even from exile. The passage comes from the end of a letter in which Seneca has been arguing that, for the Stoic wise person, virtue on its own is sufficiently "effective" (*efficax*) to ensure a happy life (*Ep.* 85.1). Now Seneca introduces the Greek sculptor Phidias as a comparison for the wise person: both can "fashion" (*efficere*) something even out of poor material. This discussion would inevitably have reminded readers of Seneca's own *Ad Helviam* as a creative response to the poor material of his exile—especially, perhaps, in light of Seneca's reference to the earlier works of the consolatory tradition as "monuments" (*monumenta*) at *Helv.*1.2.

40   **Non . . . tantum** "not only," creating a contrast between *ex ebore* and *ex aere*

Phidias: One of the greatest and most versatile Athenian artists, Phidias was an architect, painter, and (principally) sculptor, flourishing in the fifth century BCE in the time of Pericles. His best known works included two ivory-and-gold statues, of Athena Parthenos on the Acropolis, and of Zeus at Olympia.

faciebat ex aere "also" is implied; the object *simulacra* is carried over from the previous clause.

Si marmor illi The acc. *marmor* is direct object of the verb *obtulisses* shared with the following clause.

adhuc uiliorem materiam "a still cheaper material," i.e., than marble, which itself is inferior to the already mentioned ivory and bronze

optimum The superl. is drawn into the rel. clause; translate as if Seneca had written *optimum quale*, "the best sort of thing which."

illa i.e., *illa materia*

fieri here functions as the pass. of *facere*, "be made."

Sic "in the same way," drawing the analogy between Phidias and the wise person

uirtutem . . . explicabit The idea is that of exercising and exhibiting one's virtue in action.

si minus i.e., "if not"

imperator . . . miles "as a commander . . . as a soldier"

quamcumque fortunam i.e., whether good fortune or bad fortune

acceperit fut. pf., preceding in time the simple fut. of *efficiet*

Consolatio ad Polybium 13.3–4: A plea for clemency

In a work ostensibly meant to console Polybius for the death of his brother, Seneca here digresses to express his hope that Claudius will pardon him and allow him to return to Rome, just as he has pardoned others. Polybius, as Claudius' secretary, is imagined to be able to help persuade the emperor. The passage contrasts starkly with the *Ad Helviam* and its image of Seneca happy on Corsica.

3   **Interim** i.e., while Seneca remains in exile

magnum . . . solacium est indicates that Seneca is offering himself a form of consolation, with this thought about Claudius serving as a "comfort."

eius i.e., Claudius'

totum orbem peruagantem the image compares Claudius' *misericordia* to a traveler who goes around the world liberating men from exile. The thought here implicitly resembles Stoic divine reason permeating the universe.

quae "this," i.e., Claudius' *misericordia*; subject of the *cum* clause

cum here introducing a causal clause: "seeing as . . ."

ex hoc ipso angulo i.e., from Corsica; *ex* goes closely with the sense of rescue in *effoderit* and *reduxerit*.

angulo and **defixus sum** These terms give a negative characterization to Seneca's experience of exile; compare his decla-
ration elsewhere that, for the wise person, *nullus angustus est
locus* ("no place is constraining," *Helv.* 9.3).

complures acc. pl. m. We learn from Suetonius that "certain
exiles" (*exulibus quibusdam*) had been pardoned by Claudius
during this time (*Diuus Claudius*, 17.3).

multorum . . . annorum ruina "a ruin (i.e., exile) of many
years," gen. of description; *ruina* is abl. of means modifying
obrutos.

effoderit et in lucem reduxerit i.e., as if exhuming them from
the live burial of exile

Ipse refers deferentially to Claudius.

tempus quo . . . debeat "the time at which he should . . . ," an
indirect question; *quo* is abl. of time when.

ego emphatic, drawing attention to Seneca's own efforts to
behave acceptably and save Claudius from regretting his leni-
ency toward Seneca

4   **O felicem clementiam tuam, Caesar** exclamatory acc. followed by a direct address (*apostrophē*) to Claudius. The appeal to *clementia* stands in contrast to the cruelty of the previous emperor, Caligula.

nuper sub Gaio Gaius/Caligula was assassinated just two
years earlier, in 41, after a reign in which numerous "leading men" (the meaning of *principes* here) were tortured and
killed. Seneca's rhetorical point is that it is better to be an exile
under Claudius than it was to be a resident of Rome under
Caligula.

egere syncopated form of *egerunt*, third person pl. pf. indicative act. of *ago*

Scenario 2: Seneca and Nero

The *De Clementia* dates to 55–56 CE, at least a year into Nero's reign, when the emperor was around nineteen. Although this is the one surviving work of Seneca's that explicitly addresses an emperor, Seneca was not exclusively concerned with instructing Nero, but also with showing the Roman elite that he was doing so.

Already in antiquity, and continuing into the Italian Renaissance, the *De Clementia* was an influential model for writers or statesmen who wanted both to give advice and to be *seen* to be giving advice. In the modern era, a 1904 sculpture by Eduardo Barrón invites us to witness the advising scene with our own eyes, depicting Nero as Seneca's thoughtful (or reluctant?) pupil (Fig. 4).

We possess one book of the *De Clementia* plus the beginning of a second book, and it is uncertain exactly how the work proceeded beyond this (or indeed, if it was ever finished). The first book is

Fig. 4. Seneca and Nero. Bronze Sculpture, Cordoba, Spain, after Plaster Sculpture by Eduardo Barrón (1904).

devoted to explaining to Nero why clemency is often a better policy than severe punishment—an argument that has as much to do with protection of the state and protection of the emperor (an argument from utility) as it does with doing what is right (a moral argument).

One major theme of book 1 is the relationship between the emperor and his people, which is compared to the mutual dependency between mind and body: "Just as the whole body serves the mind . . . , so too, this immense multitude surrounding the life of one man is ruled by his breath and steered by his reason, and will crush itself and break itself by its own strength, unless it is thoughtfully managed" (*Clem.* 1.3.5). The imagery here recalls not only the mind-body dualism of ancient philosophy after Plato, but also specific Stoic theories about the divine breath that permeates the cosmos.

Another theme is the distinction between king and tyrant, a dichotomy that is articulated in numerous ways: "Tyrant and king share the same appearance of good fortune and the same liberties, but what distinguishes them is that tyrants become enraged for pleasure, but kings only when it is justified and necessary" (*Clem.* 1.11.3). The emphasis on pleasure as distinguishing the tyrant is interesting, in light of Seneca's opening sentence of the whole work: as we will see, Seneca mentions the pleasure Nero will feel—evidently a more honorable form of pleasure—when he inspects his own good conscience.

The selection below begins with the opening of the work (1.1), in which Seneca presents himself as a "mirror" who can show Nero the beauty of his virtuous rule so far, and the extent of his responsibilities over the empire. We then shift to a later section (1.9–10) in which Seneca retells the somewhat ambivalent example of Nero's great-great-grandfather, the emperor Augustus, who adopted clemency only late in life.

Two follow-up passages have been included to offer comparisons with the *De Clementia*: an excerpt from the *Apocolocyntosis* in which the deified Augustus speaks in a satirical council of the gods on Olympus, and a sequence from the beginning of the *De Ira* that sketches out anger's horrific consequences.

For further background on Seneca's political writings and their historical context, see "Seneca's life" and "Political works" in the Introduction. A comprehensive introduction, translation, and commentary on the *De Clementia* can be found in Braund (2008). For discussion of the work and its historical context, see Leach (2008) and Griffin (1992) 129–71.

∾ *De Clementia (book 1)*

1.1: A mirror for the prince

Seneca begins the preface by explaining the purpose of his work: he will be discussing clemency in order to help Nero observe himself and see his reign in a positive light. To secure Nero's goodwill (using the rhetorical device known as *captatio beneuolentiae*), Seneca begins with copious praise of Nero's virtuous rule. But he also hints at certain dangers that Nero will need to work hard to avoid.

1   **Nero Caesar** a very direct address to the young emperor. His full name was Nero Claudius Caesar Augustus Germanicus, changed from his birth name L. Domitius Ahenobarbus after his adoption by Claudius in 49.

    quodam modo "in a certain sense," qualifying Seneca's use of the somewhat unusual mirror metaphor

    speculi uice "the role of a mirror"; *uice* is abl. with *fungerer*. The mirror metaphor evokes many associations that are not necessarily in harmony with one another. In the *Naturales Quaestiones*, Seneca describes how the earliest human beings first saw themselves reflected in water or other natural surfaces, and observes that "mirrors were invented so that human beings could know themselves" (*inuenta sunt specula, ut homo ipse se nosset, NQ* 1.17.4); but he also recounts the increasingly luxurious materials from which mirrors came to be made and the decadent and narcissitic uses to which they were put, including cosmetics and sexual stimulation.

    fungerer The first person may suggest that Seneca himself is the "mirror."

te . . . ostenderem peruenturum "to show you . . . as destined to arrive"

uoluptatem a term suggesting the joy that the wise person always feels, but also exploiting the young man's inclination toward self-admiration

Quamuis introduces the following clause up to *extra ipsas sit*; we might paraphrase, "although virtue is its own reward."

recte factorum strongly participial: "of things done rightly"

fecisse "simply to have done them"

uirtutum pretium objective gen.: "reward for the virtues"

dignum illis . . . sit "is worthy of them (i.e., the virtues)"

ipsas i.e., the virtues

iuuat "it is pleasing for one to . . ."; the implied subject of the infinitives is a generalized third person (cf. *secum* below), though it obviously implies Nero.

inspicere et circumire an image of military inspection

conscientiam a concept of introspective self-witnessing, which Seneca often emphasizes as more important than one's external "reputation" (*opinio, fama*)

tum immittere oculos in hanc . . . multitudinem Seneca re-directs Nero's gaze from himself to his subjects, and intro-duces a more practical consideration: the risk of violence in a population that is potentially like a mob or an animal.

impotentem "uncontrolled," i.e., exercising no power over itself

in perniciem alienam suamque pariter "to the destruction of others and equally of itself," following from *exultaturam*

exultaturam, si . . . fregerit a future-more-vivid conditional, except that in the apodosis a fut. pple. stands in for fut. indica-tive; *exultaturam* agrees with *multitudinem*.

hoc iugum acc.: "this yoke (that presently keeps them in check)"

*** , et ita loqui secum Some text has been lost, and *et* is a scholar's emendation; *ita* looks ahead to the following passage.

1.2: The emperor recognizes his power

Seneca now illustrates what Nero can say to himself, in the form of
an imaginary speech or *prosōpopoeia*. The speech begins with a rhetorical question and a catalogue, in which the speaker delineates his
vast and godlike powers extending throughout the empire.

2   **Egone . . . ?** emphatic, and with a sense of disbelief

placui electusque sum refers to his divine selection as emperor (not to election by the people).

qui . . . fungerer rel. clause of purpose ("in order to serve") or
of characteristic ("as qualified to serve")

Ego . . . arbiter Supply *sum*.

gentibus dat. of reference, referring to the peoples of the
whole Roman empire

qualem . . . habeat indirect question introduced by *in mea
manu positum est*

quid cuique . . . datum uelit "what she wants given to each"

pronuntiat The subject is *Fortuna*.

laetitiae objective gen. with *causas*

pars i.e., of the empire

uolente propitioque me abl. absolute

ad "in response to"

stringentur The fut. tense, instead of potential subjunctive, is
ominous, suggesting the inevitability of violence.

quas nationes . . . excidi This and the following infinitives
(*transportari, dari, eripi, fieri* and *circumdari*) are all governed
by *oporteat*: "which nations ought to be annihilated," etc.

quibus . . . quibus dat. of indirect object (with *dari*) and dat.
of disadvantage (with *eripi*) respectively

eripi The implicit subject is *libertatem* from the previous
phrase.

quorumque capiti regium circumdari decus "and whose
heads the royal ornament (i.e., crown) ought to be placed

around." Note the playful word order, with *regium . . . decus* encircling the verb.

quae oriantur The implicit subject is *urbes* from the previous phrase.

mea iuris dictio est "it is my right to say"; governs all the preceding indirect questions (*quas nationes . . . excidi . . . oporteat, quae ruant urbes, quae oriantur*).

1.3–4: Young Nero's boast

In this second half of the *prosōpopoeia*, the Nero-speaker recounts how he has used his powers responsibly, avoiding the path of violence. He finishes by acknowledging once again his role as a servant of the gods.

3   **hac tanta facultate rerum** refers to the list of powers recounted in the previous sentences.

non . . . non . . . non . . . non anaphoric repetition, characterizing his reign negatively by a list of the impulses he has avoided since becoming emperor

ira may allude to Seneca's own arguments against anger in *De Ira*. This and the other negative qualities listed in the next lines were all characteristics of the reign of Caligula.

iuuenilis impetus acknowledges Nero's potential susceptibility, as still a young man, to behave rashly.

temeritas . . . et contumacia bad attitudes among his subjects that could have provoked Nero to retaliate

tranquillissimis quoque pectoribus "even from the calmest breasts"; dat. of disadvantage

ipsa, dira, frequens all agreeing with *gloria*

ostentandae . . . potentiae . . . gloria "(thirst for) the glory that comes from displaying one's power"; *ostentandae . . . potentiae* is a gen. gerundive phrase.

dira, sed magnis imperiis frequens "evil, yet (all too) common in great empires"

apud me "in my reign"

summa parsimonia abl. of attendant circumstances

etiam uilissimi sanguinis continues the economic metaphor of *parsimonia*: he has avoided squandering "blood of even the least value."

nemo non . . . est "there is no one . . . who is not"

cui alia desunt has a concessive force: "even if" he has no other redeeming features

hominis nomine "on account of his being human"; abl. of cause

4 **Seueritatem abditam** goes with *habeo* in the following phrase: "I keep sternness hidden away." The phrase *abditam . . . habeo* approximates the pf. tense construction of the Romance languages, with *habeo* as auxiliary verb.

sic . . . tamquam "exactly . . . as if." This sentence has often been singled out for indicating that the Roman emperor was not held to be *actually* accountable to the laws.

legibus indirect object of *redditurus sim*

quas . . . euocaui suggests that Nero has restored law and order after their neglect under the previous emperors.

rationem redditurus sim The idiom *rationem reddere* is suggestive of economic accounts, continuing the metaphor from *parsimonia* above.

aetate prima . . . ultima i.e., youth . . . old age

alium dignitati donaui . . . humilitati The idiom is rare: "I forgave (+ acc.) . . . for the sake of (+ dat.)."

quotiens equivalent to *cum* + plpf.: "whenever"

mihi peperci suggests both that carrying out punishment was troublesome to the emperor and, as emphasized later in the work, that avoiding it could help to protect him.

dis immortalibus dat. of advantage, effectively indirect object of *adnumerare*

si . . . repetant . . . paratus sum mixed conditional, using the indicative to emphasize Nero's actual readiness

1.5–6: You are your own best model

Seneca compares the beginning of Nero's reign favorably with that of the emperors who preceded him. But he now adds some words of warning: Nero's reign may have begun more peacefully than those of earlier emperors, but people are looking on and waiting to see whether this will continue in the future.

5   **hoc** "this, namely . . . ," anticipating the clauses introduced by *omnia* and *nihil*

   in fidem tutelamque tuam uenerunt alludes to the emperor's responsibility as "trustee." Note also the soundplay on *tu-*, reinforcing the connection between *tutelam* and *tuam.*

   per te "in your name," encompassing the agency of both Nero and his surrogates

   neque ui neque clam *ui* contrasts with *clam*, because *ui* implies openly observable actions.

   rei publicae dat. of disadvantage

   nulli indirect object of *concessam*; *concessam* agrees with *laudem.*

   adhuc principum "of emperors up till now." The term *princeps* (originally just "first citizen"), and its derivative, *principatus, -us,* m., are standard for referring to the emperor and his reign. Later, however, Seneca invokes a contrast between the king (*rex*)—which in this work lacks its usual negative associations in the minds of Roman audiences—and his opposite, the tyrant (*tyrannus*).

   concupisti syncopated form of *concupiuisti*

   non perdis operam i.e., the effort has been worthwhile

   aestimatores The term invites Nero to think of himself as observed by witnesses evaluating his performance—no longer just a mirror.

   gratia "gratitude." The term is central to Seneca's discussion of gift-giving in the *De Beneficiis*, and is important here for characterizing the emperor and his subjects as partners in an exchange.

nemo . . . nemo . . . Nemo The anaphoric repetition reinforces from a negative angle the sense of uniqueness already established in *bonitas ista tua singularis.*

tam . . . quam "as . . . as," drawing an analogy

nemo unus homo Seneca might have used *nullus homo* or simply *nemo*, but the full phrase with *unus* is more emphatic, and allows for strong emphasis on one-to-one friendship as an analogy for the emperor's relationship to his people.

magnum longumque eius bonum "its (i.e., the people's) great and long-lasting good," nom. in apposition to *tu*

6 **onus** The idea of power as a burden is later intensified when Seneca describes being emperor as a form of "servitude" (*seruitus, Clem.* 1.8.1).

diuum Augustum emperor 31 BCE—14 CE. This somewhat dismissive reference to Augustus will be qualified in *Clem.* 1.9 below.

Ti. Caesaris prima tempora Tiberius' reign (14–37 CE) began with relatively poor relations between the emperor and senate (cf. Tacitus *Ann.* 1.11–12).

loquitur "talks about"

quod te imitari uelit "which he would have you imitate," qualifying *exemplar*

extra te "outside of you." Nero is thus being asked to continue doing what he has done previously—like Helvia at *Helv.* 2.3 above.

naturalis . . . ad tempus sumpta a contrast between permanent and temporary characteristics

ad tempus "for the occasion"

personam a theatrical concept of identity often used by Seneca to criticize inconsistent behavior. As Seneca writes disapprovingly elsewhere, we human beings often "change our mask and put one on that is opposite of that which we removed" (*mutamus . . . personam et contrariam ei sumimus quam exuimus, Ep.* 120.22).

ficta "fictions," nom. pl. n. subject of *recidunt*

quibus . . . quaeque the two rel. clauses connected by *-que* define the implicit n. pl. subject of *procedunt*.

ut ita dicam "so to speak," qualifying the metaphorical phrase *ex solido enascuntur*, which evokes the growth of plants

ex solido "from solid ground"

tempore ipso i.e., simply by the passage of time

in maius meliusque procedunt lit. "advance into the greater and the better," i.e., become greater and better

9.1–3: Augustus and the conspirator

To demonstrate that clemency can keep the emperor and his empire safe, Seneca recalls the example of how Nero's great-great-grandfather, the emperor Augustus, responded to the rumor of a conspiracy against him led by a nobleman named Cinna. Yet in his story about how Augustus pardoned Cinna, Seneca does not simply give Nero an example of his ancestor's clemency, but emphasizes that Augustus had arrived at this policy only after a long habit of using violence.

The Cinna story recurs in a slightly different form in Cassius Dio (see Braund 2008, 258–60, 424–31), and may have been connected with ancient rhetorical exercises on the dilemmas of power. It was was also the inspiration for the French tragedy *Cinna* by Corneille (1639).

The initial passage describes how Augustus, hearing of Cinna's conspiracy against him, almost condemned him to death, just as he had condemned those who conspired against him earlier. But the emperor, Seneca explains, immediately began to question his own decision.

1   **Hoc** nom. sing. n., subject of the indirect question *quam uerum sit*; refers back to the point of the previous passage (here omitted): that when individuals are punished with death, others spring up to take their place. In the following story about Augustus, the emperor begins to realize this and decides to change his approach.

exemplo domestico Seneca here seeks to persuade by drawing on a parallel from Nero's own household, and therefore
with close connections to Nero himself. In ancient rhetoric
an *exemplum* is defined as any "recollection of a thing done,
or as if done, that is useful for making the direction of your
argument persuasive" (*rei gestae aut ut gestae utilis ad per-
suadendum id quod intenderis commemoratio*, Quintilian,
Institutio Oratoria 5.11.6).

Diuus a standard epithet for Augustus (who was deified upon
his death in 14 CE), but here juxtaposed with the all-too-mor-
tal faults that he showed as the young Octavian

quis standard usage after *si*, equivalent to *aliquis*

a principatu suo "beginning from his reign as emperor." It is
unclear whether a precise pivotal date is meant, but in 31 BCE
Octavian defeated Antony at Actium, and in 27 BCE he took
on the name Augustus; in the meantime he had also taken on
the title of *princeps*.

in communi . . . republica "while the Republic was shared,"
i.e., before he became monarch

quidem "admittedly"

gladium mouit "wielded the sword"; the image contrasts with
Nero's *constrictum apud me ferrum est* at *Clem.* 1.1.3 above.

hoc aetatis lit. "this thing of age," i.e., "this age"; *hoc* is nom.
sing. n., and is picked up by *quod*.

duodeuicensimum egressus annum the pple., agreeing with
tu, takes *annum* as direct object. This information helps us to
date the *De Clementia* to 55–56 CE (Nero was born in 37). It
would also seem to date Octavian/Augustus' violent years to
before 45 BCE (he was born in 63), though some of the events
mentioned below are from 44–42, in the aftermath of the as-
sassination of Julius Caesar on the Ides of March in 44; Seneca
bends the truth slightly to help him claim that Octavian had
done these violent things before he was Nero's age.

iam . . . iam . . . iam . . . "already . . . ," i.e., by the time he had reached Nero's present age, emphasized by the anaphoric repetition

amicorum probably the consuls Hirtius and Pansa, killed at the battle of Mutina in 43 BCE

M. Antonii consulis latus petierat Octavian had supposedly plotted against Antony during the latter's consulship in 44 BCE.

petierat syncopated form of *petiuerat*

collega proscriptionis refers to Octavian's role in the confiscations and killings of 43–42, in the Second Triumvirate along with Antony and Lepidus.

2   **annum quadragensimum transisset et in Gallia moraretur** dates the event roughly to Augustus' forties; Augustus was on campaign in Gaul in 16–13.

indicium "information (that) . . . ," introducing the indirect statement *L. Cinnam . . . struere*

L. Cinnam In fact this praenomen (Lucius) is wrong: his name was Cn. (Gnaeus) Cornelius Cinna Magnus (cf. Braund 2008, 264–65).

stolidi ingenii gen. of description

ei i.e., Augustus

ex consciis "of the guilty," equivalent to gen. of the whole

3   **se ab eo uindicare** "to avenge himself on him (Cinna)"; Augustus' first impulse, after years of practice, is for revenge and punishment.

consilium amicorum "advisory group of friends"; an informal group assembled from the emperor's retinue

illi dat. of reference, referring to Augustus

hoc detracto lit. "this thing removed," i.e., this one infraction aside, going closely with *integrum*

Cn. Pompei nepotem Cinna's mother Pompeia was Pompeius Magnus' daughter; he thus belonged to an illustrious aristocratic family.

damnandum gerundive periphrastic infinitive with *esse* implied

9.4–6: The emperor's exasperation and Livia's remedy

Seneca dramatizes Augustus' predicament by presenting the emperor speaking in solitude: first his angry reaction to Cinna's plot, then his reaction *to* his own reaction. Two contrasting speeches by Augustus are followed by an intervention from his wife Livia, who helps him to change course.

4   **inter se contrarias** "differing among themselves," referring to the fact that he begins by arguing for revenge, then argues against it. The phrase may evoke the *controuersia*, the declamatory form that involved arguing opposite sides of the case.

Quid ergo? "Well?"

Ego . . . ? a rhetorical question (the first of several)

securum ambulare "to walk free"

patiar fut. indicative

me sollicito abl. absolute, contrasting with *securum*

5   **silentio interposito** abl. absolute

multo modifies *maiore.*

quam "than," with the compar. *maiore*, and also establishing a contrast between *sibi* and *Cinnae*. The idea is that Augustus spoke more loudly now than he had in the speech of the previous lines.

perire te lit. "that you perish," i.e., "your perishing"; the infinitive goes closely with *interest.*

Quis finis a common variation on the more usual adjectival form (i.e., *qui finis*)

Quis sanguinis? supply *finis* again.

Ego sum Augustus' language intensifies with a shift from second person (in *Quid uiuis* above) to first person.

nobilibus adulescentulis dat. of reference with *expositum*

caput an evocative image: *caput* can just mean conspicuous person (as in "heads" of population), but he is literally threatened with decapitation.

in quod "against which," introducing rel. clause of characteristic or purpose

tanti gen. of value

ut . . . non peream a purpose clause; *ut . . . non* would normally be *ne*, but here *non* negates the word *peream*: "in order that I not-perish," i.e., "survive." On this reference to living, through the device of litotes (understatement), see Braund 2008, 269.

6   **Interpellauit** The emphatic verb position lends drama to Livia's surprising entry into the scene.

Liuia uxor Livia (58 BCE–29 CE), married to Augustus in 38 BCE, was both a highly visible public figure and an influential private counsellor during the reigns of Augustus and her son Tiberius. Suetonius mentions instances in which Augustus, consulting with Livia about serious matters, would speak from prepared notes (*Diuus Augustus* 84), though the present situation appears somewhat more informal. In a more extensive portrait of Livia in the *Consolatio ad Marciam*, Seneca depicts her receiving philosophical advice on grief after her son Drusus' death (*Marc.* 2–6).

admittis . . . ? the question suggests that Livia is tentative; but her advice is forceful.

medici introduces a medical analogy, as often in Seneca's advising scenes, including *Helv.* 3.1 above and *Ep.* 2.3 below.

Seueritate the opposite of clemency, as above at *Clem.* 1.1.4

nihil adverbial: "not at all"

tempta, quomodo tibi cedat clementia "try how clemency may go for you," a potential subjunctive embedded in indirect question

ignosce an emphatic imperative, underlined by the sentence's brevity

nocere . . . non potest, prodesse . . . potest asyndeton, with "but" implied between the two clauses; the parallel structure (with repetition of *potest*) enhances the contrast.

9.7–10: Interview with the would-be assassin

Following Livia's advice, Augustus summoned Cinna and forced him to listen to his thoughts, recounting the favors he had conferred on him in the past and ridiculing his present ambition to replace him as emperor.

7   **Gauisus** pf. pple. used with pres. sense ("rejoicing"); other deponent pples. can be used in a similar way, such as *ueritus* ("fearing"), *ratus* ("thinking")

sibi dat. of advantage, belonging inside the *quod* clause; goes closely with *aduocatum*

renuntiari . . . amicis . . . imperauit: "he ordered the call to his friends to be canceled"; i.e., he uninvited them

arcessît syncopated from *arcessiuit*

dismissisque omnibus e cubiculo The *cubiculum* was not exclusively a sleeping chamber, but a place for private meetings; here Augustus probably excludes Livia, secretaries, slaves, and bodyguards, who would otherwise be a constant presence.

alteram . . . cathedram i.e., in addition to the one already occupied by Augustus. The seating arrangment makes for an appearance of equality.

Hoc acc. sing. n., direct object of *peto*, anticipating the indirect command *ne . . . interpelles*

ne . . . ne asyndeton rather than *ne . . . neue*, perhaps because the second *ne* clause simply paraphrases the first

medio sermone meo abl. of time when

loquendi liberum tempus lit. "free time for speaking," i.e., time for speaking freely

8   **Ego te** The prons. are emphasized by their position, but syntactically they are the subject and object of the clause *cum . . . inuenissem*, and implicitly also of the main verb *seruaui*.

te . . . cum in hostium castris inuenissem Here *cum* is concessive. The exact situation is not certain, but perhaps refers to Cinna's siding with Sextus Pompeius during his rebellion in Sicily (35 BCE) or with Antony during the battle of Actium (31 BCE).

non factum . . . sed natum As a descendant of Pompey, Cinna was "born" an opponent of Octavian (a descendant of Julius Caesar), and to this extent had not really *chosen* to oppose him.

patrimonium . . . concessi i.e., rather than confiscating Cinna's wealth

Cum concessive

sic de te meruerim "I behaved so well towards you"

9   **ad hanc uocem** "in response to these words"

exclamasset syncopated form of *exclamauisset*

Non praestas . . . fidem "you aren't making good on your promise"

conuenerat impers.; lit. "it had been agreed," i.e., "we had an agreement"

ne interloquereris "that you would not interrupt"; the normal construction after impers. *conuenit* and other "verbs of deciding, resolving, etc." (Bennett 295.4)

Occidere, inquam, me paras repeats the accusation more emphatically, including the more vivid pres. tense of *paras* (as opposed to *constituisti* above).

diem "the date"

cui commissum esset ferrum an indirect question identifying the planned assassin

10   **defixum . . . tacentem** the pples. agree with implied *Cinnam*.

ex conuentione "in accordance with the agreement"

ex conscientia "from guilt"

Quo . . . animo "with what intention?" (cf. Braund 2008, 275)

hoc acc. sing. n.

male . . . cum populo Romano agitur i.e., the Roman people is in a sorry state

tibi goes with *obstat*

ad imperandum "on the path to power"

nuper . . . superatus es Nothing further is known about this court case, but clearly Cinna had been humiliated.

libertini hominis gratia "by the influence of a mere freedman" (trans. Braund 2008, 113)

9.11–12: I forgive you

Seneca brings the Cinna narrative to a close, abbreviating the rest of Augustus' speech and briefly summing up the outcome of his lenient treatment of Cinna. The Cinna episode resulted in lasting benefits for Augustus.

11　　**ne . . . occupem** "so as not to take up"

totam . . . orationem direct object of *repetendo*

diutius . . . quam duabus horis "for longer than two hours"; abl. of time throughout which (cf. note above on *Helv.* 20.2 *omnibus saeculis*)

locutum esse subject is the implied *Augustum*.

prius hosti i.e., in the situation referred to above at *Clem.* 1.9.8 (*cum in hostium castris inuenissem*)

parricidae a strong term, implying the killing of one's own kin; a possible allusion to Augustus' profile as *pater patriae*

ex hodierno die "from this day on"

utrum ego . . . an tu debeas indirect question introduced by *contendamus*. Seneca's formulation of this contest in friendship gives an epigrammatic ending to Augustus' speech.

detulit with implied indirect object *Cinnae*

questus "complaining"; i.e., Augustus wanted Cinna to feel comfortable actively seeking political positions

petere either with *consulatum* as implied direct object or absolutely ("to seek election"). In reality, the consulship and other offices were conferred by the emperor, not by the votes of the people.

Amicissimum agrees with implied direct object *Cinnam.*

heres solus illi fuit i.e., Cinna named only Augustus in his will, a sign of his loyalty

petitus est "was targeted"

10.1–3: Augustus lives on

Seneca draws out the lesson of the *exemplum domesticum* by pointing out to Nero how the benefits of Augustus' clemency can be seen in the excellent reputation that Augustus enjoyed during his own lifetime and continues to enjoy up to the present day. The people and senate had bestowed on Augustus the title "father of the fatherland" (*pater patriae*); Seneca alludes to this here, and also to Augustus' deification after his death.

10.1   **imperasset** syncopated form of *imperauisset*

2   **haec eum clementia . . . haec . . . haec** The anaphoric repetition allows Seneca to make several general observations about Augustus' use of clemency, culminating in the profile he presently enjoys now, in Nero's day.

     gratum agrees with implied direct object carried over from *eum.*

     quamuis . . . imposuisset i.e., despite Augustus' overall strictness as a ruler

     nondum subactis . . . ceruicibus "upon the necks . . . not yet suppressed"; *ceruicibus* is dat. with compound verb *imposuisset.*

hodieque "to this day," "even now"

illi dat. of indirect object, referring to Augustus

quae uix uiuis principibus seruit i.e., he has maintained his reputation in a way that few emperors could do in their own lifetime

3 **Deum esse** Supply *Augustum*. Seneca here refers to Augustus' posthumous deification (cf. the title *Diuus Augustus* at *Clem.* 1.9.1 above).

non tamquam iussi "not as if ordered," i.e., without duress

bene . . . conuenisse "suited well," governing the dat. *illi*

parentis nomen i.e., the title *pater patriae*, conferred on him by the people and senate in 2 BCE (cf. Augustus, *Res Gestae* 35.1)

∾ Follow-ups to the DE CLEMENTIA

Apocolocyntosis 10.1–3: The deified Augustus ashamed of his successors

The satirical tone of the *Apocolocyntosis* ("Pumpkinification"), written in late 54, just months before the *De Clementia*, offers a different perspective on the rule of Augustus as a model for the Julio-Claudian emperors. The work's narrator had mocked Claudius' slow and messy death scene and praised the new emperor Nero. He had also described how Claudius arrived at Olympus, the home of the gods, and sought permanent admission. Claudius' request is considered by a council of the gods, in which Seneca parodies the workings of the Roman senate.

Among the opponents of this request is the deified Augustus himself, who speaks here in a *prosōpopoeia*. Augustus trades upon the general perception that Claudius' rule was violent and chaotic, and he paints this as a travesty of the principate that Augustus himself had established. Augustus indeed wins the day with this speech, and at the work's end Claudius is sent to the underworld to be a slave of Caligula.

On the *Apocolocyntosis* see also on "Seneca's life" and "Political works" in the Introduction. For introduction, translation, and commentary to the *Apocolocyntosis*, see Eden (1984). The work is also discussed by Leach (2008).

1   **diuus Augustus** the epithet emphasizes his qualifications to be present on Olympus and to participate in the council of the gods.

sententiae suae . . . dicendae dat. of purpose in gerundival construction: "to voice his opinion"

loco abl. of place at which: lit. "in turn," i.e., in order; refers to the fact that Augustus was next in the rank of speakers. On the syntax, see Eden (1984) 116.

summa facundia abl. of means. Augustus will in fact employ much "eloquence," including many rhetorical devices, though he will also break into the colloquial language of satire.

p. c. = *patres conscripti* ("conscript fathers"), a standard phrase for addressing the senate

testes "(as) witnesses (that) . . . ," introducing the indirect statement *nullum me uerbum fecisse*

ex quo "from (the time) when"

semper meum negotium ago colloquial: "I always mind my own business"

Et non possum "And (yet) I cannot . . ."

pudor i.e., Augustus is not only upset but also embarrassed by the reign of Claudius. Seneca may be aware that Augustus late in his life had already expressed reluctance about letting the young Claudius be seen in public (cf. Suetonius, *Diuus Claudius* 4).

2   **In hoc** "for this?" (*hoc* is acc.), i.e., the embarrassing reign of Claudius. Augustus' language in the two rhetorical questions here closely echoes his autobiographic *Res Gestae*: e.g., *bella terra et mari ciuilia externaque toto in orbe terrarum saepe gessi* ("I often fought wars on land and sea, both civil and foreign, throughout the whole world," *RG* 3.1).

Ideo ... ut "for this purpose ..., namely, that ...?"

operibus ornaui Augustus famously claimed to have found Rome a city "of brick" (*latericiam*) and left it a city "of marble" (*marmoream*, Suetonius, *Diuus Augustus* 28).

quid dicam ... non inuenio Augustus is lost for words. This rhetorical device is an *aposiōpēsis* ("breaking off in silence"), expressing the speaker's outrage.

infra "insufficient for expressing"

Messalae Coruini A distinguished public servant during the reign of Augustus, M. Valerius Messala Corvinus appears to have uttered these words when resigning from his position as prefect of the city of Rome in 25 BCE because he was uneasy about wielding excessive power (cf. Eden 1984, 117).

illam "that well-known"

pudet imperii supply acc. *me*: "I am ashamed of my power."

3   **Hic** i.e., Claudius

muscam excitare a sudden shift to a colloquial register, typical of the satirical mode

tam facile homines occidebat, quam canis adsidit Claudius was notorious for impulsively condemning Roman citizens to death. The colloquial expression, "as easily as a dog sits," probably refers to a dog squatting to relieve itself.

4   **diue Claudi** Augustus sarcastically mocks Claudius' unworthiness to be a god.

quos quasque In an omitted section of the speech, Augustus had listed both male and female members of the Julio-Claudian dynasty killed by Claudius.

antequam ... cognosceres, antequam audires "before you could ...." Augustus is being sarcastic: Claudius was notorious for presiding as a judge over court cases, so that executing someone without a trial was a missed opportunity. Here the verbs *cognosco* and *audio* are technical terms: "hold an inquiry" and "give a hearing."

damnasti syncopated from *damnauisti*

Hoc i.e., execution without trial

In caelo non fit i.e., the murderous Claudius does not belong among the gods

De Ira 1.2.1–3: The costs of anger

Seneca's *De Ira* offers lessons for his brother Novatus, and his other contemporaries, on the dangers of anger, and the passage below, just a few pages into the work, offers a sampling of his approach. He has just argued that anger is not much different from insanity. Now he describes some of its outward signs on the human face and body. He employs some extreme rhetoric to depict the damage anger can inflict on whole societies, directing his reader to "look" around him at anger's diverse effects. Although written a decade before the *De Clementia*, and focusing on a passion (*ira*) rather than a virtue (*clementia*), it has the same basic goal: preventing acts of violent revenge.

For background on the *De Ira* see on "Seneca's life" and "Political works" in the Introduction.

1   **eius** i.e., "anger's"

si ... uelis "if you would like (to) . . . ." With this clause Seneca raises a new topic: anger's impact on the world.

effectus acc. pl. parallel to *damna*

nulla ... stetit this clause describes what "you" will discover; when you translate, supply "you will discover that . . . ."

humano generi dat. of disadvantage

pluris stetit "has come at greater cost," with *pluris* gen. of value

Videbis builds upon the visual metaphor first introduced by *intueri*. Seneca is presenting his catalogue of anger's impacts in the form of a great spectacle.

reorum mutuas sordes alludes to the black clothes donned by defendants in court in a show of mourning; *mutuas* suggests a competiton between the different aggrieved parties.

principum sub ciuili hasta capita uenalia "the heads of leading men on sale at civic auction." At public auctions a spear
was planted in the ground.

**et subiectas tectis faces nec intra moenia coercitos ignes sed
ingentia spatia regionum . . . relucentia** the first image of
"torches thrown beneath roofs" is corrected by a more expan-
sive image: "and not (only) fires confined within (city) walls
but (also) huge expanses of regions . . . alight . . . ."

2   **Aspice . . . Aspice . . . Aspice** the repeated verb continues the
visual metaphor introduced above. The repetition will be varied by an inventive set of compound verbs, each involving a
different prefix, which adds variety to the images of violence:
deiecit, exhausit, confodit, percussit, diffindere.

per multa milia "over many miles"

tot memoriae proditos duces "so many leading men handed
down to posterity"

mali exempla fati "illustrations of ill fate"; objective gen.; *exempla* is in apposition to *duces.*

alium . . . alium . . . alium . . . alium . . . alium . . . alium more
anaphoric repetition, making the third and final *Aspice* clause
the most detailed. Anger's acts include a great variety, ranging from private to public, from victim to agent, from slaves
to kings. In some cases Seneca may have specific historical
events in mind, but he keeps the descriptions anonymous and
generalized.

intra leges celebrisque spectaculum fori "amid the law
courts and the spectacle of the crowded forum"

filii parricidio "by being murdered by his son"; subjective
gen. and abl. of means

dare sanguinem iussit "forced to give blood"

aperire iugulum "to have his throat opened"

membra diffindere "to have his limbs divided"

3   **Et adhuc singulorum . . .** Seneca now expands his catalogue, transitioning from the killings of individuals to the fates of whole groups.

quid si tibi libuerit introduces *aspicere*: "what if you (will) want . . . to look at . . . ?"; with *libuerit* fut. pf. indicative

relictis in quos ira uiritim exarsit abl. absolute with the subject absorbed into relatival *quos*: "leaving behind (those) against whom anger has flared individually"

contiones . . . plebem . . . populos three types of group victim, each functioning as direct object of *aspicere*

inmisso milite abl. absolute

in perniciem promiscuam follows from *capitis damnatos*: "condemned to death in indiscriminate ruin"; *capitis* is gen. of charge; after *damnatos* there is a lacuna in the text.

Scenario 3: The Drama of Revenge

According to the established mythic tradition, the hero Jason, on the orders of his uncle, Pelias, had sailed in the first ship, the Argo, with the rest of the Argonauts, to retrieve the Golden Fleece from Colchis. (Colchis lay beyond the Black Sea; this and other locations can be tracked on the MAP in Appendix B.) Jason had succeeded in this mission only through the help of the Colchian princess Medea, daughter of king Aeetes and granddaughter of the Sun. With her daring and her abilities as a sorceress, Medea had helped Jason to escape such threats as the "Earth-born" warriors sown from the dragon's teeth, and the dragon itself that was guarding the Fleece. Jason and Medea's most violent act as they departed Colchis was to kill and dismember Medea's brother Absyrtus, who had been sent in pursuit of them. Further violence awaited them, however: in Jason's home of Iolchos, Medea had tricked Pelias' daughters into thinking that their father could be rejuvenated through boiling his body in a cauldron—with fatal consequences for Pelias, and forcing Jason and Medea to flee once again, this time to Corinth.

Fig. 5. Medea Contemplates Killing Her Children. Wall-painting from Pompeii, first century.

The plot of the *Medea* play begins in Corinth, where a new predicament faces Medea. Jason has arranged to marry the Corinthian princess Creusa, daughter of king Creon. Medea, now divorced, is to be sent into exile alone, without the two sons she and Jason have produced together. This dramatic scenario, seen already in the *Medea* of Euripides, is taken up in turn by Seneca. Certain elements of the Euripidean version are missing here: for example, Euripides has

Medea meet an Athenian visitor, Aegeus, who agrees to let Medea seek refuge in Athens, whereas Seneca omits Aegeus altogether. And Euripides begins his play with Medea's Nurse lamenting that the Argo had ever been built, whereas Seneca makes Medea herself the opening speaker, and instead has these same sentiments expressed by the Chorus. In other respects the plays are quite similar.

In the selections below taken from throughout the play, Seneca shows Medea first responding to the news that Jason has divorced her to marry Creusa, then progressively inventing and carrying out the best revenge she can think of: a bloody sacrifice of her two children in full view of Jason and the play's audience. (The scenario spoke to the first-century Roman imagination: we see Medea's planning visualized, for example, in a wall-painting from Pompeii; see Fig. 5.) En route to this revenge, we are party to an ineffectual advising scene between Medea and her Nurse, the reactions of the Chorus, who lament that Jason ever met Medea and that he even went to sea to begin with, and tense dialogues between Medea and Jason both before and after the infanticide.

Several elements of Seneca's *Medea* have close comparisons elsewhere in his tragedies. Medea's gradual plotting of her revenge, for instance, in which she goads her mind to outdo all prior crimes that she or anyone else has committed, yet only comes to the idea of killing the children late in the play, can be paralleled from the *Thyestes*, where Atreus says early in the play:

> *Nescioquid animus maius et solito amplius*
> *supraque fines moris humani tumet*
> *instatque pigris manibus—haud quid sit scio,*
> *sed grande quiddam est. Ita sic. Hoc, anime, occupa . . .*
> (*Thy.* 267–70)

> My mind swells with some great uncertain thing,
> something greater than usual and beyond the limits of
>   human custom,
> and goads my sluggish hands—what it is, I do not know,
> but it is something grand. Let it be thus. Get to it, mind
>   of mine . . .

The advising scenario that recurs in the dialogues of the *Medea*, in which the Nurse and Jason each seek in vain to assuage Medea's grief by dispensing quasi-philosophical wisdom, is in many ways *the* defining type scene of Senecan tragedy. To take one example from the *Phaedra*, the Nurse character there seeks to curb Phaedra's desire for her stepson Hippolytus, saying: "My child, control the impulses of your unleashed mind, and rein in your spirit" (*Moderare, alumna, mentis effrenae impetus, animos coerce, Pha.* 255–56). This resembles the words of Medea's Nurse closely: *Siste furialem impetum, / alumna* (*Med.* lines 157–58, below). The climax of the *Medea* scene in the fast-paced dialogue at lines 168–73 below also matches the *Phaedra* scene closely, where the heroine meets her Nurse's arguments with swift and concise rebuttals (*Pha.* 240–45). Similar "passion-restraint" scenes recur in most of the tragedies, and in each case the wisdom of the advisor is overwhelmed by the more forceful emotions and self-serving rhetoric of the heroine or hero.

Medea's state of mind appears to have been a favorite topic for philosophical discussion, especially among the Stoics, who used Euripides' Medea character as a kind of showcase for problems of moral psychology. And with some surprises. The Stoic Epictetus, a near-contemporary of Seneca, at the same time as condemning Medea's decisions and actions, points out that "she had . . . the right impression, namely, what it means not to yield one's will to anyone" (*Discourses*, 2.17.19). To this extent, although Medea served mostly to illustrate anger and irrationality at their worst, she was potentially also good to think with as a comparison for the Stoic wise person's unyielding focus on virtue.

Along the same lines, some of Seneca's scenes in the *Medea* are very suggestive for thinking about the relationship between his tragedies and his philosophical works. When the Nurse urges Medea to embrace *uirtus* ("virtue," *Med.* line 160 below), this Stoic-seeming advice is adapted by Medea to account for her preferred notion of *uirtus*, which encompasses manliness and violence. When Jason tells her that she should think more rationally or seek consolation for her grief (*Med.* lines 537–39 below), she consoles herself, yes, but by taking comfort in . . . revenge. More generally, Medea's ambition of living up to her identity as "Medea" may be understood as a mis-understanding, or a willful perversion, of the Stoic moral ideal of consistency (*constantia*)—a recurring theme traced in the *Medea* and other Senecan works by Star (2006).

For further background see "The tragedies" in the Introduc-tion. For full introduction, translation, and commentary to Seneca's *Medea* see Hine (2000). For discussion, see among others Guastella (2001), Littlewood (2004) 148–71, and Nussbaum (1997).

∾ *MEDEA*

1–18: Calling all gods

As often in Seneca's tragedies, Act 1 consists of a prologue by a soli-tary character: Medea prays to all the gods who she thinks will be offended by the news that Jason is divorcing her and remarrying. Her prayer is both an invocation, calling on the gods to be present, and a catalogue that reviews various earlier parts of the story. This includes the voyage of the Argonauts to her home of Colchis in search of the Golden Fleece, and her own established powers as a sorceress.

Meter: IAMBIC TRIMETERS (see Appendix C)

1   **Di coniugales** vocative; Medea directly addresses all the dei-ties in lines 1–9, without any larger syntactic structure except an implied *adeste* ("Be present!"); cf. line 13 below.

        genalis tori objective gen. governed by *custos*

2   **Lucina** in apposition to *tu . . . custos*. Lucina was not a well-defined goddess in Roman culture, but had associations with both marriage and childbirth, and with multiple female god-desses such as Juno and Venus.

        quaeque "and (you) who . . . ," calling obliquely upon a third deity: Minerva, who had guided the making of the Argo, the legendary first ship (here referred to as *nouam . . . ratem*)

        domituram agrees with *ratem*, and takes *freta* as direct object; the first ship would assert human control over the sea. The mo-tif of domination will be developed further below (lines 4, 11).

3   **Tiphyn** acc. sing., direct object of *docuisti* and acc. subject of
    frenare. Tiphys was the Argo's helmsman.

4   **et tu . . . dominator maris** i.e., Neptune

5   **Titan** vocative sing.; the Sun (also known as Sol, Helios, Phoe-
    bus) was Medea's grandfather.

    diuidens orbi diem i.e., giving daylight to half the world at
    a time

6   **tacitisque praebens conscium sacris iubar** describes the god-
    dess Hecate in her form as the moon, bearing witness to noc-
    turnal rites and prayers.

7   **Hecate triformis** This goddess was three-formed in various
    senses: she was represented as having three bodies, and was
    associated with the Moon in the sky, Diana on earth, and
    Hecate in the underworld (cf. Hine 2000, 113). Medea had
    been her priestess in Colchis, and she is closely associated
    with Medea's witchcraft.

    iurauit i.e., when Jason took his marriage vows to Medea

7-8 **quosque . . . / deos** "and (you) gods whom," with *quos* direct
    object of *iurauit*

8-9 **quosque Medeae magis / fas est precari** "and (you gods)
    whom it is more right for Medea to call upon in prayer." This
    introduces the nocturnal and infernal divinities of the fol-
    lowing lines, with whom Medea, as sorceress, has a special
    connection.

9   **chaos** acc. sing. n.; in a change of syntactic structure, the dei-
    ties of lines 9–12 are given in acc., as direct object of *precor*
    (line 12).

10 **auersa superis regna** "kingdoms turned away from those
    above," i.e., the underworld; *auersa regna* is acc.; *superis*
    (probably dat. of reference) has a double sense, referring both
    to those on earth (upper in relation to the underworld) and to
    the celestial gods above.

dominum . . . dominam i.e., the underworld's king (Dis = Hades, Pluto) and queen (Proserpina = Persephone)

11-12 **fide / meliore raptam** Medea alludes bitterly to the rape of Proserpina as having been committed "with better faithfulness": Dis, although abducting Proserpina to be his wife in the underworld, did not abandon her in the way that Jason now abandons Medea.

12 **uoce non fausta** abl. of means; *non fausta* is equivalent to *infausta* ("inauspicious").

13 **nunc, nunc adeste** The repetition is typical of ritual invocation; *adeste* is second person pl. pres. imperative.

sceleris ultrices deae "goddesses (who are) avengers of wrongdoing," vocative pl. f. with *sceleris* objective gen. The phrase refers to the Furies, the dog-like female deities with snakes in their hair who wielded torches and sought revenge from wrongdoers. Already common in Greek tragedy (especially Aeschylus' *Eumenides*) and Latin poetry (especially Catullus 64, in Ariadne's curse), in Senecan tragedy they bring together the desire for revenge, underworldly power, and the psychology of madness (*furor*).

crinem acc. of respect referring to body-part, with *squalidae*: "filthy haired"

solutis . . . serpentibus abl. of description modifying *squalidae*: "defiled with disheveled serpents" (trans. Hine 2000, 115)

15 **amplexae** agrees with *deae*, and takes *facem* as direct object.

16-17 **thalamis . . . meis / quales stetistis** translate *quales stetistis* first: Medea asks the Furies to be present and to be horrendous, just as they were at her own wedding. The wedding torches at her own wedding had been wielded ominously by the Furies, because she and Jason had killed her brother Absyrtus to help their escape back to Greece; Medea seeks similar ill omen at the wedding of Jason and his new wife.

17-18   **letum . . . letumque** both direct object of *date*

18   **socero** i.e., Creon, king of Corinth and father of Jason's bride

       regiae stirpi may refer to Creon's household more generally, though it may also foreshadow Medea's killing of her and Jason's children *as if* they were now part of Creon's royal line. Medea, however, will come to the idea of killing her children only gradually.

40–50: I'm not a girl anymore

As Medea's prologue-soliloquy continues, we encounter another common mode of Senecan tragedy: the self-address scene, in which a character addresses herself or her *animus*. Here Medea, reviewing the crimes she committed as a young woman to help bring Jason back to Greece, urges herself on to greater extremes as she prepares her exit from Corinth.

In Seneca's prose works, self-address is often a tool for steering one's mind toward improved moral consistency (*constantia*), but Medea seeks "improvements" that are altogether different from those sought by a philosopher.

     Meter: IAMBIC TRIMETERS

40   **Per uiscera ipsa** lit. "through the very guts," i.e., even carving a path through the body. The phrase picks up on a comparison of her future victims to sacrificial animals in the previous line (here omitted).

       supplicio dat. of purpose

41   **si uiuis, anime** She challenges her mind to show signs of life and signs of courage.

       quid standard usage after *si*, equivalent to *aliquid*

       antiqui . . . uigoris gen. of the whole with *quid*; *antiqui* ("pristine") alludes to Medea's previous feats when she and Jason were escaping from Colchis.

42 **pelle femineos metus** She seeks to overcome the emotions apparently typical of women.

 Caucasum . . . indue lit. "put on the Caucasus," i.e., take up your native identity as a barbarian. For the Caucasus mountains, see the MAP in Appendix B.

 mente either instrumental abl. or abl. of place where

44–45 **uidit . . . uidebit** lit. "has seen . . . will see," i.e., witness

 Phasis, Pontus, Isthmos metonyms referring to Colchis and Corinth respectively. See the MAP in Appendix B.

45–46 **effera ignota horrida, / tremenda** asyndeton; all these adjs. agree with *mala.*

46 **caelo . . . terris** both dat. of agent with gerundive

47 **uulnera et caedem** general references to the killings that facilitated Jason's escape from Colchis

47–48 **uagum / funus per artus** "a death wide-ranging through (scattered) limbs," alluding to the killing of her brother Absyrtus, whose limbs were scattered on the sea (see note on lines 16–17 above)

49 **haec** acc. pl. n.; refers to the deeds mentioned in the previous two lines.

50 **maiora . . . scelera** invokes the common theme in Senecan tragedy of committing ever greater crimes. Medea is distinctive, however, in seeking to outdo her *own* crimes, as if in revenge against Jason for having made her do them.

 post partus contrasts Medea's present maturity as a mother with her earlier identity as *uirgo*; the emphasis on her maternity also hints at her future crimes directed against her children.

155–76: Rejecting sensible advice

Act 2 had begun with Medea preparing to ask Creon for a brief reprieve to her banishment—just long enough for her to get her revenge. But now her Nurse intervenes to dissuade her, in a "passion-restraint" scene consisting of a battle of *sententiae*. The dialogue, fiercely fought in alternating lines (*stichomythia*) and alternating half-lines (*antilabē*), only increases Medea's determination to live up to her role as "Medea."

Meter: IAMBIC TRIMETERS

155 **Leuis est dolor, qui . . . potest** Medea seeks to emphasize the magnitude of her grief, echoing her own words, *grauior exurgat dolor*, at line 49 in the prologue above.

156 **clepere sese** In earlier lines (here omitted), the Nurse had urged her to keep silent and conceal her anger.

   non latitant "cannot be kept hidden"

   mala nom. pl. n. substantive "sufferings"

157 **furialem impetum** hints at Medea's resemblance to the Furies.

158 **uix . . . quies** i.e., things are bad enough for you as it is, even if you were not to raise a protest

159 **Fortuna fortes metuit** This *sententia* distorts the proverbial expression, "Fortune helps the brave" (e.g., Terence, *Phormio* 203: *fortes fortuna adiuuat*; cf. Hine 2000, 135).

160 **Tunc est probanda** "(*uirtus*) should be put to the test (only) then . . ."; *tunc* introduces the condition *si locum uirtus habet*. The Nurse's response begins the *stichomythia* between her and Medea.

161 **Numquam potest . . . locus** As the *stichomythia* continues, Medea contradicts the Nurse with a *sententia* that gives a new inflection to the Nurse's own terms (*uirtus, locus*). This formulation resembles the central tenet of Stoicism concerning the invincibility of virtue, except that by *uirtus* Medea means something more like "manliness, courage," which in her case involves violent criminal acts.

162   **rebus . . . adflictis** dat. of advantage, or indirect object: "for
        your shattered state of affairs"

        uiam i.e., a way out

163   **Qui** "he who"; Medea explains that she has nothing left to lose.

        desperet nihil either "should not despair at all" (*nihil* as adv.)
        or "should not despair of anything" (*nihil* as acc. noun); with
        desperet jussive subjunctive

164–65 **Abiere Colchi . . . tibi** The Nurse impresses upon Medea the
        absence of resources that had aided her in the past.

165   **opibus e tantis** "from such great resources," i.e., from what
        she had accumulated with Jason

166   **Medea superest** "Medea remains"

        hic "here," referring to herself; she portrays herself as a con-
        troller of elemental forces.

168   **pater** Medea abandoned her father Aeetes while escaping
        from Colchis, and successfully eluded his armies.

169   **sint licet terra edita** "(no), even though they [i.e., the *arma*]
        be brought forth from the earth." This alludes to the "Earth-
        born" warriors in Colchis, which grew from the dragon's
        teeth; Medea had helped Jason to defeat them in battle.

170   **Moriere** second person fut. indicative

        Cupio i.e., *cupio moriri*

        Paenituit fugae i.e., she regards her previous flight, from Col-
        chis to Greece, as a mistake

171   **Fiam** i.e., *Medea fiam*. This verse is often quoted in support
        of the idea that Seneca's Medea has a self-conscious sense that
        she will be taking upon herself the preexisting literary char-
        acter of "Medea."

        Cui sim "for whom (i.e., for which father) I am (a mother)"; a
        cutting reference to Jason

173   **moras** i.e., a way to slow down her avenger. She probably al-
        ludes to her murder of Absyrtus, which had slowed down the
        Colchians pursuing her and Jason.

174-75 **minis / animosque minue** The soundplay of *min-* and *-nim-*
        adds urgency to the Nurse's advice.

175   **tempori aptari** "to adapt yourself to the situation"

176   **Fortuna ... potest** another quasi-philosophical *sententia* em-
        phasizing the mind's invulnerability to external conditions

301–8: Blame the boat

Act 2 had concluded with Creon reluctantly permitting Medea to
spend one more day in Corinth before going into exile. Now the
Chorus, in a typical Senecan interlude, reflects on the larger sequence of events that conspired to bring Medea to Greece in the first
place: Jason's voyage on the first ever ship, the Argo. The Chorus
also exhibits a deeply ambivalent attitude to technological progress
in general, drawing attention to the violation of natural boundaries.

The identity of the Chorus in Seneca's *Medea* is indeterminate, in
contrast with Euripides' more precise identification of his Chorus as
women of Corinth. Euripides' Chorus is also, to begin with, sympa-
thetic to Medea's plight, whereas Seneca's Chorus is overtly hostile
not only to the Argo, but also to Medea personally.

Meter: ANAPAESTIC DIMETERS

301   **Audax nimium qui** i.e., *nimium audax fuit is qui . . . .* Seneca
        echoes an ode of Horace on the same theme of human techno-
        logical audacity: "That man had a heart of oak and threefold
        bronze around his chest, who first entrusted to the ferocious
        sea his fragile ship" (*illi robur et aes triplex / circa pectus erat,
        qui fragilem truci / commisit pelago ratem / primus*; *Carmina*
        1.3.9–12). Horace's poem had begun from his anxiety about
        a sea-journey being undertaken by Virgil from Greece back
        to Italy, and proceeded to catalogue all the boundaries vio-
        lated by human beings, and provoking divine retribution: fire
        stolen by Prometheus, the air invaded by Daedalus, and the
        underworld entered by Hercules. To readers familiar with Au-
        gustan poetry, Seneca's Chorus may seem to hint at parallels
        between the voyage of the Argo and these other myths, each

concluding in the gods' punishment of human daring. Certainly the Augustan echo intensifies the dramatic impact that Seneca's play would have upon its cultivated audience.

primus "for the first time"

301–2   **freta . . . perfida** acc. pl.

302   **rupit** an image of violence characterizing the ship's cutting through the water

303   **terrasque . . . uidens** i.e., losing sight of his home shores as he sails away

304   **animam . . . credidit** "entrusted his life." This emphasis on trust and risk-taking continues throughout the passage.

305   **dubio . . . cursu** he hadn't yet learned navigation.

306   **tenui . . . ligno** recalls the ancient idea that the sailor is only a finger's breadth (the thickness of the ship's hull) away from death.

307–8   **inter . . . uices** follows from the pple. *ducto* in the abl. absolute construction of the following line: "with too-slender boundary drawn . . . between . . . ."

361–79: The Argo's price

Later in the ode, the Chorus asserts that the consequences of the Argo's voyage include Medea herself, and a world transformed by travel.

Meter: ANAPAESTIC DIMETERS

361a   **huius** agrees with *cursus*, gen. (The numbering of lines 361a, 361b, 365a, 365b simply accommodates the fact that these lines were divided differently in earlier printed editions; on the anapaestic half-lines, see note on line 361b below.)

pretium this term's double sense of "prize" and "cost" will be played out in the characterization of the Golden Fleece, and especially Medea, as treasures but also as evils (cf. *malum* at line 362 below).

361b   This half-line varies the meter, with one anapaestic foot instead of two (a variation repeated in lines 365a, 367, 372). See also Appendix C on ANAPAESTIC DIMETERS.

362   **maiusque mari Medea malum** The alliteration draws attention to the role of Medea in the story; *mari* is abl. of comparison; *Medea* is in apposition to *maius malum*.

363   **merces . . . digna** in apposition to *Medea*

prima . . . carina abl. governed by *digna*

364   **Nunc iam** "now already," signalling a shift of focus to the present world of the Roman empire, which gives evidence of how the effects of the first ship have been played out. This is a remarkable shift of perspective in the Chorus.

364-65a   **omnes / patitur leges** refers to the Roman conquest of the seas.

365b-67   **non . . . quaeritur Argo** "there is no need for an Argo"

compacta, referens, inclita all nom. sing. f., agreeing with *Argo*

365b   **Palladia compacta manu** "built by the hand of Athena" (see note on lines 2–3 above)

366   **regum . . . remos** "the oars of kings"; a grandiose reference to the Argonauts, anticipating line 368, with its reference to the modern-day everyman

369   **motus** i.e., *motus est*

urbes nom. pl.

370   **terra . . . noua** abl. of place where; in poetry no prep. is needed.

371   **nil** direct object of *reliquit*

qua fuerat sede "in the place where it had been"

373-74   **Indus . . . bibunt** describes people drinking from foreign rivers, a metonym indicating their displacement from their own regions as they travel along major trade routes. For the rivers Rhine, Elbe, and Araxes, see the MAP in Appendix B.

373   **gelidum** agrees with *Araxen* (Greek acc. sing.).

374   **Albin** acc. sing.

375–79 **uenient . . . ultima Thule** In the early modern period these
        lines were taken to foretell the discovery of the Americas by
        European explorers (cf. Hine 2000, 154).

375   **annis . . . seris** "in a later time"

376   **quibus** abl. of time when; the antecedent is *saecula*.

        uincula rerum "the bonds that hold the world together";
        uincula is acc.

377–78 **laxet, pateat, detegat** subjunctives in rel. clause of charac-
        teristic

379   **nec sit terris ultima Thule** The semi-mythical Thule was the
        most distant known land in the north (perhaps Iceland; see
        MAP in Appendix B). The Chorus here points to a time when
        Thule will no longer be *ultima*. The case of *terris* is perhaps
        dat. of possession ("most distant to [known] lands").

537–50: Finding Jason's weak spot

This exchange between Medea and Jason comes from the end of
a long dialogue between the estranged couple in Act 3. Although
Jason seeks to console Medea on her banishment, there is also some
tension as she here requests to be allowed to take the children with
her into exile.

In a striking aside in the final two lines of the passage, Medea
comments on the value of the children to Jason and apparently decides for the first time that the children themselves must be the material for her revenge.

Meter: IAMBIC TRIMETERS

537–38 **Sana, placida** both probably acc. pl. n. substantives ("inter-
        nal accusatives") with the meaning determined by the cor-
        responding verb: "sane thoughts," "calm words"; alternatively,
        they are nom. sing. f. functioning adverbially.

537   **meditari** the verb has associations with the spiritual exercises
       that philosophers use for training themselves to endure mis-
       fortune (see on "Techniques of philosophical training" in the
       Introduction). Jason's advice has further associations with
       consolation (especially *solamen* at line 539).

538-39 **quod . . . solamen** i.e., *aliquod . . . solamen*; standard usage
       after *si*

539   **pete** takes *solamen* from the previous clause as its implied ob-
       ject.

540-41 **Contemnere . . . soletque** Medea reminds Jason that she can
       endure the poverty that comes with exile, alluding to the fact
       that she went into exile from Colchis with Jason, and endured
       hardships with him then.

541   **tantum** "only," introducing *liceat*

541-42 **fugae . . . comites** "as companions of my flight"; *comites* is acc.

542   **liceat** "let it be permitted (for me)," with *mihi* implied

543   **profundam** subjunctive in rel. clause of purpose
       noui gnati i.e., from his new wife Creusa

545   **pietas** in this instance, a father's duties to his sons
       istud direct object of *pati*; with *istud* ("that [outcome]") Jason
       refers in a hostile tone to Medea's taking the children with her.

545-46 **ut possim** dependent on *non . . . cogat*: "could not compel me
       to be able"

546   **ipse memet** the prons. add decisive emphasis to both subject
       and object.
       et rex et socer both terms refer to Creon, in his two distinct
       capacities.

547   **haec . . . hoc** both prons. refer to the idea of Jason's keeping the
       children; their gender and number are determined by assimi-
       lation to the respective predicate nouns *causa* and *leuamen*.

547-48 **perusti pectoris / curis** "for the cares (dat. of advantage) of a
       heart that has been scorched"

548   **queam** potential subjunctive

548-49 **spiritu ... / ... membris, luce** asyndeton, emphasizing Jason's willingness to endure any other suffering; all three are abl. of separation governed by *carere*.

549 **Sic natos amat? ...** in her aside, Medea now refers to Jason in the third person, and with great sarcasm. Although this is not absolute proof that Seneca's play was performed rather than just read, the text requires that we imagine an audience as present; the audience (or perhaps the reader) is here disarmingly enlisted by Medea as a confidante.

550 **bene est** "good news!"

tenetur i.e., as if snared in a trap

uulneri ... locus "a place for a wound"

670–93: She's planning something evil

This monologue by the Nurse arises at the beginning of Act 4, where the Nurse is alone but acts as a kind of messenger: she is in emotional turmoil, because she has seen Medea gathering materials for witchcraft. Her speech serves as a preface to the rest of the Act, in which Medea herself invokes evil forces and assembles the poisons that will help her to destroy Creusa and Creon. The emphasis on Medea as a sorceress owes much to Ovid's depiction of Medea in book 7 of his *Metamorphoses*.

Meter: IAMBIC TRIMETERS

670 **Pauet animus, horret** The Nurse describes her sense of foreboding, even though she remains unclear on exactly *what* Medea is planning.

671 **immane quantum augescit** i.e., *immane est quantum augescit*, with *quantum* adverbial; the subject of *augescit* is *dolor*.

semet emphasizes the autonomy of Medea's self-propelling grief. Compare the virtual personification of *dolor* at *Helv.* 2.1 above.

672 **uim ... praeteritam** "the strength it had before now"

673 **uidi** The implied direct object is *Medeam*.

aggressam deos Medea's use of magic is essentially "an attack on the gods of the upper world" (Hine 2000, 177). Compare her ambition to rival the gods at 166–67 above: *Medea superest*: *hic . . . uides / . . . deos.*

674   **caelum trahentem** alludes to a typical ability of witches to draw the moon down from the sky.

674–75   **maius his, maius parat / Medea monstrum** The anaphoric repetition and alliteration add intensity; *his* is abl. of comparison; *monstrum* (here acc., modified by *maius*) can refer to anything prodigious or ill-omened. For the alliteration with *m-*, compare 362 above.

675   **ut** "when"

676   **penetrale** Medea has a secret place for preparing magic, probably inside her house, though its location is left indefinite.

677–78   **effundit, explicat** The repeated prefix *e(x)-* introduces an image of her disclosing secret materials.

678   **etiam ipsa** "even she herself." Medea had used magic in several episodes of the Argonautic myth, but apparently never as strong as this; the tense of *timuit* indicates that she previously feared to use them, but now brings them to bear with greater assurance.

679   **turbam malorum** "swarm of evils." The gesture may echo the mythical first woman, Pandora, opening her jar, letting all evils out into the world. The term *turba* is applied to a mass of snakes at line 685 below.

arcana secreta abdita acc. pl. n. substantives, in apposition to *turbam*; the asyndeton enhances the sense of a rapid succession of evils.

680   **triste laeua . . . sacrum manu** an ornate line giving the two adjs. and then their corresponding nouns in the same order. *Laeuus* in poetry indicates ill-omen (though in Roman augury the left side was lucky).

681   **pestes uocat . . .** The Nurse begins a catalogue of different kinds of poison, demonstrating Medea's universal mastery of magic materials.

681-83   The heat of *feruentis . . . Libyae* in Africa is contrasted with the *frigore Arctoo* of Mt. Taurus in Asia Minor, and sand (*harena*) is contrasted with snow (*niue*). For Libya and Taurus, see the MAP in Appendix B.

683   **frigore Arctoo** abl. of cause with *rigent*

684   **magicis cantibus** abl. of means. Songs and spells were a central part of Medea's sorcery.

685   **squamifera** a rare compound adj., here used to encompass the entire class of scaly creatures

         latebris . . . desertis abl. absolute

         adest this term hints at the language of invocation, as used by Medea at line 13 above: *nunc, nunc adeste.*

686   **hic** "here"

687   **quibus** dat. of disadvantage, going closely with *mortifera*

688   **stupet** The subject is again the *serpens.*

689   **nodis . . . aggestis** "in bunched coils"

690   **cogitque in orbes** "and contorts (its body) into circles"

         inquit The Nurse now quotes Medea's words.

691   **ima . . . tellus** i.e., the underworld, which Medea here sees as an insufficient source for her magic

692   **caelo** abl. of separation. Medea will in fact employ birds, among other things, in her magic.

         iam iam The repetition conveys urgency.

693   **fraude uulgari** abl. of comparison: "than ordinary treachery." Once again Medea shows an ambition to outdo previous crimes.

849–69: Her rage is visible

This choral ode comes in the aftermath of Medea's spell-casting (in Act 4), when Creusa and Creon are dying offstage, something as yet unknown to the Chorus. The Chorus has seen Medea's agitated behavior, and although they don't know exactly what she has planned, they know it can't be good.

In lines omitted at the end of this passage, the Chorus also prays to Phoebus, the sun god, to set earlier than usual and thus to end Medea's last day in Corinth quickly—but to no avail.

Meter: IAMBIC CATALECTIC DIMETERS

849-51 **Quonam . . . rapitur?** -*nam* adds emphasis to the interrog.: "Where *on earth* . . . is she being carried to?"

maenas nom., referring to Medea. The figure of the maenad (i.e., "bacchant," raging female devotee of Dionysus/Bacchus) introduces associations with temporary insanity and violence. In Euripides' *Bacchae*, the maenad Agave inadvertently kills her own son, Pentheus—a parallel that bodes ill for Medea's children.

851 **impotenti** "uncontrolled"

853 **ira** abl. of agent (anger personified) with *citatus*

854 **caput** direct object of *quatiens*

856 **regi** dat. with *minatur*

857 **quis credat exulem?** i.e., *quis credat eam esse exulem?* Medea is not behaving in accord with her status as a banished nobody.

858-61 **Flagrant . . . colorem** The sudden changes in complexion suggest inner turmoil.

860 **uagante forma** abl. absolute, "her appearance fluctuating"

861 **seruat** The subject is Medea.

863-65 **ut tigris . . . Gangeticum nemus** a simile that owes something to Ovid, who compares Procne, as she kills her son Itys, to a *Gangetica . . . tigris* ("tiger of the Ganges," *Metamorphoses* 6.636–37; cf. Hine 2000, 197)

863   **orba** As Hine (2000, 197) notes, this detail is an addition to the Ovidian simile by Seneca; it corresponds nicely to Medea's situation, as she has been prohibited from taking her children into exile.

natis abl. of separation

867   **non amores** "nor (does she know how to rein in) her loves"

868   **ira amorque** i.e., her anger at being divorced and her love for both Jason and the children

868-69   **causam / iunxere** "have made common cause" (trans. Hine 2000, 197); the metaphor comes from the law courts.

904–15: You ain't seen nothin' yet

At the beginning of Act 5, a Messenger had reported the grisly deaths of Creusa and Creon, and the Nurse urged Medea to leave Corinth immediately to avoid recriminations. But Medea responded by asking, *Egone ut recedam?* ("Me? Withdraw?," *Med.* 893), and she embarked upon a violent soliloquy. Now, partway into the soliloquy, she explains that she is only just getting warmed up.

Meter: IAMBIC TRIMETERS

904   **quidquid admissum est adhuc** i.e., her killing of Creusa and Creon; this whole clause is the subject of *uocetur* in the following line.

905   **hoc age!** probably a self-directed exhortation: "get on with it!"

faxo sciant the archaic *faxo* (a form with a fut. sense, though explanations vary) governs the subjunctive: "I will make (sure) they know."

906   **uulgaris notae** gen. of description: "of common type"

907   **quae commodaui scelera** i.e., *ea scelera quae commodaui*, with *ea scelera* functioning as the subject of *fuerint* in the previous line

prolusit casts the royal murders as simply Medea's warm-up act. But note that the "agent" of the crimes is not Medea herself but her *dolor*.

908   **per ista** "in those (murders)," referring to her killing of Creu-
       sa and Creon

       manus . . . rudes "my uneducated hands"

908-9 **quid . . . magnum** "what (that was truly) great?"; direct object
       of *audere*

909   **puellaris furor** echoes her earlier words *haec uirgo feci* at line
       49 above.

910   **Medea nunc sum** asserts her maturation in the role of "Me-
       dea." Compare *Medea fiam* at line 171 above.

911-13 **iuuat, iuuat . . . iuuat . . . iuuat** With these repetitions Medea
       seeks to establish beyond doubt (including perhaps her *own*
       doubt) that she is glad she killed her brother Absyrtus when
       she and Jason were fleeing Colchis.

912-13 **arcano patrem / spoliasse sacro** refers to when she had as-
       sisted Jason in the stealing of the Golden Fleece, against the
       wishes of her father; *spoliasse* is syncopated from *spoliauisse*.

913-14 **in exitium senis armasse natas** alludes to the more recent
       episode in Jason's home city of Iolchos, in which Medea had
       deceitfully led the daughters of the aged Pelias to boil their
       father to death.

914   **materiam** Medea directly addresses her *dolor* and treats it as
       an artisan in need of new material to work with. Compare
       Seneca's depiction of the wise person as an artisan at *Ep.* 85.40
       above.

915   **non rudem** "not inexperienced"; her apprenticeship is now
       over.

926–36: A brief return of maternal affection

Further into her long soliloquy, Medea suddenly recoils from her plan to kill the children, and in this passage she briefly seeks to dissuade herself from going ahead with it. But the children's innocence soon loses out to Medea's desire for revenge.

Meter: IAMBIC TRIMETERS

926   **pepulit** She uses pf. tense here to describe a sudden, surprising event: "has struck." The third-person description here and in the following lines is common in depictions of bodily reaction in Senecan tragedy (as at 670 above); here the third-person mode partially distances the speaker Medea from her body's reaction.

927   **loco** abl. of separation: "from its position"

928   **materque . . . redit** a remarkable description of Medea's two conflicting roles

       tota may be nom. or abl. (it is metrically indeterminate), and thus may agree with either *mater* or *coniuge*.

       coniuge expulsa abl. absolute

929-30 **egone ut . . . fundam . . . ?** "Am I to pour out . . . ?" The construction *ego* + (*ut*) + subjunctive is common for rhetorical questions uttered in a self-exhortation.

       liberum syncopated from *liberorum*

930   **melius** acc.; an imperative such as *fac* is implied. The urge to do something morally better is a temporary deviation from her urge to do something greater in violence.

931   **incognitum istud facinus** i.e., the infanticide her *demens furor* has been planning; *istud* has a strong second-person sense here ("of yours").

932   **a me quoque** "even from me," i.e., despite her more general profile as an evildoer

       quod scelus miseri luent? The question upholds the children's innocence.

933   **Iason genitor** i.e., "Jason('s being their) father." The children are guilty by association.

934   **Medea mater** i.e., "Medea('s being their) mother"; further "guilt" by association

934-35 **non sunt mei; / . . . mei sunt** Medea gives two distinct and contradictory reasons for why the children should die: (1) Jason's removal of them from her (together with their adoption into Creon's household) *and* (2) their association with her, their evildoing mother.

936   **et frater fuit** Medea thus appeals again to her murder of her young and innocent brother Absyrtus as a precedent that makes her killing of her children not so exceptional after all.

1008–13: Double infanticide

Toward the end of her soliloquy, Medea saw a vision of the ghost of her dead brother Absyrtus calling for revenge, which eliminated all doubt from her mind. She immediately killed the first son, and her hesitation in killing the second son was simply a matter of waiting for Jason to arrive, so that he could be a spectator. Now Jason pleads with her to stop.

Meter: IAMBIC TRIMETERS

1008 **poenae satis** *poenae* is either dat. of purpose ("enough to serve as punishment") or gen. of the whole ("enough punishment").

1009 **una caede** "by a single killing," going closely with *satiari*

1010 **nullam** i.e., *nullam caedem*: "no (killing at all)"

      petisset syncopated form of *petiuisset*

      ut . . . perimam, tamen concessive: "even though I kill . . . , nevertheless"

1011 **nimium** goes closely with *angustus*.

1012 **quod** i.e., *aliquod*, standard usage after *si*

pignus The term is often applied to a child, who serves as the "surety" of a marriage; Medea seems to refer here to any unborn child of Jason's she might be carrying.

1013   **uiscera** echoes her self-command above at line 40: *Per uiscera ipsa quaere supplicio uiam.*

1018–27: Kill me instead

In the play's final passage, Jason tries offering up his own life to prevent Medea from killing the second son. But Medea, who is standing in the flying chariot that she once received from her grandfather, the Sun, kills the child and bids Jason a cruel farewell.

Meter: IAMBIC TRIMETERS

1018   **Infesta** vocative sing. f., addressing Medea

memet Jason emphatically seeks to substitute himself for the second child.

Misereri iubes i.e., in asking to be killed, Jason is asking for the soft option

bene est, peractum est "all's well, it's finished." This appears to be the moment when Medea finishes killing the second child. The phrase *peractum est* echoes an expression from the theater or amphitheater, referring to the end of a show.

dolor vocative: Medea addresses her grief as if it a person present, as at line 914 above.

1020   **quae . . . litarem** rel. clause of characteristic. Medea frames her killing as a form of sacrifice offered up to assuage her own grief.

huc "up here," i.e., to where Medea stands in her flying chariot

1021   **ingrate** a reminder that Medea sees Jason as failing to recognize her services to him in Colchis

coniugem agnoscis tuam? Medea forces Jason to recognize her, and to remember her violent powers. The term *agnoscis* plays upon the traditional "recognition" (Greek *anagnōrisis*) moment in ancient tragedy, in which a character discovers the unhappy truth about his or her situation.

1022   **sic fugere soleo** "this is how I always flee." This refers to the chariot as Medea's conventional method of escaping from tight situations, and also to her record of going into exile triumphant.

       uia once again echoes her earlier self-address at line 40 above: *quaere . . . uiam.*

1023-24 **colla . . . iugo / summissa praebent** "offer their necks submissive to the yoke": the dat. *iugo* works closely with both *summissa* and *praebent.*

1024   **recipe** the line probably accompanies Medea's giving back to Jason the children's corpses.

       parens sarcastic

1027   **nullos esse . . . deos** in light of what has happened to him, Jason questions the existence of divine justice. The reference to gods in this, the play's final line, echoes (and contrasts with) Medea's prayer to *di coniugales* (etc.) in line 1 above, and also develops the idea that she has displaced the gods (compare line 167) or attacked them (line 673).

       qua ueheris "where you will be carried," i.e., "wherever you drive [your chariot]")

Scenario 4: Letters to a Friend

In the *Epistulae Morales*, written over the last three years of his life (62–65), Seneca gives the impression that he was either locked away in philosophical study or journeying around the Italian countryside, while Lucilius was for much of this period occupied far away in Sicily. In conjunction with this situation, the themes of separation, distance, and travel are woven into many of the letters, and the selected letters below offer advice on the moral aspects of travel, with "travel" understood in more than one sense.

    In letter 2 below, Seneca draws comparisons between travel and reading, as if we "travel" from one book to another, which means that certain warnings about traveling too frequently must also apply to Lucilius as he accumulates books. In letter 40, as we will see, he writes more directly about how handwritten letters can bridge the gap between one friend (Lucilius in Sicily) and another (himself in Rome). Then, in letter 49, we follow Seneca on his real travels in the vicinity of Pompeii and Naples, where he describes the emotional experience of being reminded of Lucilius (his friend was a native Pompeian). In letter 55, sent from the same region, he also explores the ruins of a villa once owned by a recluse named Servilius Vatia, and raises the question of whether Vatia's luxurious location can really match the "location" provided by the mind (*animus*), in which the philosopher can live a truly happy life and communicate with his friends, however distant. (For Pompeii, Naples, and the other locations in Campania, see the inset MAP in Appendix B.)

For further background, see on "Seneca's life" and "The *Epistulae Morales*" in the Introduction. For additional commentary on letter 2 see Motto (2001); and on letters 40 and 55, see Summers (1910). For discussion of the *Epistulae Morales* in general, see Edwards (2008), Wilson (2008), and Ker (2009) 147–76. On the Campanian letters in particular, see Henderson (2004) and Ker (2009) 325–28, 342–60.

ᴥ *EPISTULAE MORALES 2*

In his first letter (omitted here), Seneca had urged Lucilius to make better use of his time, emphasizing how precious and irreplaceable time is as a resource for attending to his spiritual health. Here, in his second letter, he shifts topic, first to travel, then to reading. The focus on reading, which will continue for the rest of letter 2, implicitly raises the question of what Lucilius is supposed to get from being a reader of Seneca's letters themselves.

1–2: About your reading habits . . .

Seneca opens by greeting Lucilius and applauding his avoidance of travel, but he then criticizes his friend's habit of reading many authors. Both these activities, and their inherent dangers, are portrayed in vivid terms. Travel itself also provides a metaphor for reading.

SENECA LVCILIO SVO SALVTEM The verb *dicit* is implied;
the use of *suo* and the omission of the other parts of Lucilius' name
signal Lucilius as a close friend. Seneca's letters are preserved without any further information about when or where each letter was
written (unlike those of Cicero, which appear to have been published
with indications of date and location).

1   **ex iis quae audio** Seneca implies that he has external sources
       of information about Lucilius in Sicily, evidently from people
       who had either traveled there or received news. As an imperial
       administrator, Lucilius was to some extent in the public eye.

       bonam spem de te concipio i.e., regarding Lucilius' progress
       toward spiritual wellbeing and wisdom

       Aegri animi . . . est gen. of characteristic: "is (the symptom)
       of an unwell mind "

       ista iactatio refers pejoratively to the kind of travel mentioned
       in the previous sentence.

       primum argumentum . . . existimo with *esse* implied; this
       introduces, as a predicate, the infinitive *posse* ("the ability [to]
       . . .").

       secum morari an image of introspective or self-directed con-
       cern. Seneca's frequent use of reflex. phrases is closely con-
       nected with his philosophical regimen of self-care and self-
       transformation.

2   **illud autem uide** "watch *this*, however, namely . . . ," with *illud*
       anticipatory, introducing the prohibition *ne . . . habeat*

       ista lectio Here *ista* has a strong second-person sense: "that
       reading you mentioned."

       omnis generis gen. of description qualifying *uoluminum*

       uagum et instabile these terms (like others in the following
       lines) suggest that Seneca treats reading as analogous to spa-
       tial movement, or even as a specialized form of "travel."

       Certis ingeniis inmorari et innutriri "to linger upon and be
       nourished by reliable minds." The case of *ingeniis* is probably

dat. with the nearer verb *inmorari*, though with *innutriri* we would expect an abl. of means.

quod ... sedeat rel. clause of characteristic, or of purpose

Nusquam est qui ubique est the epigrammatic statement of proverbial wisdom again characterizes reading as a form of spatial movement.

Vitam ... exigentibus dat. of reference: "to/for those consuming their life ..."

hoc nom. sing. n.: "this, namely ... ," anticipating the substantive clause *ut ... habeant*

idem accidat necesse est standard subjunctive construction after *necesse est*: "it is necessary that the same thing happen"

ingenio dat. with compound verb *applicant*

3–4: Watch your "diet"

In reading, as in all things, frequent changes are always harmful, whereas careful "digestion" can be good. Although Lucilius may like to browse his bookshelves like a buffet, Seneca suggests an alternative: reread the best authors, with a view to extracting practical advice for each day.

3   **Non prodest cibus ...** to illustrate his point about the dangers of cursory reading, Seneca appeals to a series of comparisons from different areas of human experience: food, medicine, and horticulture.

qui The antecedent is *cibus*.

statim modifies *emittitur*; the reference is to excretion or vomiting.

aeque ... quam "as greatly as"

remediorum ... mutatio The phrase echoes *locorum mutationibus* at *Ep.* 2.1 above, but now applies the concept of *mutatio* to new areas of activity.

non uenit ... ad cicatricem "does not heal to a scar"

nihil tam utile est ut in transitu prosit Seneca distils the lesson to be drawn from the above comparisons. This is reinforced by the ring-composition of the long sentence, which begins and ends in two forms of the same verb (*prodest* and *prosit*).

planta an ambiguous term; it probably denotes a "plant" being transplanted, though it is not inconceivable that it refers to a "sole of the foot" that is prevented from healing.

Distringit here not transitive but absolute: "is a distraction"

cum legere non possis . . . quantum legas This striking formulation, almost like a riddle, reorders the same two verbs to generate the opposite meaning; the rhetorical figure is called *antithesis* (Latin *contentio*). In his *De Tranquillitate Animi* (*Tranq.* 9), Seneca criticizes ostentatious book-collecting more fully.

quantum habueris with *tantum* implicit, "(as much) as you have acquired"; *habueris* is probably fut. pf. indicative rather than pf. subjunctive.

4   **modo . . . hunc . . . modo illum** "now this . . . now that"

inquis Seneca introduces an element of dialogue, as if Lucilius is defending himself.

euoluere The image is of Lucilius opening papyrus rolls one after another.

Fastidientis stomachi gen. of characteristic; compare *aegri animi* at *Ep.* 2.1 above. Together with *degustare*, this returns to the earlier comparison of reading to eating; food continues as a dominant image in the rest of the passage.

quae a sentence-connecting rel.: "these things"; the antecedent is *multa*.

Probatos "proven authors." Seneca's advice here was often excerpted during the Middle Ages, sometimes with reference to favoring an approved set of Christian authors over broader reading of pagan authors, sometimes just to emphasize selectivity in general.

si . . . libuerit . . . redi a fut. more vivid conditional (with *libuerit* fut. pf. indicative) in which the apodosis is an imperative rather than the more usual fut. indicative

quando standard usage after *si*, for *aliquando*

Aliquid cotidie Seneca here outlines one aspect of the *cotidiana meditatio* ("daily practice") that is a focus of the letters. Of the two specific topics mentioned here, *paupertas* and *mors*, the present letter itself will address *paupertas* below.

auxili gen. of the whole with *Aliquid . . . aliquid*: "some assistance"

aduersus mortem i.e., against one's fear of death

ceteras pestes such as exile, perhaps. Compare *Ep.* 85.40 above.

percurreris fut. pf. indicative

quod . . . concoquas rel. clause of characteristic, or purpose

5–6: Be happy with little

Seneca concludes by recounting some moral advice about *paupertas* ("poverty, frugality") that he has distilled or digested. Surprisingly, this advice comes from his readings in the works of Epicurus, not Stoic authors.

5   **Hoc ipse quoque facio** i.e., Seneca practices what he preaches. As often in the letters, he portrays himself as a progressing student rather than as someone who has already acquired wisdom.

Hodiernum hoc est "today's (excerpt) is this . . . ." Seneca here initiates a routine that he will continue in many of his letters: he concludes with a quotation from what he has been reading.

apud Epicurum "in (the writings of) Epicurus." It may be a surprise that Seneca, a Stoic, would be excerpting from Epicurus (341–270 BCE), since the Epicureans regarded "pleasure" (Latin *uoluptas*; Greek *hēdonē*) as the highest good, in contrast with the Stoics, who privileged "virtue" (Latin *uirtus*;

Greek *aretē*). But there was also much overlap between the two schools on basic morality, as Seneca makes clear in the next few lines. Seneca may have conceived of the idea of writing the *Epistulae Morales* from philosophical letters written by Epicurus, and it is possible that this quotation comes directly from a lost Epicurus letter. For further information on these schools of philosophy, see "The Stoics: Life according to nature" in the Introduction.

et in aliena castra "even into the opposition's camp"

non tamquam transfuga, sed tamquam explorator the military language evokes a "war" of doctrines, as with *castra* above.

honesta . . . res est "is a virtuous thing"

laeta paupertas "cheer(il)y (accepted) poverty"

6   **Illa** i.e., the *laeta paupertas* referred to by Epicurus; Seneca begins to explicate the quotation.

Quid . . . refert "What does it matter . . . ?," introducing the indirect questions in *quantum . . . quantum . . . quantum*

illi dat. of possession, going closely with *iaceat*: "(how much) he has lying (around)"

pascat aut feneret these terms refer respectively to holdings in cattle (and perhaps land), and the lending of money for interest.

alieno dat. sing. n. substantive, "another's (wealth)"; dat. with compound verb

acquirenda a negative concept, both because it involves becoming dependent on the future, which is uncertain, and because it involves unrestrained desire for things of no intrinsic value (i.e., "indifferents")

modus The concept of measure is associated with the more general philosophical question of what is and isn't valuable, and how to limit desires for things that are "indifferent." Below Seneca offers two answers, making reference to the principles of necessity and sufficiency.

primus i.e., *primus diuitiarum modus est*

proximus i.e., *proximus diuitiarum modus est*

Vale the standard greeting at the end of a letter

∾ *EPISTULAE MORALES 40.1: Our letters unite us*

Seneca begins letter 40 by thanking Lucilius for writing to him often, and then explains the effect that seeing Lucilius' letters has on him whenever he opens them. He touches on familiar themes of epistolography: a desire for frequent letters, a sense of "presence" between absent friends, and the superiority of letters over visual portraits.

The letter also points toward the theme of philosophical friendship conducted between two minds over a long distance, which will be a focus in *Ep.* 55.8–11 and *De Amicitia* fragment 59 below.

In the rest of letter 40 (here omitted), Seneca goes on to discuss which rhetorical style is best suited for teaching philosophy.

1   **Quod** "for the fact that," following from *gratias ago*

quo uno modo potes "in the only manner (in which) you can." Being in Sicily, Lucilius had no other way of keeping in touch than through letters.

te mihi ostendis recalls Seneca's promise to Nero that he will show Nero to himself (*te tibi ostenderem*) at *Clem.* 1.1.1. The phrase signifies something more than simply self-representation—perhaps something more like revelation.

ut non . . . simus "without our being"

imagines i.e., portrait busts. As Seneca goes on to explain, portraits are less dynamic representations of someone than handwriting. Elsewhere he observes that "a portrait is a dead thing" (*imago res mortua est, Ep.* 84.8). Contrast his qualified use of *imago* as a positive model for remembering friends in *De Amicitia* fragment 59 below.

desiderium . . . solacio these terms strikingly suggest that remembering absent friends is directly analogous to the process of consolation.

falso atque inani i.e., portraits deceive us into thinking that our absent friends are present, but no reality lies behind this impression

quanto . . . ? a rhetorical question; *quanto* is abl. of degree of difference.

litterae probably means "letters" in the sense of handwritten text, but also implies "epistles" more generally as a form of communication.

uera . . . ueras The anaphoric repetition emphasizes the contrast with *falso* above.

uestigia . . . notas The terms primarily refer to handwriting. Although ancient letters were often dictated to slaves or freedmen secretaries, autograph letters could express greater intimacy, and Seneca indicates clearly that this was the habit between him and Lucilius.

manus epistulae impressa "the hand impressed upon the letter"; *epistulae* is dat. following the compound verb.

agnoscere The infinitive functions essentially as an acc. n. sing. noun in apposition to *id*: "this thing, . . . namely, recognition." This is recognition in a strong sense, suggesting the dynamic self-revelation that comes through an epistolary correspondence, not just through recognition of handwriting.

✺ *EPISTULAE MORALES 49.1–3: Memories triggered by a visit to Pompeii*

This passage is from the beginning of Seneca's first letter sent from the region of Campania, which includes Naples and Lucilius' hometown of Pompeii. (See inset MAP in Appendix B). It appears that Pompeii was also the place where Seneca had seen Lucilius off when he sailed to Sicily to take up his position as an administrator there.

Seneca greets Lucilius as usual, but then explains how a recent visit to Lucilius' home region suddenly reminded him of the past and elicited an uncharacteristically emotional response. Seneca's reminiscences soon turn into a more general reflection on the brevity of life and the irrecoverability of the past.

The anxieties expressed here seem to be connected to the fact that Seneca has ignored his own advice in *Ep.* 2.1 above against traveling around too much, and has let his emotions temporarily get the better of him.

In the rest of letter 49 (here omitted), Seneca goes on to discuss the philosophical concept of the "good" (*bonum*).

1 **Est . . . supinus et neglegens qui** "(that man) is inactive and inattentive who . . . ." Seneca here makes criticisms of an indefinite person; but the criticisms will soon turn out to apply to himself.

in amici memoriam "into remembering a friend"; *amici* is objective gen.

ab aliqua regione admonitus The power of places to serve as triggers of memory was a favorite topic in ancient theories of rhetoric and poetic inspiration.

nostro Seneca still speaks somewhat generally, though his anecdote will soon become personal.

sicut dolorem lugentium *dolorem* is direct object of *renouat* at the end of the sentence. The comparison with experiences of grief and melancholy points to the negative emotional aspects of this kind of reminiscence.

etiam si mitigatus est tempore "even if it has been soothed by time," alluding to the commonplace notion of "time the healer." The subject *dolor* is implied.

seruulus The diminutive intensifies the emotion.

familiaris amisso "close to the deceased"

Ecce Campania . . . Seneca dramatically announces his arrival in Campania. For other locations in Campania see *Ep.* 55 below.

Neapolis and **Pompeiorum tuorum** both objective gen. with *conspectus*

tuorum because Lucilius originates from there

incredibile est quam recens desiderium "it is unbelievable how fresh a longing . . . ." This is technically the beginning (i.e., main) clause of the sentence; but Seneca preposes **Ecce . . . conspectus** to create a dramatic impact

fecerint The subjects are *Campania* and *conspectus*.

tui objective gen. with *desiderium*

totus can be taken adverbially: "entirely."

Cum maxime an idiom: "right at this very moment." Seneca describes the past event of his parting from Lucilius as if it were happening in the present.

conbibentem . . . resistentem both agree with implicit object *te*.

affectibus tuis . . . exeuntibus dat. object of *resistentem*

inter ipsam coercitionem lit. "amid the very suppression," i.e., "even as you sought to curb them (i.e., the tears)"

non satis adds a gentle critique of Lucilius' failure to control his emotions at the time, thus perhaps blaming some of Seneca's own present emotions on those of his friend.

2   **Modo** this adv. ("just now") becomes the focus of Seneca's meditation on time in the following lines.

amisisse te i.e., when Lucilius departed for Sicily

si recorderis "if one should reminisce." This introduces Seneca's autobiographical recollections that follow.

apud Sotionem philosophum "before Sotion the philospher." Seneca evidently studied with Sotion when very young. This is the first of several memories here from successive moments in Seneca's life, proceeding from his childhood after he first arrived in Rome through to his retirement from public oratory.

causas agere coepi refers to Seneca's first forensic speeches. The successive moments, referring to Seneca's loss of his desire (*uelle*) and then his ability (*posse*), are hard to pinpoint. As an orator was still capable of arousing the jealousy of Caligula even in the late 30s, after his return from his sojourn to Egypt.

magis apparet respicientibus "is more obvious (to us) looking back (i.e., in retrospect)"

ad praesentia intentos "focused on things present"

fallit The subject is still *uelocitas temporis*.

adeo . . . transitus lenis est "so gentle is the passing"

3   **transît** syncopated from *transiuit*

eodem loco abl. of place where

est . . . aspicitur . . . iacet The subject of these verbs is *quidquid temporis transît.*

in idem profundum "into the same abyss," i.e., the flat category of "the past." Elsewhere Seneca writes, "whatever of our lifetime is behind, death holds," (*quidquid aetatis retro est mors tenet, Ep.* 1.2).

∾ *EPISTULAE MORALES* 55

This letter evidently belongs to the same journey through Campania begun in letter 49 above. In an intervening letter, Seneca had described his brief trip to the luxury resort of Baiae, from which he beat a hasty retreat (*Ep.* 51). Now he describes how he visited the site of a once luxurious villa near Cumae, just to the north of Baiae (see Fig. 6 below and the inset in the MAP in Appendix B). The letter begins with an account of his visit, but concludes in a meditation on Lucilius' absence from Campania, and his presence in Seneca's mind.

A section of the letter describing the luxurious villa in greater detail (*Ep.* 55.6–7) has been omitted here.

1–2: A "stroll" along the seashore

Seneca begins by greeting Lucilius and recalling a recent outing in which he was carried in a litter. The litter was ostensibly for health reasons. In recent letters Seneca had described his ill health, including respiratory problems that sometimes made him feel as though he was dying.

Seneca's outing took him along a narrow, sandy isthmus between the sea and a small lake to where the villa of a deceased Roman aristocrat, Servilius Vatia, is located.

1   **a gestatione . . . uenio** "I am fresh from an expedition on my litter . . ."

     quam si tantum ambulassem quantum sedi "than if I had walked as much (as far) as I sat"; *ambulassem* is syncopated from *ambulauissem*. Seneca had been sitting on the litter, but suggests (paradoxically) that this had exhausted him.

     et diu ferri "even being carried for a long time" (i.e., not even walking)

     nescio an The phrase functions adverbially (translate: "probably") and here does not introduce an actual indirect question.

     eo . . . quia "because of the fact that . . ."; *eo* is abl. of cause.

     maior agrees with *labor*.

     quae The antecedent is *naturam*.

     per nos . . . per nos "on our own legs . . . with our own eyes"

     nobis probably "us old men"; dat. with compound *indixere*

     indixere syncopated from *indixerunt*

     deliciae Seneca playfully incriminates himself (and perhaps Lucilius too) as having been made weak by over-indulgence.

     quod diu noluimus posse desîmus i.e., we had already been lazy about taking long walks, and now the state of our old and sick body prevents us from being able to take long walks even if we had wanted to

2   **Mihi tamen** Despite having admitted to laziness and weakness, Seneca now characterizes his more respectable motives for litter travel.

concutere ... discuteretur ... iactatio These terms refer to the litter's ability to shake up the body in a helpful way, whether by clearing bile from the throat or by easing his breath itself.

discuteretur subject is *bilis*

illum i.e., *spiritum*

quam acc. subject of *profuisse*; the antecedent of *quam* is *iactatio*.

inuitante ipso litore begins Seneca's transition to describing the landscape.

litore, quod ... curuatur For this shore-line, see Fig. 6.

mari ... lacu abl. of means with *cluditur*

uelut angustum iter "like a narrow causeway," i.e., as if the *litus* were a man-made path. The landscape described here is still visible at the modern site, where an inland lake makes the beach an isthmus (out of frame to the left, in Fig. 6).

Fig. 6. The Villa of Servilius Vatia (ruins above), approached along the shore from Cumae.

3–5: But was it *life*?

Stopping outside Vatia's villa, Seneca describes how he reflected on that man's life of solitude and leisure. He describes contemplating the villa, recalling how Vatia had secluded himself during the reign of Tiberius. Vatia's lifestyle had some superficial resemblances to the philosophical life, but Seneca points out that his solitude was of a different kind altogether.

3   **Ex consuetudine . . . mea** "in keeping with my habits." This alludes to the fact that Seneca often begins his letters with anecdotes from his external experiences, then proceeds to develop these into meditations on moral life or philosophy.

an equivalent to *num* introducing an indirect yes/no question

mihi . . . bono double dat., "beneficial for me"; i.e., offering some moral lesson

aliquando Vatiae fuit Servilius Vatia was a wealthy aristocrat and ex-praetor who appears to have lived out his days (cf. *consenuit*) at the villa during the latter part of Tiberius' reign in the 30s CE. The ruins of the villa survive today in the grounds of the Villa Vazia resort; see the detailed images at http://www.villavazia.com. Seneca's letter is the sole surviving text that makes reference to Vatia's villa.

ille praetorius diues "that well-known rich ex-praetor." Vatia had evidently decided that his political career was complete after his praetorship, without proceeding to the consulship.

nulla alia re quam otio "for no other reason than for leisure/retirement"; abl. of cause

felix habebatur "was esteemed lucky"

exclamabant homines In some lines omitted here, Seneca explains how Vatia, by withdrawing to his villa, avoided the fates of many other aristocrats who were killed or ruined during Tiberius' reign.

solus scis uiuere a phrase with more than one meaning, including "you alone know how to live (the good life)" and "you alone know how to stay alive"

4   **latere** the term has overtones of hiding like an animal, and of
       the Epicurean maxim, "Live unnoticed" (Greek *lathe biōsas*).

       Numquam aliter . . . quam ut lit. "never in any other manner
       . . . than that . . .," i.e., "never . . . without," introducing the
       subjunctive *dicerem*

       Vatia uiuo abl. absolute

       Vatia hic situs est This is meant to sound like Vatia's epitaph;
       in other words, his life was *uita mortua* ("a living death").

       adeo goes closely with *sacrum* and *uenerabile*, and anticipates
       the result clause *ut . . . placeat.*

       quid standard usage after *si*, for *aliquid*

       illi i.e., *philosophiae*

       mendacio abl. of means: "by falsehood," i.e., "falsely"

       placeat The subject is *(ali)quid.*

       hominem seductum . . . existimat uulgus "the common peo-
       ple reckons that a man who has secluded himself (*hominem
       seductum*) is . . .," introducing the four attributes *Otiosum . . .
       securum . . . se contentum . . . sibi uiuentem.* The statement in-
       cludes an audible emphasis on *se-* and *sibi* (although in *seduc-
       tum* and *securum* the *se(d)-* prefix actually means "separate,"
       not "self"); the effect is to point to the ideal of self-reliance and
       self-sufficiency.

       quorum nihil "none of which"; the antecedent of *quorum* is
       the four attributes just listed.

       Ille i.e., the *sapiens*

       quod est primum "what is of prior importance," i.e., simply
       knowing how to "live" (a morally good life) is a prerequisite to
       knowing how to live for oneself

5   **qui . . . quem . . . qui . . . qui** The anaphoric repetition allows
       Seneca to pile up negative characterizations of solitude sought
       for the wrong reasons, obviously all applicable to Vatia.

       fugit must be pf., on analogy with *relegauit*, etc. in the follow-
       ing phrases.

metu abl. of cause

ille i.e., the person defined in the prior *qui* clauses

quod est turpissimum "the most disgraceful thing of all"

uentri, somno, libidini The terms contrast with *sibi*; in other words, Vatia serves his bodily needs, not his moral health.

qui nemini i.e., *qui nemini uiuit*. This punctuates Seneca's brief, summarizing *sententia*: Vatia's devotion to the body means he is not living for himself, or for anyone else.

Adeo goes closely with *magna*.

constantia et in proposito suo perseuerantia Self-consistency is a favorite ideal of Seneca (as in his advice to Helvia at *Helv.* 2.3 above), but as he explains here, it can be present for the wrong reasons.

inertia quoque pertinax "even stubborn inactivity"

8–11: You're right here, Lucilius!

After his description of Vatia's villa (sections 6–7, here omitted), Seneca concludes the letter with a reflection on the absence of Lucilius. For although Lucilius is far away in Sicily, in other ways Seneca feels exceptionally close to his friend, thanks to the powers of the mind.

The letter evidently offers a solution to the acute sense of separation that Seneca described above on his visit to Pompeii at *Ep.* 49.1. With its emphasis on mutual recognition mediated by letters, it also echoes *Ep.* 40.1.

8   **non multum . . . locus confert** "location does not contribute much"

sibi commendet omnia rel. clause of characteristic: "can make all things agreeable to itself"; i.e., can find satisfaction in surroundings of any kind, even if less than comfortable. Elsewhere Seneca says to Lucilius about travel, "You need to change your mind, not the sky overhead" (*animum debes mutare, non caelum, Ep.* 28.1).

Vidi . . . uidi The anaphoric repetition emphasizes the verb, and conveys a sense of wonder at the paradoxes he has witnessed.

in uilla hilari et amoena i.e., in living conditions just like those enjoyed by Vatia

maestos "(people) gloomy"

occupatis similes "(people) resembling busybodies"

Quare . . . Quare note the different functions for this word in the two instances here: "Therefore . . . Why . . . ?"

non est quod "there is no reason why," introducing subjunctive *existimes* ("you should think")

parum bene compositum "insufficiently well positioned"

cogitationes . . . mitte Seneca invites Lucilius to undertake a mental or spiritual exercise, directing his attention to his absent friend. On remembering absent friends, compare *Ep.* 40.1 above and also *De Amicitia* fragment 59 below.

9   **cum amicis absentibus** i.e., with friends from whom we are separated by great distance. In lines omitted here, Seneca goes on to explain how being in the same city as our friends often gives us the illusion of proximity, when in fact our daily occupations prevent us from having much contact with them.

11   **hic** i.e., *animus*

mecum . . . mecum . . . mecum Seneca offers Lucilius a vision of mutual proximity effected through the mind.

stude . . . cena . . . ambula i.e., a whole day's varied activities

in angusto uiuebamus, si . . . esset . . . clusum a mixed conditional, with the indicative *uiuebamus* suggesting an actual state of affairs that they have now overcome

cogitationibus dat. of disadvantage with *clusum*

Video te Seneca perhaps plays on a traditional notion of letters as communicating an *imago praesentiae* ("image of co-presence") between the correspondents. This sentence may be meant to recall, and to correct, the melancholy reminiscence described at *Ep.* 49.1 above.

cum maxime "at this very moment"

adeo tecum sum ut "I am so *with* you that . . ."

non epistulas sed codicellos The correction suggests that, as a result of the two friends' spiritual communion across space, the correspondence has been replaced by a much more intimate form of communication, passing notes written on wooden tablets joined together (or perhaps even a single sheet of wood), rather than sending letters written on papyrus rolls. The term *codicelli* is the diminutive of *codex*, which Seneca mentions elsewhere was the archaic term for "multiple tablets joined together" (*plurium tabularum contextus, De Brevitate Vitae* 13.4). For Seneca's sentiment, compare Catullus 50, describing how the poet and his friend Licinius had passed poems to one another.

∾ Follow-up to the EPISTULAE MORALES

De Amicitia (fragment 59.5–6 Vottero): A technique for keeping an absent friend in mind

Only a few pages of Seneca's work *Quomodo Amicitia Continenda Sit* ("How Friendship Is to Be Maintained"), otherwise known as *De Amicitia*, survive in the manuscripts. This passage comes from a fragment of the work in which Seneca describes how we can use our own "mental energy" (*animi uelocitas*) continually to refresh our memory of a friend when he or she is on an overseas journey, keeping before our eyes a detailed mental representation of the person.

This theory offers useful background to Seneca's practical exercise of friendship with Lucilius in the *Epistulae Morales*.

5   **eradit** an evocative metaphor, suggesting that the mind is like a monument from which an inscription (a memory) is being struck out

ius "duty"; the term seems to continue the metaphor of an inscription being struck out; the quasi-legal obligations we have toward our friend are apparently forgotten.

haec picks up *peregrinatio* from the previous sentence.

excidit pf. of *excido* ("fall out"), not *excīdo* ("cut out")

quoque "even," emphasizing *notitia*

Quod sentence-connecting rel., nom., subject of *possit*; it refers to the result described in the whole preceding sentence.

omni abl. with *ope*

resistamus . . . reducamus hortatory subjunctives

6   **animo** abl. of means

e uiuo petita, non euanida et muta The better image is taken from, and retains, the dynamism of the living person (which Seneca will go on to illustrate below). The implicit contrast may be with *imago* as an ancestor portrait or death mask. Compare also Seneca's outright rejection of *imagines* as hollow representations at *Ep.* 40.1 above.

"Sic ille . . . ferebat" a half line from book 3 of Virgil's *Aeneid*, where Aeneas describes how Hector's widow Andromache, on seeing Aeneas' son Ascanius, is reminded of her dead son Astyanax, calling him "alas the only image left over for me of my Astyanax" (*o mihi sola mei super Astyanactis imago*). Observing Ascanius' gestures, Andromache recalls: "This is how he moved his eyes, his hands, his mouth (i.e., just like you)" (*sic oculos, sic ille manus, sic ora ferebat, Aen.* 3.489–90). Here Seneca adapts the formula *sic* + impf. indicative as the basis of a spiritual exercise for remembering the absent friend.

illi "to it," i.e., to our mental portrait; dat. with compound verb

quae magis . . . pertinent i.e., things that are less about physical gestures and more about his moral habits as a friend. In the following lines Seneca particularly emphasizes the friend's habits with respect to giving and receiving advice (*consilium*) and gifts (*beneficia*).

hortabatur . . . deterrebat The verbs refer to persuasion and dissuasion, two equally important aspects of friendly advice.

in accipiendo . . . in mutando for these gerundives supply *consilio* from the previous phrase as the implicit object.

perdere lit. "to waste," i.e., to give without repayment; the object is *beneficia* from the previous phrase.

eo uultu . . . quo solent "with the same expression on his face . . . as (people) usually have when they . . ."

in harum usu tractatuque objective gen. The idea is one of continually living with, and maintaining familiarity with, the friend's virtues, in the same way that we would if he had been physically present.

Illustration Credits

1   Family Tree of the Annaei at the Time of the *Consolatio ad Helviam* (42 CE). © 2011 Bolchazy-Carducci Publishers.

2   Double Herm of Seneca and Socrates, 3rd c. Berlin, Staatliche Museen, Antikensammlung, Inv. Sk 391. Courtesy of Bildarchiv Preussischer Kulturbesitz / Art Resource, NY.

3   Medieval Ruin in the Mountains of Corsica, the So-called "Tower of Seneca" (Torre di Seneca). Source: Wikimedia Commons.

4   Seneca and Nero. Bronze Sculpture, Cordoba, Spain, after Plaster Sculpture by Eduardo Barrón (1904). Source: Wikimedia Commons.

5   Medea Contemplates Killing Her Children. Wall-painting from Casa dei Dioscuri, Pompeii, 1st c. Museo Archeologico Nazionale, Naples. Source: Wikimedia Commons.

6   The Villa of Servilius Vatia (ruins above), Approached along the Shore from Cumae. Photo by author.

7   (Appendix 2) Map of Seneca's World, Together with the World of the *Medea*. © 2011 Bolchazy-Carducci Publishers.

Appendix A

∾ *Timeline*

BCE

50s	Seneca the Elder born
46	Suicide of Cato the Younger
44	Death of Julius Caesar (Ides of March)
43	Battle of Mutina. Death of Cicero
43–42	Second Triumvirate. Proscriptions by Octavian and Antony
31	Battle of Actium (Octavian defeats Antony)
27	Octavian becomes "AUGUSTUS"
c. 13	Conspiracy of Cinna
c. 5	Seneca the Younger born

CE

c. 5	Seneca brought to Rome
14	Death of AUGUSTUS. Accession of TIBERIUS
20s?	Seneca the Elder's *Controversiae, Suasoriae*
30s	Seneca the Younger in Egypt
37	Death of TIBERIUS. Accession of GAIUS/CALIGULA
	Seneca quaestor. Seneca nearly executed by Caligula
c. 39	Death of Seneca the Elder
c. 40	*Consolatio ad Marciam*
41	Death of CALIGULA. Accession of CLAUDIUS
	De Ira. Seneca banished to Corsica

42	*Consolatio ad Helviam*
43	*Consolatio ad Polybium*
49	Seneca recalled from exile to serve as Nero's teacher
early 50s?	Seneca begins writing tragedies
54	Death of CLAUDIUS. Accession of NERO
	Apocolocyntosis. Seneca serves as Nero's advisor, speechwriter, etc.
55	*De Clementia*
58	Seneca accused by P. Suillius Rufus
59	Death of Agrippina
62	Death of Burrus. Seneca withdraws from Nero's court. Nero divorces Octavia, marries Poppaea
62–65	*Epistulae Morales. Naturales Quaestiones*
64	Great Fire of Rome. Persecution of Christians
65	Pisonian Conspiracy. Deaths of Seneca, Lucan, Mela, Gallio, etc.
68	Death of NERO
69	Year of the four emperors (GALBA, OTHO, VITELLIUS, VESPASIAN)
69–98	Flavian dynasty (VESPASIAN, TITUS, DOMITIAN)
110s	Tacitus, *Annales*
120s	Suetonius, *De Vita Caesarum*
c. 202–230	Cassius Dio, *Roman History*

Appendix B

~ *Map of Seneca's World, Together with the World of the* MEDEA

Key to sites:

Araxes R.: cf. *Med.* 373

Black Sea (Pontus): cf. *Med.* 44

Caucasus Mts.: cf. *Med.* 43

Britain: Seneca loans money

Egypt: Seneca visits in the 30s CE

Elbe R.: cf. *Med.* 374

Colchis: Jason meets Medea; they escape with Golden Fleece

Cordoba: Seneca born c. 5 BCE

Corinth: Jason divorces Medea, marries Creusa

Corsica: Seneca in exile, 41–49 CE

Iolchos: Jason's home

Libya: cf. *Med.* 682

Phasis R.: cf. *Med.* 44

Pompeii: Seneca visits, *Ep.* 49

Rhine R.: cf. *Med.* 374

Rome: Seneca arrives c. 5 CE

Sicily: Lucilius administrator, early 60s CE

Taurus Mts. : cf. *Med.* 683

Ultima Thule?: cf. *Med.* 379

Villa Vatiae: Seneca visits, *Ep.* 55

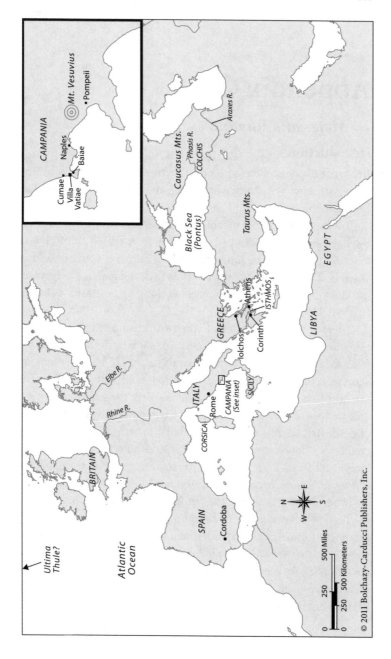

© 2011 Bolchazy-Carducci Publishers, Inc.

Appendix C

∾ *Meter and Rhythm*

Introduction

In his use of poetic meter and prose rhythm Seneca presupposes the same basic laws of quantity with which you may already be familiar from Latin poetry.

Briefly reviewed, the rules of quantity are as follows: Assume that a syllable is **short** (marked ⌣) unless you have reason to think it is long. A syllable will be **long** (marked −) only if it contains a long vowel or diphthong (**naturally long**), as in *dī* and *quae*, or if its vowel is followed by two or more consonants (**long by position**), as in the first syllable of *conscius*.

There are some exceptions to the two-consonant rule: combinations in which fricatives (*f*) or stops (*p, ph, b, t, th, d, c, ch, g*) are followed by liquids (*l, r*) or (rare) nasals (*m, n*) can be either long or short (e.g., the first syllable in *sacris*); *h* does not count as a consonant (e.g., the first syllable in *inhospitalem* is short); the sequences *qu, gu,* and *su* (where *u* is pronounced "w") counts as single consonants (e.g., the first syllable in *sequetur* is short); *x*, being pronounced "ks," counts as a double consonant (e.g., the second syllable in *uindex* is long); and *i* and *u* are often consonantal (e.g., the first syllable of *coniugales* is long, because *i* is consonantal, being pronounced "y").

In Seneca's verse we see the famliar process of **elision**, in which the final syllable of a word ending in a vowel or in vowel + *m* will disappear for metrical purposes when the next word begins with a vowel or with *h* + vowel (e.g., *manesqu[e] impios; caed[em] et; ignot[a] horrida*). Scholars are divided over how to pronounce elided syllables, but probably the elided vowel is not to be pronounced at all (though nasalization may remain as residue of *m*).

We also see **prodelision**, in which the *e-* in *est*, "is," will disappear for metrical purposes when preceded by a word ending in a vowel or in vowel + *m* (e.g., *nulla [e]st*; *telum [e]st*); this effectively creates a single word (*nullast*; *telumst*—they are sometimes printed this way in modern editions).

Iambic trimeters

The basic metrical unit of speech in Senecan tragedy is the iamb (⏑ –), which for practical purposes is best pronounced with a slight emphasis on the second syllable, as in English "below." The basic meter of each line is three pairs of iambs, adding up to an iambic trimeter.

No line will ever have six simple iambs, however, because the line structure includes certain flexibilities and constraints. Depending on their positions in the verse, some iambs can be substituted by spondees (– –), and some single syllables can be resolved into two short syllables, resulting in dactyls (– ⏑ ⏑), anapaests (⏑ ⏑ –), or pro-celeusmatics (⏑ ⏑ ⏑ ⏑). The final syllable of the line is classified as *anceps* ("doubtful," marked ×): it can be either one long or one short syllable. The resulting possibilities can be represented as follows:

```
1                    2                3
⏑                    | ⏑              | ⏑
—    —    ⏑    —  | —    —    ⏑   —  | —    —    ⏑    ×
⏑⏑   ⏑⏑       ⏑⏑ | ⏑⏑   ⏑⏑          ⏑⏑ | ⏑⏑
```

Below lines 1–9 of the *Medea* have been scanned as an example. Macrons are given to help you see those syllables that are naturally long.

```
 –    –    ⏑   –|–    –    ⏑   ⏑   ⏑|–    –    ⏑  ×
```
Dī coniugālēs tūque geniālis torī,

```
 –    –  ⏑    –   | –     –    ⏑   ⏑   ⏑|–   –      ⏑  ×
```
Lūcīna, custōs quaeque domitūram freta

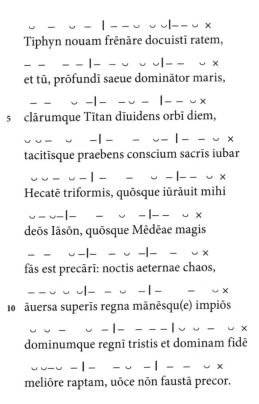

```
   ◡   —   ◡   —   |  —  —  ◡   ◡  ◡|— —  ◡  ×
Tiphyn nouam frēnāre docuistī ratem,

   —  —     —  —  |—  —  ◡    ◡  ◡|—  —    ◡  ×
et tū, prōfundī saeue dominātor maris,

   —  —     ◡  —|—   —  ◡  —   |—  —  ◡ ×
5  clārumque Tītan dīuidens orbī diem,

   ◡  ◡ —    ◡    —|  —   —   ◡—  |—  —  ◡  ×
tacitīsque praebens conscium sacrīs iubar

   ◡  ◡  —  ◡  —  |  —    —   ◡   —|— —  ◡  ×
Hecatē triformis, quōsque iūrāuit mihi

   ◡  —  ◡—|—     —   ◡   —|— —    ◡  ×
deōs Iāsōn, quōsque Mēdēae magis

   —   —     ◡ —|—   —  ◡  —|—  —    ◡  ×
fās est precārī: noctis aeternae chaos,

   —  —  ◡   ◡  ◡|—   —  ◡   —  |—     —    ◡ ×
10  āuersa superīs regna mānēsqu(e) impiōs

   ◡   ◡  —     ◡  —  |—   — — —|◡  ◡  —    ◡  ×
dominumque regnī tristis et dominam fidē

   ◡  ◡—◡   —  |  —    —  ◡   —  |  —  —    ◡  ×
meliōre raptam, uōce nōn faustā precor.
```

As you may have noticed, it is the syllables substituted with ◡◡ that are the most difficult to process as you read, because two syllables occupy the position normally occupied by one. With some practice, however, these can be easily spotted: above, they occur in the <u>first two</u> syllables of *genialis, domituram, docuisti, dominator, tacitisque, Hecate, superis, dominumque, dominam,* and *meliore.* Note also the patterns that emerge in Seneca's use of these. In the first four lines, ◡◡ recurs always in the fourth foot, and in some later lines (6, 7, 11, 12) it recurs in the first foot.

Several other features of Seneca's technique are worth noting. For example, virtually every line ends in a two-syllable word. Elision is less frequent, so when it appears (e.g., *manesqu[e] impios* in line 10) it makes an impact. Seneca also uses enjambment (i.e., the running over of a clause onto the next line) to add to the drama: here, the enjambments of lines 6–7, 7–8, 8–9 suggest a gradual breakdown in Medea's control over her emotions.

Metrical effects also work in conjunction with other sound effects, such as alliteration (e.g., *c* and *qu* in line 2; *m* in line 8) and repetition of words (e.g., *quosque* in lines 7–8). The repetition of *dominus* and its derivatives four times in this passage (lines 2, 4, and twice in 11) helps to highlight the contests of power in which Medea is caught up.

Anapaestic dimeters

The most frequent lyric meter used by the Chorus in Senecan tragedy is based on the unit of the anapaest ($\smile\smile-$), which is best pronounced with a slight emphasis on the first syllable, as in English "diligence." The anapaests are arranged in two pairs to make up the anapaestic dimeter. In Greek tragedy, this meter was associated most closely with the entrances and exits of the Chorus. In Seneca it has been generalized to serve as the meter of at least half the choral odes.

As with the iambic trimeter above, the anapaestic dimeter seldom consists of four simple anapaests, because of the flexibilities and constraints built into the line structure. Any anapaest can be substituted with a spondee, and some anapaests can be substituted with dactyls. The resulting possibilities can be represented below, although it should be noted that the sequence $\smile\smile\ \smile\smile$ is in practice always avoided.

```
1                    2
—      —     | —        —
∪∪  — ∪∪ —  | ∪∪  —  ∪∪  ×
     ∪∪      |      ∪∪
```

Below lines 301–8 of the *Medea* have been scanned as an example.

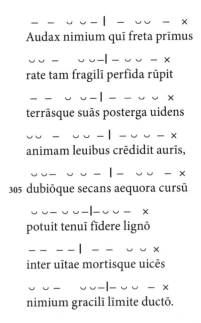

⏜ ⏜ ⏑ ⏑ – | – ⏑ ⏑ – ×
Audax nimium quī freta prīmus

⏑ ⏑ –   ⏑ ⏑–| – ⏑ ⏑ – ×
rate tam fragilī perfida rūpit

⏜ ⏜ ⏑ ⏑ –| – – ⏑ ⏑ ×
terrāsque suās posterga uidens

⏑ ⏑ – ⏑ ⏑ – | – ⏑ ⏑ – ×
animam leuibus crēdidit aurīs,

⏑ ⏑– ⏑ ⏑ – |– ⏑ ⏑ – ×
305 dubiōque secans aequora cursū

⏑ ⏑– ⏑ ⏑ –|– ⏑ ⏑ – ×
potuit tenuī fīdere lignō

⏜ ⏜ – –| – – ⏑ ⏑ ×
inter uītae mortisque uicēs

⏑ ⏑ –   ⏑ ⏑–|– ⏑ ⏑ – ×
nimium gracilī līmite ductō.

The key to scanning this meter is being able to spot the "pure" anapaests (⏑ ⏑ –) as you read. In the passage above, these are: *nimium,
rate tam, fragili, -que suas, -ga uidens, animam, leuibus, dubio, -que
secans, potuit, tenui* (though *tenui* could also be read as a spondaic
two-syllable word, with *u* read as a consonant, pronounced "w"),
-que uices, nimium, and *gracili.*

It also helps to recognize the dactyls, which in this passage follow
a striking pattern, being all in the third foot of the line: *qui freta, perfida, credidit, aequora, fidere, limite.* There are some other consistent
patterns in Seneca's anapaests: every line ends with a two-syllable
word; there is no elision and little use of enjambment; and boundaries are more clearly marked within the line (e.g., the middle of the
dimeter always corresponds to breaks between words).

The exact line breaks in Seneca's anapaests are sometimes dis-
puted by scholars. A few lines of the selection in this volume (*Medea*
361b, 365a, 367, 372) appear to be short lines, consisting of a single

pair of anapaests rather than the usual dimeter. These are regularly spaced, coinciding with pauses in the sense, and provide a kind of punctuation for the ear through the surprise of a shorter line.

Iambic catalectic dimeters

In the selections from the *Medea* in this volume, the one other lyric meter used by Seneca is the iambic catalectic dimeter, a rare but very straightforward pattern. An iambic dimeter consists of two pairs of iambs, but a process called *catalexis* cuts this short by one syllable.

As in the iambic trimeter, the verse structure includes both flexibilities and constraints. Here are the variations and constraints seen in the *Medea* ode:

```
1                    2
ᴗ                    |
—    —    ᴗ    —  |    ᴗ    —    ×
ᴗᴗ                   |
```

Below lines 849–52 have been scanned as an example:

```
    —    —      ᴗ  –| ᴗ    –  ×
```
Quōnam cruenta maenās

```
    —    —    ᴗ  –| ᴗ  –  ×
```
850 praeceps amōre saeuō

```
  ᴗ ᴗ  –      ᴗ    – | ᴗ – ×
```
rapitur? quod impotentī

```
ᴗ ᴗ  –    ᴗ  – | ᴗ – ×
```
facinus parat furōre?

Many of the same effects discussed above for the iambic trimeter are relevant here, such as enjambment (seen here in lines 850–51, with dramatic effect) and alliteration (e.g., *f* in line 852). As with the anapaestic dimeter above, the selection in this volume includes two lines that are further shortened (by one syllable) and coincide with pauses in the sense (*Medea* 857, 865).

Prose rhythm

Even when he is not writing poetry, Seneca's arrangement of words (*compositio*) is carefully contrived, and in many cases he appears to have taken into consideration how the arrangement will sound.

Like most Latin prose artists, Seneca places special rhythmical emphasis on the ends of each clause-length or sentence-length unit (the unit called a *colon*; pl. *cola*). These rhythmical endings are called *clausulae* because they bring the unit to a "close." "Colometric" analysis (the analysis of *cola* and their internal rhythms) is a sometimes imprecise art, because there is some dispute about identifying where *cola* end, and therefore whether a given phrase is a *clausula* or not. Still, it is clear that different authors show a preference for specific *clausulae*, and often these are easy to see—and hear!

Seneca exploits many of the popular *clausulae* such as double trochee ($-\smile \mid -\times$) or double spondee ($--\mid -\times$), but he most often strives for a double cretic ($-\smile-\mid-\smile\times$) or cretic + spondee ($-\smile-\mid -\times$), or a version of these in which a long syllable is substituted with two shorts. (Note that as in notation of poetic meters, the symbol × denotes an *anceps*, "doubtful," syllable, that can be either long or short.)

In what ways could *clausulae* be important in Seneca? One tantalizing hint arises at the end of a letter about premature death, where he concludes: "As in a story, so too in life: it is not how long, but how well it was acted, that matters. It is irrelevant in what place you cease. Cease wherever you want: just make sure to put a good end on it (*tantum bonam clausulam impone*)" (*Ep.* 77.20). Here Seneca draws on the reader's assumptions about the importance of good endings (*clausulae*) in drama, and perhaps in rhetoric, too, and sees this as a clue to the importance of having a good death. This will not answer every question you may have about *clausulae*, but it shows how the *clausula* may be significant within Seneca's thinking about correspondences between literary form and meaning. Compare his privileging of brevity and encapsulation discussed under "Three stylistic tendencies" in the Introduction above.

Whether or not you decide to hunt for *clausulae*, it is always worth reading Seneca's prose out loud, and even to "scan" the long and short syllables in a selected sequence, such as this sentence from *Helv.* 1.2, where *clausulae* have been underlined and identified in parentheses:

⏑ – ⏑⏑ ⏑ ⏑‖–⏑⏑ – ⏑ ×
1 Fleant itaque di<u>ūtius et gemant</u>,
    (*clausula*: dactyl + cretic = so-called "*ēdite rēgibus*")

– – –⏑– – – – – – – –‖– ⏑ –|–⏑ ×
2 quōrum dēlicātās mentēs ēneruāuit <u>longa fēlīcitās</u>,
    (double cretic)

⏑ – ⏑ – ⏑ – – –⏑– – – –‖– –|– ×
3 et ad leuissimār(um) iniūriārum mōtūs <u>conlābantur</u>:
    (double spondee)

– – – – – – – ⏑⏑ ⏑– –‖– ⏑|– ×
4 at quōr(um) omnēs annī per calamitātēs <u>transiērunt</u>,
    (double trochee)

⏑ – ⏑ ⏑ ⏑ ⏑ – ⏑ – –⏑– –‖– ⏑–|– ⏑ ×
5 grauissima quoque fort(ī) et inmōbilī con<u>stantiā perferant</u>.
    (double cretic)

– ⏑ ⏑ –⏑ ⏑ – –‖–⏑ – ⏑ ×
6 ūn(um) habet adsidu(a) infē<u>līcitās bonum</u>, ("hypodochmius")

– – ‖– –|– ×
7 quod quōs <u>semper uexat</u> (double spondee)

⏑‖– ⏑ – |– ×
8 no<u>uissim(ē) indūrat</u>. (cretic + spondee)

There is a striking recurrence here of a few *clausulae*, such as the double cretic. Note also that *cola* that come in syntactic pairs (2 + 3, 4 + 5, 7 + 8) have comparable numbers of syllables with one another (*isocolon*), and also that in lines 2 through 8 each *colon* is successively shorter (syllable count: 18, 17, 16, 14, 13, 6, 6).

Several further effects can be noticed here, which combine sound with syntactic structure. For example, there is a prevalence of spondees adding to the passage's emphasis on suffering and perseverance;

there is a recurring pattern of relative pronoun in one clause followed by superlative in the next (*quorum . . . leuissimarum, quorum . . . grauissima, quos . . . nouissime*); the *cola* tend to conclude in verbs; and almost every verb in the passage has a different prefix, some giving a picture of moral weakness (*eneruauit, conlabantur*), others of endurance (*transierunt, perferant, indurat*).

This sample, taken at random, scarcely exhausts the kind of formal complexity that can be found in Seneca's prose. There is much more to find.

Further reading

On Latin meter in general, a good basic introduction is A. Keller and S. Russell, *Learn to Read Latin* (New Haven 2003) 176–80; more advanced is A. Mahoney, *Allen and Greenough's Latin Grammar* (Newburyport, MA, 2001) §§602–29.

On Senecan meter see E. Fantham, *Seneca's Troades: A Literary Introduction with Text, Translation, and Commentary* (Princeton 1982) 103–115 and R. J. Tarrant, *Seneca's Thyestes* (Atlanta 1985) 27–33.

On Latin prose rhythm in general, see D. A. Russell, *An Anthology of Latin Prose* (Oxford 1990) xxii–xxv.

Vocabulary

ā *or* **ab,** *prep.* + *abl.*, from, away from; from the time of; by

abauus, -ī, *m.*, great-great-grandfather

abdō, -ere, -didī, -ditum, to remove, conceal

abeō, -īre, -īuī *or* **-iī, -itum,** to go away

abscondō, -ere, -didī, -ditum, to conceal; *of swords*, bury (up to the hilt)

absum, -esse, āfuī, āfutūrus, to be absent; be away, removed

āc *or* **atque,** *conj.*, and

accēdō, -ere, -cessī, -cessum, to be added, accrue, (to) + *dat.*

accendō, -ere, -cendī, -censum, to kindle, inflame

accidō, -ere, -cidī, —, to happen (to), befall, + *dat.*

accipiō, -ere, -cēpī, -ceptum, to receive; hear

accūsō (1) to accuse

acquīrō, -ere, -quīsīuī, -quīsītum, to acquire

acuō, -ere, acuī, acūtum, to sharpen

ad, *prep.* + *acc.*, to(ward); for the purpose of; in response to

adeō, *adv.*, so much, to such an extent

adfectus, -ūs, *m.*, feeling

adferō. *See* **afferō**

adflictātiō, -ōnis, *f.*, torment

adflīgō, -ere, -flixī, -flictum, to crush, ruin; **adflictus,** *pple.*, wretched, destitute

adgredior, adgredī, adgressus sum, to advance, attack

adhūc, *adv.*, up till now; still

adiciō, -ere, -iēcī, -iectum, to add (to) + *dat.*

adimō, -ere, -ēmī, -emptum, to take away (from) + *dat.*

adminiculum, -ī, *n.*, prop, support

admittō, -ere, -mīsī, -missum, to allow, allow in

admoneō, -ēre, -monuī, -monitum, to advise, remind

adnumerō (1) to count up

adquiescō, -ere, -quiēuī, -quiētum, to find rest, find comfort, (in) + *abl.*

adsīdō, -ere, -sēdī, —, to sit down

adsiduus, -a, -um, *adj.*, constant

adsuescō, -ere, -suēuī, -suētum, to become accustomed (to) + *dat.*

adsum, -esse, -fuī, -futūrus, to
be present; + *dat.*, to be at
hand for, support

aduentus, -ūs, *m.,* arrival

aduersus, *prep.* + *acc.,* against

adulescens, -entis, *m.,* young
man

adulescentulus, -ī, *m.,*
diminutive, young (little)
man

aduocātus, -ī, *m.,* counsellor,
advocate

aduocō (1) to summon

aeger, -gra, -grum, *adj.,* sick,
unwell

aegrē, *adv.,* with difficulty,
badly

aequē, *adv.,* equally; **aequē . . .
quam,** as much . . . as

aequor, -oris, *n.,* level surface;
(surface of) the sea

aerumna, -ae, *f.,* trouble,
hardship

aes, aeris, *n.,* bronze

aestimō (1) to reckon, evaluate

aetās, -tātis, *f.,* age, time of life

aeternitās, -tātis, *f.,* eternity,
immortality

aeternus, -a, -um, *adj.,* eternal,
everlasting

aether, -eris, *n.,* heavens, the
upper sky

affectus. *See* **adfectus**

afferō, -ferre, attulī, adlātum,
to bring to, deliver

aggerō, -ere, -gessī, -gestum, to
heap up

**aggredior, aggredī, aggressus
sum,** to attack

**agnoscō, -ere, -gnōuī,
-gnōtum,** to recognize

agō, -ere, ēgī, actum, to do;
drive; act; deal; **causās
agere,** to plead cases; **grātiās
agere,** to give thanks; **uītam
agere,** to live (a) life

alacer, alacris, alacre, *adj.,*
happy, cheerful

Albis, -is, *m.,* the Elbe (river in
Germany)

āles, ālitis, *adj.,* winged

aliēnus, -a, -um, *adj.,* another's

aliquandō, *adv.,* at some time

aliquis, aliquid, *pron.,*
someone, something;
anyone, anything

aliter, *adv.,* in another way;
aliter . . . quam, in another
way . . . than

alius, -a, -ud, *pron./adj.,* other,
another (one, thing); **alius . . .
alius,** one . . . another

alleuō (1) to lift up

alō, -ere, -uī, altum *or* **alitum,**
to nourish

alter, altera, alterum, *pron./
adj.,* the other (of two); **alter
. . . alter,** the one . . . the
other

alternus, -a, -um, *adj.,*
alternating

altum, -ī, *n.,* the deep sea

altus, -a, -um, *adj.,* deep; high,
lofty

alumna, -ae, *f.,* nursling, foster-
daughter

ambulō (1) to walk

amīcitia, -ae, *f.,* friendship

amīcus, -a, -um, *adj.*, friendly

amīcus, -ī, *m.*, friend

āmittō, -ere, -mīsī, -missum, to lose

amoenus, -a, -um, *adj.*, pleasant, charming

amor, -ōris, *m.*, desire, passion

āmoueō, -ēre, -mōuī, -mōtum, to remove, keep away

amplector, amplectī, amplexus sum, to embrace

amplius, *adv.*, more, further

an, *conj. giving second half of an alternative question,* or; *conj. introducing indirect yes/no question, equivalent to* -nē *in direct question,* whether

angulus, -ī, *m.*, corner, narrow spot

angustus, -a, -um, *adj.*, narrow, constraining

anima, -ae, *f.*, soul, life-breath, life

animal, -ālis, *n.*, animal

animus, -ī, *m.*, mind; intention, attitude; *pl.*, spirit

annus, -ī, *m.*, year

ante, *prep.* + *acc.*, before

antequam, *conj.*, before

antīquus, -a, -um, *adj.*, ancient; past, former; old-fashioned

Antōnius, -iī, *m.*, Antony

aperiō, -īre, -peruī, -pertum, to open

appāreō, -ēre, -uī, -itum, to appear (to) + *dat.*

applicō, -āre, -āuī *or* -uī, -ātum *or* -itum, to apply (to) + *dat.*

apprehendō, -ere, -ndī, -nsum, to grasp, seize

aptō (1) to fit, adapt, (to) + *dat.*

apud, *prep.* + *acc.*, with, before; at the house of; *with an author's name,* in

Araxēs, -is, *m.*, the Araxes (river in Armenia)

arbiter, arbitrī, *m.*, judge, decider

arca, -ae, *f.*, money chest, coffer

arcānus, -a, -um, *adj.*, secret, hidden

arcessō *or* accersō, -ere, -īuī, -ītum, to send for, summon

Arctōus, -a, -um, *adj.*, pertaining to Arctos (northern constellation), northern

Argō, -ūs, *f.*, the Argo (ship)

argūmentum, -ī, *n.*, mark, sign, proof

arma, -ōrum, *n. pl.*, arms, weapons

armō (1) to arm

ars, artis, *f.*, art, skill; bonae artēs, good morals, philosophy

artus, -ūs, *m.*, limb

aspiciō, -ere, -spexī, -spectum, to look at, see

at, *adv.*, but; by contrast

ater, atra, atrum, *adj.*, black

atque. *See* āc

attingō, -ere, -tigī, -tactum, to touch upon, reach

attonitus, -a, -um, *adj.*, astonished, startled

auctor, -ōris, *m.*, author

auctōritās, -tātis, *f.*, authority

audacter, *adv.*, boldly

audax, *gen.* **-ācis,** *adj.*, bold, daring

audeō, -ēre, ausus sum, to dare (to) + *infinitive*

audiō, -īre, -īuī *or* **-iī, -ītum,** to hear; listen

āuertō, -ere, āuertī, āuersum, to turn away; **āuersus,** *pple.*, turned away, averse

auferō, -ferre, abstulī, ablātum, to take away

augescō, -ere, —, —, to begin to grow

Augustus, -ī, *m.*, Augustus

auidus, -a, -um, *adj.*, greedy

aura, -ae, *f.*, breeze

aureus, -a, -um, *adj.*, golden

autem, *adv.*, but, however; and

auunculus, -ī, *m.*, maternal uncle

auxilium, -iī, *n.*, help, assistance

bene, *adv.*, well; **bene est,** all is well

beneficium, -iī, *n.*, good service, gift; **beneficiō,** *abl. with gen. noun*, thanks to

benignitās, -tātis, *f.*, kindness, generosity

bibō, -ere, bibī, —, to drink

bīlis, -is, *f.*, bile, fluid

bonitās, -tātis, *f.*, goodness

bonum, -ī, *n.*, good, advantage, blessing; **bonō esse,** to be a good (to) + *dat.*

bonus, -a, -um, *adj.*, good

cadō, -ere, cecidī, casum, to fall

caedēs, -is, *f.*, slaughter, murder

caedō, -ere, caesī, caesum, to cut down, slaughter

caelum, -ī, *n.*, sky, heavens

Caesar, -aris, *m.*, Caesar (referring to the present emperor)

calamitās, -tātis, *f.*, disaster, misfortune, ruin

Campānia, -ae, *f.*, Campania (region south of Rome)

canis, -is, *m.*, dog

cantus, -ūs, *m.*, song, spell

capiō, -ere, cēpī, captum, to take (up); capture; **consilium capere,** to take advice

caput, -itis, *n.*, head; **capitis damnāre,** to condemn to capital punishment, to death

careō, -ēre, -uī, castum, to be without, lack, + *abl.*

carīna, -ae, *f.*, keel; ship

carmen, -minis, *n.*, song, spell

cārus, -a, -um, *adj.*, dear, beloved

castra, -ōrum, *n. pl.*, camp

cathēdra, -ae, *f.*, chair, arm-chair

Caucasus, -ī, *m.*, the Caucasus (= the Caucasian mountain range)

causa, -ae, *f.*, cause, reason; **causās agere,** to plead cases

cēdō, -ere, cessī, cessum, to go; yield, give way

celeber, -bris, -bre, *adj.*, crowded

cēnō (1) to dine

certō (1) to compete

certus, -a, -um, *adj.*, sure, certain; reliable

ceruix, -īcis, *f.*, neck

cēterī, -ae, -a, *pl. adj.*, (the) other

cēterum, *adv.*, but; for the rest

chaos, *n. indecl.*, chaos, disorder

cibus, -ī, *m.*, food

cicātrīcōsus, -a, -um, *adj.*, covered in scars

cicātrix, -trīcis, *f.*, scar

Cinna, -ae, *m.*, Cinna

circumdō, -dare, -dedī, -datum, to place around + *dat.*

circumeō, -īre, -īuī *or* -iī, -itum, to go around, inspect

circumfundō, -ere, -fūdī, -fūsum, to pour around

circumspiciō, -ere, -spexī, -spectum, to look around; consider

cito, *adv.*, quickly

citō (1) to stir up, exite

cīuīlis, -e, *adj.*, civil, civic

cīuitās, -tātis, *f.*, city, citizenry

clādes, -is, *f.*, disaster, ruin

clam, *adv.*, in secret

clārus, -a, -um, *adj.*, conspicuous, bright; famous, illustrious

Claudius, -iī, *m.*, Claudius

claudō *or* clūdō, -ere, clūsī, clūsum, to close, shut (off), hem in

clēmentia, -ae, *f.*, clemency, mercy

clepō, -ere, clepsī, cleptum, to steal; conceal

clūdō. *See* claudō

Cn. = Gnaeus, -ī, *m.*, Gnaeus

coaceruō (1) to heap up

cōdicellī *or* cōdicillī, -ōrum, *m. pl.*, writing tablet, booklet, brief note

coepī. *See* incipiō

coerceō, -ēre, -uī, -itum, to confine

coercitiō, -ōnis, *f.*, confinement, suppression

cōgitātiō, -ōnis, *f.*, thought

cōgitō (1) think, consider

cognoscō, -ere, -gnōuī, -gnōtum, to learn; hold a judicial hearing

cōgō, -ere, coēgī, coactum, to force, compel

Colchī, -ōrum, *n. pl.*, the Colchians; *metonym for* Colchis

collēga, -ae, *m.*, colleague

collum, -ī, *n.*, neck

color, -ōris, *m.*, color, complexion

comes, -itis, *m.*, partner, companion

commendō (1) to adapt, make agreeable, (to) + *dat.*

committō, -ere, -mīsī, -missum, to entrust (to) + *dat.*

commodō (1) to make fit; arrange

commūnis, -e, *adj.*, shared, common

compactus. *See* compingō

comparō (1) to prepare,
procure; arrange
compellō, -ere, -pulī, -pulsum,
to drive to, compel
compescō, -ere, -uī, —, to curb,
restrain
compingō, -ere, -pēgī,
-pactum, to fit together
complōrō (1), to lament for
complūrēs, -ium, *pl. adj.*,
several
compōnō, -ere, -posuī,
-positus, to arrange, put in
order; compose
comprendō *or* comprehendō,
-ere, -ndī, -nsum, to grasp
completely
comprimō, -ere, -pressī,
-pressum, to suppress
computō (1) to calculate
conbibō, -ere, -bibī, —, to
drink down, swallow
concēdō, -ere, -cessī, -cessum,
to concede, give, (to) + *dat.*
concipiō, -ere, -cēpī, -ceptum,
to take up, conceive
concoquō, -ere, -coxī, -coctum,
to boil up; digest
concupiō, -ere, -īuī *or* -iī,
-ītum, to desire greatly
concurrō, -ere, -currī,
-cursum, to come together;
clash
concutiō, -ere, -cussī, -cussum,
to shake up
condiciō, -ōnis, *f.*, situation,
circumstances
condō, -ere, -didī, -ditum, to
bury, suppress, conceal

conferō, -ferre, -tulī, -lātum,
to bring together; bestow,
contribute
confodiō, -ere, -fōdī, -fossum,
to stab, pierce
confugiō, -ere, -fūgī, —, to flee
for refuge
coniciō, -ere, -iēcī, -iectum, to
throw together
cōnītor, -ī, cōnīsus *or* cōnixus
sum, to strive, struggle
onward
coniugālis, -e, *adj.*, of marriage
coniunx, -iugis, *f.*, wife
conlābor, -ī, conlapsus sum, to
fall in ruins, collapse
conlocō (1) to place
conscientia, -ae, *f.*, private
knowledge, conscience;
guilt
conscius, -a, -um, *adj.*,
witnessing
conscius, -iī, *m.*, co-
conspirator, guilty party
cōnscrībō, -ere, -scrīpsī,
-scrīptum, to enroll; **patrēs
cōnscrīptī**, *m. pl.*, conscript
fathers, senators
consenesco, -ere, -senuī, —, to
grow old
consequor, -ī, consecūtus
sum, to go after, seek to
accomplish
consīderō (1) consider,
contemplate
consilium, -iī, *n.*, plan, advice;
deliberation; advisory group;
consilium capere, to take
advice

consistō, -ere, -stitī, -stitum, to stop, halt

consōlātiō, -iōnis, *f.,* consolation, comforting

consōlātor, -ōris, *m.,* consoler

consōlor, -ārī, consōlātus sum, to console, comfort; alleviate

conspectus, -ūs, *m.,* view, sight

conspiciō, -ere, -spexī, -spectum, to see, perceive, observe

constantia, -ae, *f.,* steadfastness, consistency

constat, -stāre, —, —, *impers.,* it is known, agreed

constituō, -ere, -stitī, -stitūtum, to arrange; decide

constringō, -ere, -strinxī, -strictum, to draw together, bind, tie up

consuētūdō, -dinis, *f.,* habit, custom; **ex consuētūdine,** according to habit

consul, -sulis, *m.,* consul

consulātus, -ūs, *m.,* consulship

contemnō, -ere, -tempsī, -temptum, to scorn, dismiss as of little value

contendō, -ere, -ndī, -ntum, to strive, compete

contentus, -a, -um, *adj.,* content, satisfied, (with) + *abl.*

contineō, -ēre, -uī, contentum, to hold or keep together; restrain, repress

continuō, *adv.,* immediately, automatically

contiō, -ōnis, *f.,* assembly, gathering of the people

contrā, *adv.,* in the opposite direction

contrā, *prep.* + *acc.,* against

contrārius, -a, -um, *adj.,* opposing, contrary, contradictory

contrucīdō (1) to cut to pieces, butcher

contumācia, -ae, *f.,* arrogance, disobedience

conualescō, -ere, -ualuī, —, to recover health, gain strength

conueniō, -īre, -uēnī, -uentum, to be suitable, befit, + *dat.*

conuenit, -ire, *impers.,* it is agreed, there is an agreement (that) + **ut/nē**

conuentiō, -ōnis, *f.,* agreement; **ex conuentiōne,** according to the agreement

conuersor, -ārī, conversātus sum, to live, spend time (with)

cor, cordis, *n.,* heart

corpus, -oris, *n.,* body

Coruīnus, -ī, *m.,* Corvinus

cotīdiē, *adv.,* daily

crēber, -bris, -bre, *adj.,* frequent

crēdō, -ere, -didī, -ditum, to believe; trust, entrust (to), + *dat.*

creō (1) to produce

crescō, -ere, crēuī, crētum, to grow

crīmen, -inis, *n.,* charge, crime

crīnis, -is, *m.,* hair

cruentus, -a, -um, *adj.*, bloody

cruor, -ōris, *m.*, blood

crux, crūcis, *m.*, cross, rack

cubiculum, -ī, *n.*, bedroom, private room

cubīle, -is, *n.*, bed

cuique = *dat. of* quisque

culpa, -ae, *n.*, guilt

cum, *conj.*, when; because; although; cum maximē, at this very moment

cum, *prep.* + *abl.*, with

Cūmae, -ārum, *f. pl.*, Cumae (city in Campania)

cumba, -ae, *f.*, skiff, small boat

cupiditās, -tātis, *f.*, desire

cupiō, -ere, -īuī, -ītum, to desire, wish

cūra, -ae, *f.*, care; anxiety

cūrātiō, -ōnis, *f.*, healing, therapy

currus, -ūs, *m.*, chariot

cursim, *adv.*, hastily, superficially

cursus, -ūs, *m.*, course, motion

curuō (1) to bend, curve

custōdiō, -īre, -īuī *or* -iī, -ītum, to guard, protect

custōs, -ōdis, *m.*, guardian

cutis, -is, *f.*, (the) skin

damnō (1) to condemn (to death); capitis damnāre, to condemn to capital punishment, to death

damnum, -ī, *n.*, damage

dē, *prep.* + *abl.*, about, concerning; from; dē industriā, on purpose

dēbeō, -ēre, -uī, -itum, to owe; ought (to) + *infinitive*

dēbilis, -e, *adj.*, maimed, disabled

dēbilitās, -tātis, *f.*, disability

decet, -ēre, *pl.* decent, decuit, *impers.*, it suits, befits, + *acc. of person*, (to) + *infinitive*

decus, -coris, *n.*, splendor; ornament

dēdō, -ere, dēdidī, dēditum, to give over, commit, surrender, (to) + *dat.*

dēfendō, -ere, -ndī, -nsum, to defend, protect

dēferō, -ferre, -tulī, -lātum, to bring down; hand over, pass on, deliver (*information*)

dēfīgō, -ere, -fīgī, -fixum, to fasten, fix; dēfixus, *pple.*, transfixed

dēgustō (1) to take a taste of

dēiciō, -ere, -iēcī, -ectum, to cast down

deinde, *adv.*, then, next

dēlectō (1) to please, delight

dēlicātus, -a, -um, pleasing, alluring; addicted to pleasure

dēliciae, -ārum, *f. pl.*, pleasures, luxuriousness

dēmens, -entis, *adj.*, mad, out of one's mind

dēmentia, -ae, *f.*, madness

densus, -a, -um, *adj.*, thick

dēprehendō *or* dēprendō, -ere, -ndī, -nsum, to seize; discover

dērigō *or* dīrigō, -ere, -rexī, -rectum, to direct

dēscendō, -ere, -scendī,
  -scensum, to go down,
  descend; sink
dēserō, -ere, -seruī, -sertum, to
  leave, abandon
dēsīderium, -iī, *n.*, longing
dēsinō, -ere, dēsiī, —, to cease
  (to) + *infinitive*
dēspērō (1) to despair, be
  without hope; despair of
dēsum, deesse, dēfuī,
  dēfutūrus, to be lacking (to)
  + *dat.*
dētegō, -ere, -texī, -tectum, to
  uncover
dēterreō, -ēre, -uī, -itum, to
  scare off, discourage
dētrahō, -ere, -traxī, -tractum,
  to draw away, remove
dēuertō, -ere, -tī, -sum, to turn
  away
deus, *gen.* deī, *nom. pl.* dī, *m.*,
  god
dextra, -ae, *f.*, right hand
dīcō, -ere, dīxī, dictum, to say
dictiō, -ōnis, *f.*, saying; iūris
  dictiō, saying of right, right
  to say
dīdūcō, -ere, -dūxī, -ductum,
  to draw apart, separate
diēs, diēī, *m.*, day; daylight;
  date
difficilis, -e, *adj.*, difficult
diffindō, -ere, -fidī, -fissum, to
  cleave, divide
dignitās, -tātis, *f.*, social
  position
dignus, -a, -um, *adj.*, worthy
  (of) + *abl.*

dīmittō, -ere, -mīsī, -missum,
  to send away, dismiss
dīrus, -a, -um, *adj.*, horrible,
  ominous
discēdō, -ere, -cessī, -cessum,
  to depart
discō, -ere, didicī, —, to learn
discors, *gen.* discordis, *adj.*,
  dissonant, disordered
discurrō, -ere, -currī, -cursum,
  to run in different directions
discutiō, -ere, -cussī, -cussum,
  to shake up, break up
dīsertus, -a, -um, *adj.*, eloquent
dispōnō, -ere, -posuī,
  -positum, to arrange
disserō, -ere, -seruī, -sertum,
  to speak; discuss
dissimulō (1) to pretend (that
  something is not the case)
distringō, -ere, -strinxī,
  -strictum, to pull in
  different directions
diū, *adv.*, for a long time
dīuersus, -a, -um, *adj.*, varied,
  differing
dīues, *gen.* dīuitis, *adj.* wealthy;
  m., wealthy man
dīuidō, -ere, -uīsī, -uīsum, to
  divide up, apportion
dīuīnus, -a, -um, *adj.*, divine
dīuitiae, -ārum, *f. pl.*, wealth
diūtius, *adv.*, for a longer time;
  compar. of diū
dīuus, -a, -um, *adj.*, deified,
  divine
dō, dare, dedī, datum, to give
doceō, -ēre, -uī, doctum, to
  teach

doleō, -ēre, -uī, -itum, to feel pain, ache

dolor, -ōris, *m.,* grief; pain

domesticus, -a, -um, *adj.,* of the household, of one's own household

domina, -ae, *f.,* mistress

dominātor, -ōris, *m.,* subjugator

dominus, -ī, *m.,* master

domō, -āre, -uī, -itum, to subjugate, tame

domus, -ī, *f.,* home, household

dōnō (1) to give, present

dubitō (1) to doubt; hesitate

dubius, -a, -um, *adj.,* doubtful

dūcō, -ere, dūxī, ductum, to lead

dulcis, -e, *adj.,* sweet

dum, *conj.,* while; until

duo, duae, duo, *numeral,* two

duodēuice(n)simus, -a, -um, *adj.,* eighteenth

dux, ducis, *m.,* leader

ē. *See* **ex**

ebur, -oris, *n.,* ivory

ecce, *interj.,* behold!

ecquid, *adv. introducing rhetorical question,* Is it not the case that . . . ?

ēdō, -ere, ēdidī, ēditum, to bring forth

effectus, -ūs, *m.,* effect, outcome

efferō, -ferre, extulī, ēlātum, to bring out; carry out for burial

efferus, -a, -um, *adj.,* wild, savage

efficax, *gen.* **efficācis,** *adj.,* effective, consequential

efficiō, -ere, -fēcī, -fectum, to fashion; bring it about

effingō, -ere, -finxī, -fictum, to fashion, sculpt

effodiō, -ere, -fōdī, -fossum, to dig up, excavate

effundō, -ere, -fūdī, -fūsum, to pour forth

ego, *gen.* **meī,** *pron.,* I, me

ēgredior, -ī, ēgressus sum, to go beyond, pass out of

ēiulātus, -ūs, *m.,* wailing

ēligō, -ere, -lēgī, -lectum, to choose, select; elect

ēmittō, -ere, -mīsī, -missum, to send forth, expel

ēn, *interj.,* behold!

ēnascor, -ī, -nātus sum, to sprout up, be born

ēneruō (1) deprive of energy, weaken

enim, *particle,* for; you see

epistula, -ae, *f.,* letter

ērādō, -ere, -rāsī, -rāsum, to scrape off, erase (from) + *abl.*

ergō, *adv.,* therefore; **quid ergō?,** what, then?, well?

ēripiō, -ere, -ripuī, -reptum, to tear out, tear away, rescue

ērubescō, ērubescere, ērubuī, —, to blush, be embarrassed, (to) + *infinitive*

ērudiō, -īre, -īuī *or* **-iī, -ītum,** to polish, educate

et, *conj.,* and

etiam, *adv.,* also; even

etiamnunc, *adv.*, still, even now

ēuādō, -ere, -uadī, -uāsum, to come out, walk forth

ēuānidus, -a, -um, faint

ēuellō, -ere, -uellī, -uulsum, to pluck out (from) + *dat.*

ēueniō, -īre, -uēnī, -uentum, to come out, turn out, (that) + **ut** + *subjunctive*

ēuocō (1) to call forth

ēuoluō, -ere, -uoluī, -uolūtum, to unroll

ex *or* ē, *prep.* + *abl.* from, from out of; *following a number or amount*, of; according to: **ex conuentiōne**, according to the agreement, **ex consuētūdine**, according to habit

exardeō, -ēre, —, —, to blaze, flare up

excerpō, -ere, -cerpsī, -cerptum, to pick out

excidō, -ere, -cidī, —, to fall out (from memory)

excīdō, -ere, -cīdī, -cīsum, to cut out

excipiō, -ere, -cēpī, -ceptum, to take out, make an exception of

excitō (1) to stir up, excite

exclāmō (1) to cry out, exclaim

excolō, -ere, -coluī, -cultum, to cultivate

exemplar, -āris, *n.*, model

exemplum, -ī, *n.*, example, instance

exeō, -īre, -īuī *or* -iī, -itum, to go out, come out

ex(s)ertō (1) to stick out

exhauriō, -īre, -hausī, -haustum, to drain out, empty

exigō, -ere, -ēgī, -actum, to drive out; demand; make conform (to) + **ad** + *acc.*; **uītam exigere,** spend one's life

exilium, -iī, *n.*, exile

existimō (1) to reckon, judge, think

exitium, -iī, *n.*, death, destruction

expectō (1) to await; expect

expediō, -īre, -īuī, -ītum, to extricate, free up; **expedītus,** *pple.*, unencumbered, easy

expellō, -ere, -pulī, -pulsum, to drive out, displace

expers, *gen.* -pertis, having no part (in), free (from), + *gen.*

explicō, -āre, -plicuī, -plicātum *or* -plicitum, to unfold, manifest

explōrātor, -ōris, *m.*, scout, spy

expōnō, -ere, -posuī, -positum, to set out; make vulnerable; *of infants,* expose

exsāniō (1) to drain, cleanse

exstinguō, -ere, -stinxī, -stinctum, to extinguish, abolish

exsul, -ulis, *m.*, exile, person in exile

extemplō, *adv.*, immediately, without delay

extenuō (1) to make thin

extorqueō, -ēre, -torsī, -tortum, to twist out, wrest away (from) + *dat.*

extrā, *prep.* + *acc.*, outside (of)

extrahō, -ere, -traxī, -tractum, to remove, extract

exul. *See* **exsul**

exulcerātiō, -ōnis, *f.*, aggravation (of a sore)

exultō (1) to leap up

ex(s)urgō, -ere, -surrexī, —, to rise up, grow

facile, *adv.*, easily

facilis, -e, *adj.*, easy; easygoing

facinus, -noris, *n.*, deed, misdeed

faciō, -ere, fēcī, factum, to do; make; **faxō,** *archaic form with fut. sense,* I will bring it about (that) + *subjunctive*

facultās, -tātis, *f.*, capability, resources, power

facundia, -ae, *f.*, eloquence

fallō, -ere, fefellī, falsum, to deceive

falsō, *adv.*, deceptively

fāma, -ae, *f.*, reputation, fame

familiāris, -e, *adj.*, familiar, well-known

familiāriter, *adv.*, closely, intimately

fāre. *See* **for**

fās, *n. indecl.*, what is right (by divine law); **fās est,** it is right (to) + *infinitive*

fastīdiō, -īre, -īuī, -ītum, to feel disgust, be fussy

fateor, -ērī, fassus sum, to say; admit, confess

fatīgō (1) to tire out

fātum, -ī, *n.*, fate

faucēs, -ium, *f. pl.*, the throat

fauōrābilis, -e, *adj.*, popular, beloved

faustus, -a, -um, *adj.*, happy, auspicious

fax, facis, *f.*, torch; firebrand

faxō. *See* **faciō**

fēlix, *gen.* **fēlīcis,** *adj.*, fortunate, prosperous

fēmineus, -a, -um, female, womanly

fēnerō (1) to lend at interest

ferē, *adv.*, usually

ferō, ferre, tulī, lātum, to bear; carry; endure

ferox, *gen.* **-ōcis,** *adj.*, fierce

ferrum, -ī, *n.*, iron; weapon, sword

ferueō, -ēre, —, —, to be burning hot; **feruens,** *pple.*, burning hot

ficta. *See* **fingō**

fidēlis, -e, *adj.*, faithful, loyal

fidēliter, *adv.*, reliably

fidēs, fideī, *f.*, faith, trust; promise; trustworthiness

fīdō, -ere, fīsus sum, to trust (in) + *dat.*

fīdūcia, -ae, *f.*, trust, reliance, confidence

fīlia, -ae, *f.*, daughter

fīlius, -iī, *m.*, son

fingō, -ere, finxī, fictum, to fashion, contrive; **fictus,** *pple.*, fictitious, made-up

fīnis, -is, *m.*, end; boundary

fīō, fierī, factus sum, to become; come about; be done, be made

flagrō (1) to blaze

flamma, -ae, *f.*, flame

flātus, -ūs, *m.*, blast, gust

fleō, -ēre, -ēuī, -ētum, to weep; lament for

flōreō, -ēre, -uī, —, to bloom, flourish

(for), fārī, fātus sum, to speak

forma, -ae, *f.*, form, appearance; beauty

formīdō, -inis, *f.*, fear, dread

forsan, *adv.*, perhaps

fortis, -e, *adj.*, strong; brave, courageous

fortiter, *adv.*, bravely

fortūna, -ae, *f.*, fortune, chance (*neutral*); good fortune; misfortune

Fortūna, -ae, *f.*, Fortune (goddess, personification)

forum, -ī, *n.*, forum

fragilis, -e, *adj.*, fragile, breakable

frangō, -ere, frēgī, fractum, to break

frāter, frātris, *m.*, brother

frāternus, -a, -um, *adj.*, of a brother

fraus, fraudis, *f.*, deceit, trickery

frēnō (1) to rein in, restrain

frequens, -entis, *adj.*, frequent, common

frequenter, *adv.*, frequently

fretum, -ī, *n.*, strait, sea

frīgus, -goris, *n.*, cold, frost

fructus, -ūs, *m.*, enjoyment

fruor, -ī, fructus sum, to enjoy + *abl.*

fuga, -ae, *f.*, flight, exile

fugiō, -ere, fūgī, —, to flee, escape

fugō (1) to put to flight, displace

fulmen, -minis, *n.*, lightning bolt

fundāmentum, -ī, *n.*, solid basis, foundation

funditus, *adv.*, from the foundation

fundō (1) to found

fundō, -ere, fūdī, fūsum, to pour out

fūnerō (1) to bury with funeral rites

fūnestus, -a, -um, *adj.*, funereal, deathly

fungor, fungī, functus sum, to perform, execute, + *abl.*

fūnus, -eris, *n.*, funeral, burial; death, murder

furiālis, -e, *adj.*, fury-like, furious

furo, -ere, —, —, to rage; **furens,** *pple.* raging, out of one's mind

furor, -ōris, *m.*, madness, frenzy

Gāius, -iī, *m.*, the emperor Gaius/Caligula

Gallia, -ae, *f.*, Gaul

Gangēticus, -a, -um, *adj.*, of the Ganges (river in India)

gaudeō, -ēre, gāuīsus sum, to rejoice (that) + **quod**

gelidus, -a, -um, *adj.*, icy cold
(gelū), *abl.* **gelū,** *n.*, frost, icy
  cold
geminī, -ae, -a, *adj.*, twin
gemitus, -ūs, *m.*, sigh, groan
gemō, -ere, -uī, -itum, to sigh,
  groan
genae, -ārum, *f. pl.*, cheeks;
  eyes
geniālis, -e, *adj.*, relating to
  generation, birth; nuptial
genitor, -ōris, *m.*, begetter,
  father
gens, gentis, *f.*, family; nation;
  pl., the nations, the people of
  the empire
genus, -eris, *n.*, kind, type; race
gestātiō, -ōnis, *f.*, being carried
  on a litter
gladius, -iī, *m.*, sword
glōria, -ae, *f.*, glory; thirst for
  glory
gnātus, -ī, *m.*, son; *archaic form
  of* **nātus**
gracilis, -e, *adj.*, slender
gradus, -ūs, *m.*, step
grandō, -dinis, *m.*, hail
grātia, -ae, *f.*, gratitude, favor;
  grātiās agere, to give thanks
  (to) + *dat.* (that) **quod** +
  indicative; **grātiā,** *abl. with
  gen. noun*, for the sake of
grātiōsus, -a, -um, *adj.*, in
  favor, well-regarded
grātus, -a, -um, *adj.*, grateful
grauis, -e, *adj.*, heavy; serious
gustus, -ūs, *m.*, taste; **ad
  gustum,** corresponding to
  the first taste

habeō, -ēre, -uī, -itum, to have,
  hold; keep; regard
habitātor, -ōris, *m.*, inhabitant
haesitō (1) remain undecided,
  hesitate
harēna, -ae, *f.*, sand
hasta, -ae, *f.*, spear
hauriō, -īre, hausī, haustum,
  to draw out; drink down,
  consume
Hecatē, *gen.* **Hecatēs,** *f.*, Hecate,
  the Moon
Helvia, -ae, *f.*, Helvia (mother
  of Seneca)
hērēs, -ēdis, *m.*, heir
hīc, *adv.*, here
hic, haec, hoc, *pron./adj.*, he,
  she, it; this
hilaris, -e, *adj.*, cheerful
hinc, *adv.*, on this side
hodiē, *adv.*, today
hodiēque, *adv.*, even today
hodiernus, -a, -um, *adj.*, of
  today; the present
homō, -inis, *m.*, human being
honestus, -a, -um, *adj.*, noble,
  virtuous
honor, -ōris, *m.*, honor;
  political office
hōra, -ae, *f.*, hour
horreō, -ēre, -uī, —, to bristle;
  shudder (at)
horreum, -ī, *n.*, warehouse
horridus, -a, -um, *adj.*, terrible,
  terrifying, making one bristle
horror, -ōris, *n.*, terror,
  shuddering, bristling
hortor, -ārī, -atus sum, to
  encourage, exhort

hospitium, -iī, *n.,* hospitality; a
place to stay
hostīlis, -e, *adj.,* of the enemy
hostis, -is, *m.,* stranger; enemy;
pl., (the) enemy
hūc, *adv.,* this way
humānus, -a, -um, *adj.,*
human
humilis, -e, *adj.,* lowly, near the
ground
humilitās, -tātis, *f.,* lowliness

iaceō, -ēre, -uī, —, to lie
iaciō, -ere, iēcī, iactum, to
throw; **fundāmenta iacere,**
to lay foundations
iactātiō, -ōnis, *f.,* throwing
around, agitation, shaking
up
iactus, -ūs, *m.,* casting down;
fall
iam, *adv.,* now; already; **iam
prīdem,** for a long time
already
Iāsōn, -ōnis, *m.,* Jason
īdem, eadem, idem, *pron./adj.,*
the same (one, thing)
ideo, *adv.,* for that reason,
therefore
ignāuus, -a, -um, *adj.,*
cowardly
ignis, -is, *m.,* fire
ignoscō, -ere, ignōuī, ignōtum,
to forgive + *dat.*
ignōtus, -a, -um, *adj.,*
unknown, unheard of
ille, illa, illud, *pron./adj.* he,
she, it; that
illīc, *adv.,* in that place

illinc, *adv.,* on that side
illō, *adv.,* to that place
illūc, *adv.,* that way
imāgō, -inis, *f.,* portrait; image
imitor (1) to imitate
immānis, -e, *adj.,* monstrous
immensus, -a, -um, *adj.*
measureless, huge
immineō, -ēre, -uī, —, to hang
over, be eager for, + *dat.*
immitto, -ere, -mīsī, -missum,
to send in; send forth, cast
immo, *adv. correcting a
previous statement,* (not only
that but) in fact
immortālis, -e, *adj.,* immortal
impediō, -īre, -īuī, -ītum, to
obstruct
imperātor, -ōris, *m.,* general
imperium, -iī, *n.,* power,
authority; empire
imperō (1) to command, + *dat.*;
be emperor
impetus, -ūs *m.,* impulse,
initiative; onset; attack
impius, -a, -um, *adj.,* unholy,
wicked
**impōnō, -ere, -posuī,
-positum,** to place upon +
dat.
impotens, *gen.* **-entis,** *adj.,*
reckless, having no self-
control
īmus, -a, -um, *adj.,* bottom,
below
in, *prep.* + *abl.,* in; *prep.* +
acc., into, against, for the
purpose of
inānis, -e, *adj.,* empty, useless

inbuō, -ere, -uī, -ūtum, to drench, imbue, (with) + *abl.*

incipiō, -ere, incēpī *or* **-coepī, inceptum** *or* **-coeptum,** to begin (to) + *infinitive*

inclitus, -a, -um, *adj.,* illustrious, renowned

incognitus, -a, -um, *adj.,* unknown

incrēdibilis, -e, *adj.,* unbelievable; **incrēdibile est . . . quam,** it is unbelievable . . . how

incursō (1) rush onward, attack

indicium, -iī, *n.,* information, report

indīcō, -ere, -dixī, -dictum, to declare, inflict, (upon) + *dat. of person*

indignātiō, -ōnis, *f.,* indignation, outrage

indulgens, -entis, *adj.* indulgent; loving

indulgentia, -ae, *f.,* indulgence; love

indulgeō, -ēre, -dulsī, -dulsum, to be kind, allow; give oneself over (to) + *dat.*

induō, -ere, -uī, -ūtum, to put on, assume

indūrō (1) to make hard, toughen

Indus, -a, -um, *adj.,* Indian

industria, -ae, *f.,* diligence; **dē industriā,** on purpose

iners, *gen.* **inertis,** *adj.,* inactive, sluggish

inertia, -ae, *f.,* inactivity

infēlīcitās, -tātis, *f.,* lack of good fortune, unhappiness

infestus, -a, -um, *adj.,* hostile, hateful

infinītus, -a, -um, *adj.,* limitless

infrā, *prep.* + *acc.,* beneath; inferior to

ingenium, -iī, *n.,* inborn nature; mind; rhetorical style; author

ingens, *gen.* **ingentis,** *adj.,* huge

ingerō, -gerere, -gessī, -gestum, to pile up

ingrātus, -a, -um, *adj.,* ungrateful

inhospitālis, -e, *adj.,* inhospitable

inimīcus, -a, -um, *adj.,* hostile, inimical

inimīcus, -ī, *m.,* an enemy, opponent

inīquus, -a, -um, *adj.,* unfair, unjust

iniūria, -ae, *f.,* injury

inmittō. *See* **immittō**

inmōbilis, -e, *adj.,* unmovable

inmoror (1) to linger (upon) + *dat.*

innītor, -ī, innixus *or* **innīsus sum,** to lean (upon) + *abl.*

innocens, *gen.* **-entis,** *adj.,* harmless, innocent

innocentia, -ae, *f.,* causing no harm, innocence

innūtriō, -īre, -īuī, -ītum, to nourish

inprimō, -ere, -pressī,
-pressum, to press upon +
dat.

inquiētō (1) to disturb

inquiētus, -a, -um, *adj.*, restless

inquinō (1) to pollute

inquit, he or she says, said

inritus, -a, -um, *adj.*, futile,
without result

insideō, -ēre, -sēdī, -sessum, to
settle upon, occupy, + *dat.*

insidiae, -iārum, *f. pl.*, ambush,
treachery

insidiātor, -ōris, *m.*, conspirator

inspiciō, -ere, -spexī,
-spectum, to look upon,
observe

instābilis, -e, *adj.*, unsteady

instar, *n. indecl.* + *gen.* in the
likeness of, serving as

instituō, -ere, -stituī,
-stitūtum, to set up; decide,
determine, (to) + *infinitive*;
instruct

instruō, -ere, -struxī,
-structum, to draw up;
instruct

insurgō, -ere, -surrexī,
-surrectum, to rise up

integer, -gra, -grum, *adj.*,
untouched, intact

integrō (1) to renew

intendo, -ere, -ndī, -ntum, to
focus on, attend to; intentus,
pple., focused (on) + ad +
acc.

inter, *prep.* + *acc.*, between;
among

interdum, *adv.*, sometimes

interest, -esse, interfuit, —,
impers., it is in the interest
(of) + *gen. of person* (that)
+ *acc.* + *infinitive*; there is
a difference (whether) +
utrum + *subjunctive*

interiaceō, -ēre, -iacuī, —, to
lie between

interim, *adv.*, meanwhile

interloquor, -ī, interlocūtus
sum, to interrupt by
speaking

interpellō (1) to interrupt

interpōnō, -ere, -posuī,
-positum, to place between

interuallum, -ī, *n.*, gap, break

intimus, -a, -um, *adj.*, inner,
intimate

intrā, *prep.* + *acc.*, inside,
within

intrō (1) to enter

intueor, -ērī, intuitus sum, to
look at, contemplate

intus, *adv.*, within

inueniō, -īre, -uēnī, -uentum,
to find, discover; invent

inuītō (1) to invite, beckon

ipse, ipsa, ipsum, *pron./adj.*
himself, herself, itself; the
very (one, thing)

īra, -ae, *f.*, anger, wrath

īrascor, īrascī, īrātus sum, to
grow angry (at) + *dat.*

irrītō (1) to rouse, stimulate

is, ea, id, *pron./adj.*, he, she, it;
that (one, thing)

iste, ista, istud, *pron./adj.*, that
(horrible) one; that one (of
yours)

Isthmos, -ī, *m.,* the Isthmus (of Corinth)

ita, *adv.,* thus, in this way; *in combination with* **quemadmodum,** in the same way, so too

itaque, *adv.* and so, therefore

iter, itineris, *n.,* journey

iterum, *adv.,* again, for a second time

iubar, -aris, *n.,* radiance, brightness

iubeō, -ēre, iussī, iussum, to order (to) + *infinitive*

iucundus, -a, -um, *adj.,* pleasing

iūdicium, -iī, *n.,* trial; judgment

iugulus, -ī, *m.,* throat

iugum, -ī, *n.,* yoke

iungō, -ere, iunxī, iunctum, to join

iūrō (1) to swear (by)

iūs, iūris, *n.,* law; right; duty; **iūris dictiō,** saying of right, right to say

iuuenīlis, -e, *adj.,* youthful, of a young man

iuuō (1) to help; delight; **iuuat,** it is pleasing (to) + *infinitive*

L. = Lūcius, -iī, *m.,* Lucius

labor, -ōris, *m.,* work, effort

lacrima, -ae, *f.,* tear

lacus, -ūs, *m.,* lake

laetitia, -ae, *f.,* happiness, prosperity

laetus, -a, -um, *adj.,* happy, prosperous

laeuus, -a, -um, *adj.,* left; unlucky, of ill omen

lāmentātiō, -ōnis, *f.,* lamentation

lancinō (1) to tear apart

latebra, -ae, *f.,* hiding place, lair

lateō, -ēre, -uī, —, to lie hidden

latitō (1) to stay hidden

latus, -eris, *n.,* side; flank (of body)

laus, laudis, *f.,* praise

laxō (1) to relax, loosen

lectiō, -ōnis, *f.,* reading

legō, -ere, lēgī, lectum, to read

lēnis, -e, *adv.,* gentle

lētum, -ī, *n.,* death

leuāmen, -minis, *n.,* alleviation, relief

leuis, -e, *adj.,* light

leuiter, *adv.,* lightly

leuō (1) to lighten, alleviate

lex, lēgis, *f.,* law

libenter, *adv.,* willingly

liber, librī, *m.,* book

līber, -era, -erum, *adj.,* free

līberālis, -e, *adj.,* pertaining to a free man; liberal

līberī, *gen.* **līberōrum** *or* **līberum,** *m. pl.,* children

lībertās, -tātis, *f.,* freedom

lībertīnus, -ī, *m.,* freedman

libet, -ēre, libuit *or* **libitum est,** *impers.,* it is pleasing (for) + *dat. of person* (to) + *infinitive*

libīdō, -dinis, *f.,* lust, desire

Libya, -ae, *f.,* Libya, *metonym for* Africa

licet, -ēre, licitum est, *impers.*,
  it is permitted, possible,
  (for) + *dat. of person* (to)
  + *infinitive or subjunctive*;
  licet *with subjunctive verb*,
  although, even if
lignum, -ī, *n.*, wood
līmes, -mitis, *m.*, boundary;
  path
lingua, -ae, *f.*, tongue
litō (1) to sacrifice
litterae, -ārum, *f., pl.*, writing,
  literature; epistle, epistles
lītus, -oris, *n.*, shore
Līuia, -ae, *f.*, Livia (wife of
  Augustus)
locus, -ī, *m., pl.* **loca, -ōrum,** *n.*,
  place, location, position
longinquus, -a, -um, *adj.*, long;
  distant
longus, -a, -um, *adj.*, long;
  long-lasting
loquor, -ī, locūtus sum, to
  speak; talk about
Lūcīlius, -iī, *m.*, Lucilius
Lūcīna, -ae, *f.*, Lucina (goddess
  of birth, marriage, etc.)
luctus, -ūs, *m.* grief,
  mourning
lūgeō, -ēre, lūxī, lūctum, to
  grieve, mourn
lūmen, -minis, *n.*, light; *pl.*,
  eyes
luō, -ere, luī, —, to release;
  atone for
lustrō (1) to wander around
lux, lūcis, *f.*, light
luxuria, -ae, *f.*, luxury,
  extravagance

M. = Marcus, -ī, *m.*, Marcus
maenas, -adis, *f.*, maenad,
  bacchant
maestus, -a, -um, *adj.*, full of
  sadness, melancholy
magicus, -a, -um, *adj.*, magic
magis, *adv.*, more, *compar. of*
  magnoperē
magnoperē, *adv.*, greatly
magnus, -a, -um, *adj.*, great
māior, maius, *gen.* **māiōris,**
  adj., greater; *compar. of*
  magnus
māiōrēs, -ōrum, *m. pl.*, (the)
  ancestors
male, *adv.*, badly
malignus, -a, -um, *adj.*,
  spiteful; stingy
malum, -ī, *n.*, bad thing, woe
mancipium, -ī, *n.*, slave; piece
  of property
maneō, -ēre, mansī, mansum,
  to remain; await
mānēs, -ium, *m. pl.*, spirits
  of the dead; gods of the
  underworld
manus, -ūs, *f.*, hand
mare, maris, *n.*, (the) sea
marmor, -oris, *n.*, marble
māter, mātris, *f.*, mother
māteria, -ae, *f.*, material
maximē, *adv.*, especially;
  cum maximē, at this very
  moment
maximus, -a, -um, *adj.*,
  greatest; *superl. of* **magnus**
Mēdēa, -ae, *f.*, Medea
medicāmentum, -ī, *n.*,
  medicine, treatment

medicus, -ī, *m.*, doctor

meditor (1) to think over, meditate upon; practice

medius, -a, -um, *adj.*, middle; the middle of

mehercules, *adv.*, by Hercules!

melior, melius, *gen.* meliōris, *adj.*, better; *compar. of* bonus

membrum, -ī, *n.*, limb

mēmet = intensive form of mē

memor, *gen.* memoris, *adj.*, remembering, mindful (of), + *gen.*

memorābilis, -e, *adj.*, worthy of remembering

memoria, -ae, *f.*, memory, remembering; memoriae (*dat.*) prōditus, passed on to memory

memorō (1) to recall, recount

mendācium, -iī, *n.*, lies, falsehood

mens, mentis, *f.*, mind

mensa, -ae, *f.*, table

mercēs, -cēdis, *f.*, merchandise, cargo

mereō, -ēre, -uī, -itum, to earn, deserve; serve, act deservingly

Messala, -ae, *m.*, Messala

-met, *intensifying suffix on pers. prons.*

metuō, -ere, -uī, —, to fear

metus, -ūs, *m.*, fear

meus, -a, -um, *adj.*, my

mīles, mīlitis, *m.*, soldier

mille, *pl.* mīlia, *numeral*, a thousand; mīlia (passuum), thousands (of paces), miles

minae, -ārum, *f. pl.*, threats

minor, -ārī, -atus sum, to threaten + *dat. of person*

minuō, -ere, -uī, -ūtum, to decrease

minus, *adv.*, less, *compar. of* paulum; non minus . . . quam, no less . . . than

miser, misera, miserum, *adj.*, wretched, miserable

misereor, -ērī, miseritus sum, to feel pity

miseriae, -ārum, *f. pl.*, miseries, woes

misericordia, -ae, *f.*, pity, mercy

mītigō (1) make mild

mītis, -e, *adj.*, mild, kind

mittō, -ere, mīsī, missum, to send; shoot

moderor, -ārī, moderātus sum, to control, mitigate

modo, *adv.*, just now; modo . . . modo, one moment . . . the next

modus, -ī, *m.*, way, manner; measure

moenia, -ōrum, *n. pl.*, walls, fortifications

monstrō (1) to show

monstrum, -ī, *n.*, monster, monstrosity, evil portent

monumentum, -ī, *n.*, monument

mora, -ae, *f.*, delay

morior, -īrī, mortuus sum, to die

moror (1) to delay, spend time

mors, mortis, *f.*, death

mortālis, -e, *adj.,* mortal; *m.,*
mortal being, human being
mortifer, -fera, -ferum, *adj.,*
bringing death, deadly
mortuus, -a, -um, *adj.,* dead
mōtus, -ūs, *m.,* movement,
motion; disturbance
moueō, -ēre, mōuī, mōtum, to
move; set in motion
mucrō, -ōnis, *m.,* sharp edge,
sword point
muliebris, -e, *adj.* of women,
feminine
multī, -ae, -a, *pl. adj.,* many
multitūdō, -dinis, *f.,* number;
multitude; mob
multō, *adv.,* much
multum, *adv.,* much
multum, -ī, *n.,* much
mūrus, -ī, *m.,* wall
musca, -ae, *f.,* fly
mūtātiō, -ōnis, *f.,* change
mūtō (1) to change
mūtus, -a, -um, *adj.,* mute,
speechless
mūtuus, -a, -um, *adj.,*
reciprocal, retaliatory

-nam, *intensifying suffix on*
interrogs., at all, on earth
namque, *adv.,* for
nanciscor, -ī, nactus sum, to
obtain, meet with, find
narrō (1) to tell (of)
nascor, -ī, nātus sum, to be born
nāta, -ae, *f.,* daughter
nātālis, -is, *m. with* **diēs**
implied, day of birth;
birthday

nātiō, -ōnis, *f.,* nation
nātūra, -ae, *f.,* nature
nātūrālis, -e, *adj.,* natural
nātus, -ī, *m.,* child, son
-ne, *interrog. particle indicating*
yes/no question
nē, *conj.,* lest, that not; *after*
verbs of fearing, that; **nē . . .**
quidem, not even
Neapolis, -is, *f.,* Naples
nec *or* **neque,** *adv.,* and not; **nec**
. . . nec, neither . . . nor
necessārius, -a, -um, *adj.,*
necessary, unavoidable
necesse, *n. indecl.,* necessary;
necesse est, it is necessary
(to) + *infinitive,* it is
necessary (that) + *subjunctive*
nefās, *n. indecl.,* something
contrary to divine law,
unspeakable crime, evil
neglegens, *gen.* **-entis,**
negligent, inattentive
negōtium, -iī, *n.,* work
nēmō, —, *dat.* **nēminī,** *m.,* no
one
nemus, -moris, *n.,* wood, grove
nepōs, -pōtis, *m.,* nephew;
grandson
Nerō, -ōnis, *m.,* Nero
nesciō, -īre, -īuī *or* **-iī, -ītum,**
to not know (how to) +
infinitive; **nesciō an,** I don't
know whether, i.e., probably
nex, necis, *f.,* death, slaughter
nihil *or* **nīl,** *n. indecl.,* nothing;
adv., not at all
nimbus, -ī, *m.,* rain cloud, rain
storm

nimis *or* nimium, *adv.*,
excessively, too

nisi, *conj.*, unless, except

nix, niuis, *f.*, snow

nōbilis, -e, *adj.*, noble;
belonging to the senatorial
aristocracy

nōdus, -ī, *m.*, knot, coil

nōlō, nolle, nōluī, —, to not
want, refuse

nōmen, -minis, *n.*, name

noceō, -ēre, nocuī, nocitūrus,
to harm + *dat.*

nōn *adv.*, not

nondum, *adv.*, not yet

noscō, -ere, nōuī, nōtum, get to
know; *in pf. tense, with pres.
meaning*, know

noster, -stra, -strum, *adj.*, our

nota, -ae, *f.*, mark, sign;
character

notābilis, -e, *adj.*, discernible,
recognizable

nōtus, -a, -um, *adj.*, known,
renowned; *pf. pple.* of
noscō

nouissimē, *adv.*, first, before
others

nouus, -a, -um, *adj.* new;
novel

nox, noctis, *f.*, night

nullus, -a, -um, *adj.*, no

numerus, -ī, *m.*, number

numquam, *adv.*, never

nunc, *adv.*, now

nuntiō (1) to report

nuper, *adv.*, recently

nusquam, *adv.*, nowhere

nūtus, -ūs, *m.*, nod, approval

ob, *prep.* + *acc.*, on account of,
because of

obdūcō, -ere, -dūxī, -ductum,
to cover over

oblectāmentum, -ī, *n.*,
entertainment, pleasure

oblectō (1) entertain

oblīterō *or* oblitterō (1) to blot
out, erase

oblitescō, -ere, -uī, —, to go
into hiding

obruō, -ere, -ruī, -rutum, to
cover over, overwhelm, bury

obsequium, -iī, *n.*, compliance,
obedience

obstō, -āre, -stitī, -stātum, to
stand in the way (of) + *dat.*

obuersor, -ārī, -atus sum, to
come before the mind (of)
+ *dat.*

occidō, -ere, -cidī, —, to fall, be
killed

occīdō, -ere, -cīdī, -cīsum, to
slay

occupātiō, -ōnis, *f.*, activity,
distracting task

occupō (1) to take possession
of, seize; fill, take up;
occupātus, *pple.*, busy,
occupied

Ōceanus, -ī, *m.*, Ocean (the all-
encompassing river)

oculus, -ī, *m.*, eye

offerō, -ferre, obtulī, oblātum,
to put before, offer (to), +
dat.

officium, -iī, *n.*, duty

omnis, -e, *adj.*, every; all

onus, oneris, *n.*, burden

opera, -ae, *f.,* work; effort;
  operam dare, to endeavor
  (that) + **ut/nē** + *subjunctive*
oportet, -ēre, -uit, —, *impers.,*
  it is right or fitting (to) +
  infinitive
ops, opis, *f.,* power, support; *pl.,*
  resources, riches
optimus, -a, -um, *adj., superl.*
  of **bonus**
opus, operis, *n.,* task, work;
  opus est, there is a need (for)
  + *abl.*
ōrātiō, -ōnis, *f.,* speech
orbis, -is, *m.,* circle; world
orbus, -a, -um, *adj.,* deprived
  (of) + *abl.*
ordō, -dinis, *m.,* order
orior, -īrī, ortus sum, to come
  into existence; rise, arise
ornāmentum, -ī, *n.,*
  adornment; source of pride
ornō (1) to adorn
ōs, ōris, *n.,* mouth; face
ōs, ossis, *n.,* bone
osculum, -ī, *n.,* kiss
ostendō, -ere, -tendī, -tensum,
  to show
ōtiōsus, -a, -um, *adj.,* leisurely
ōtium, -iī, *n.,* leisure

p. c. = patrēs conscriptī, *m. pl.,*
  conscript fathers, senators
paenitet, -ēre, paenituit, —,
  impers. there is regret (for) +
  acc. of person (about) + *gen.*
  of thing
Palladius, -a, -um, *adj.,* of
  Pallas Athena

pallor, -ōris, *m.,* pallor
parcō, -ere, pepercī, —, to
  spare, go easy on, + *dat.*
pārens, -entis, *m./f.,* parent
pāreō, -ēre, -uī, -itum, to obey
  + *dat.*
pariō, -ere, peperī, partum, to
  bring forth, give birth to
pariter, *adv.,* equally
parō (1) to prepare, make ready;
  acquire; **parātus,** *pple.,*
  ready (to) + *infinitive*
parricīda, -ae, *m.,* a parricide,
  someone who kills kin
parricīdium, -iī, *n.,* parricide,
  killing of kin
pars, partis, *f.,* part, portion
parsimōnia, -ae, *f.,* frugality,
  thrift
partus, -ūs, *m.,* birth, giving
  birth
parum, *n. indecl.,* little, too little
paruus, -a, -um, *adj.,* small
pascō, -ere, pāuī, pastum, to
  put out to feed
pateō, -ēre, -uī, —, to be open
  (to), available (for), + *dat.*
pater, patris, *m.,* father; **patrēs**
  conscriptī, *m., pl.,* conscript
  fathers, senators
patienter, *adv.,* bravely, with
  endurance
patientia, -ae, *f.,* endurance,
  patience
patior, patī, passus sum, to
  suffer; endure; allow (to) +
  infinitive
patria, -ae, *f.,* fatherland,
  country

patrimōnium, -iī, *n.*,
   inheritance, family estate
paueō, -ēre, pāuī, —, to be
   afraid, terrified
paulum, *adv.*, less
pauper, *gen.* **-eris,** *adj.*, poor
paupertās, -tātis, *f.*, poverty
pax, pācis, *f.*, peace
p. c. = patrēs conscriptī,
   m. pl., conscript fathers,
   senators
pectus, -toris, *n.*, chest, breast
pellis, -is, *f.*, skin, fleece
pellō, -ere, pepulī, pulsum, to
   drive; assault; drive out
penetrāle, -is, *n.*, inner space
per, *prep.* + *acc.*, through, by
   means of
peractum est. *See* **perigō**
peragrō (1) to wander through,
   traverse
percurrō, -ere, -currī,
   -cursum, to run through
percussor, -ōris, *m.*,
   executioner, assassin
perdō, -ere, -didī, -ditum, to
   lose; waste; destroy
peregrīnātiō, -ōnis, *f.*, travel
   abroad
pereō, -īre, -īuī *or* **-iī, -itum,** to
   perish
pererrō (1) to wander over
perferō, -ferre, -tulī, -lātum, to
   endure to the end
perfidus, -a, -um, *adj.*,
   treacherous
perīculum, -ī, *n.*, danger, peril
perigō, -ere, -ēgī, -actum, to
   carry to completion, finish

perimō, -ere, -ēmī, -emptum,
   to do away with, kill
perniciēs, -eī, *f.*, destruction,
   ruin
perpetuus, -a, -um, *adj.*,
   continual, unending
perrumpō, -ere, -rūpī,
   -ruptum, to break through
Persa, -ae, *m.*, Persian
perseuērantia, -ae, *f.*,
   persistence
perseuērō (1) to persist (in) +
   infinitive
persōna, -ae, *f.*, mask, theatrical
   role
perspiciō, -ere, -spexī,
   -spectum, to inspect
   thoroughly, penetratingly
pertinax, *gen.* **-ācis,** persistent,
   tenacious
pertineō, -ēre, -uī, —, to relate,
   be relevant
peruagō (1) to wander through
peruenīō, -īre, -uēnī, -uentum,
   to come the whole way;
   arrive
peruius, -a, -um, *adj.*, passable,
   pervious, pierced
perūrō, -ere, -ussī, -ustum, to
   burn up, scorch
pēs, pedis, *m.*, foot
pestis, -is, *f.*, plague, pestilence
peto, -ere, -īuī *or* **-iī, -ītum,** to
   seek
Phasis, -idis, *m.*, the Phasis
   (river in Colchis)
Phīdiās, -ae, *m.*, Phidias (the
   famous Greek sculptor)
philosophus, -ī, *m.*, philosopher

pietās, -tātis, *f.,* dutifulness; affection for kin

pignus, -noris, *n.,* pledge, token, proof; child

placeō, -ēre, -uī, -itum, to be pleasing

placidus, -a, -um, *adj.,* calm, peaceful

planta, -ae, *f.,* sprout, cutting; sole of foot

plebs, plēbis, *m.,* the common people

plēnus, -a, -um, *adj.,* full (of) + *gen.*

plicō, -āre, plicuī, plicātum *or* **plicitum,** to fold, double up

plūs, *adv.,* more, *compar. of* **multum**

plūs, *gen.* **plūris,** *adj./ substantive,* more; *compar. of* **multus**

poena, -ae, *f.,* punishment

Pompeiī, -ōrum, *m. pl.,* Pompeii

Pompēius, -iī, *m.,* Pompey

pōnō, -ere, posuī, positum, to place; set up; put aside

pontus, -ī, *m.,* the sea

Pontus, -ī, *m.,* Pontus, the Black Sea

populus, -ī, *m.,* people, population

portus, -ūs, *m.,* harbor, haven

possideō, -ēre, -sēdī, -sessum, to have and hold, possess

possum, posse, potuī, —, to be able (to), can, + *infinitive*

post, *prep.* + *acc.,* after

posterga, *adv.,* behind; = **post terga,** behind the back

potens, -tentis, *adj.,* powerful

potentia, -ae, *f.,* power

potius, *adv.,* rather

pōtō (1) to drink

praebeō, -ēre, -uī, -itum, to offer (up) (to) + *dat.*

praeceps, *gen.* **-cipitis,** *adj.,* headlong, hasty

praeceptum, -ī, *n.,* instruction; argument

praedicō (1) to proclaim

praesens, *gen.* **-ntis,** *adj.,* present

praesidium, -iī, *n.,* protection; garrison

praestō, -āre, -stitī, —, to give, present (to); *followed by direct object and acc. predicate adj.,* to make

praeter, *prep.* + *acc.,* besides, apart from

praetereō, -īre, -īuī *or* **-iī, -itum,** to pass by; **praeteritus,** *pple.,* past

praetōrius, -a, -um, *adj.,* ex-praetor

precor (1) to pray; call upon in prayer + *acc. of person or god*

premō, -ere, pressī, pressum, to oppress, crush

pretium, -iī, *n.,* price, value; prize, reward

prex, precis, *f.,* prayer, pleading

prīdem, *adv.,* long ago; **iam prīdem,** for a long time already

prīmum, *adv.,* first

prīmus, -a, -um, *adj.,* first, initial

princeps, -cipis, *m.,* leading man; princeps, emperor

principātus, -ūs, *m.,* principate, rule as emperor

prior, *gen.* **priōris,** *adj.,* prior, before

prīuātus, -a, -um, *adj.,* private

prius, *adv.,* first, before

prō, *prep.* + *abl.,* instead of; in proportion to

probō (1) to try, put to the test; prove; approve of

prōcēdō, -ere, -cessī, -cessum, to go forward, advance; succeed

prōcinctus, -ūs, *m.,* readiness; **in prōcinctū,** at the ready

prōclāmō (1) to call out, cry out

procul, *adv.,* far, distant

prōdō, -ere, -didī, -ditum, to hand over, pass on; **memoriae** (*dat.*) **prōditus,** passed on to memory

prōferō, -ferre, -tulī, -lātum, to bring forth, apply

prōficiō, -ere, -fēcī, -fectum, to make progress

prōfugiō, -ere, -fūgī, —, to flee

prōfundō, -ere, -fūdī, -fūsum, to pour forth

prōfundum, -ī, *n.,* abyss

prōfundus, -a, -um, *adj.,* deep

prōlēs, -is, *f.,* offspring, progeny

prōlūdō, -ere, -lūsī, -lūsum, to play beforehand, prelude

prōmiscuus, -a, -um, *adj.,* without differentiation

prōmittō, -ere, -mīsī, -missum, to send forth; promise, propose

prōmō, -ere, prompsī, promptum, to bring forth

prōnuntiō (1) to make known, proclaim

properō (1) to hurry

propitius, -a, -um, *adj.,* favoring

prōpositum, -ī, *n.,* what was proposed, plan

propter, *prep.* + *acc.,* because of

prōscriptiō, -ōnis, *f.,* proscription, confiscation

prōsum, prodesse, prōfuī, profutūrus, to be beneficial (to) + *dat.*

prōtinus, *adv.,* immediately, directly

pūblicus, -a, -um, *adj.,* of the people, public; **rēs pūblica,** the state, republic

pudet, -ēre, puduit, —, *impers.* there is shame (for) + *acc. of person* (about) + *gen. of thing*

pudor, -ōris, *m.,* shame

puellāris, -e, *adj.,* girlish

puer, puerī, *m.,* boy

pugiō, -ōnis, *m.,* dagger

pulcher, pulchra, pulchrum, *adj.,* fine, noble; beautiful

quā, *adv.,* where

quadrāge(n)simus, -a, -um, *adj.,* fortieth

quaerō, -ere, quaesīuī *or* **quaesiī, quaesitum,** to search (for); investigate

quālis, -e, *adj.*, of what sort

quam, *adv.* than; how; **tam . .
. quam** as . . . as; **aequē . . .
quam,** as much . . . as

quamdiū, *adv.*, as long as

quamuis, *adv.*, however much;
conj. + *subjunctive*, however
much, although

quando, *adv.*, where; *after* **sī,**
ever

quantus, -a, -um, *adj.*, how
great

quārē, *adv.*, why; on account
of what (which) thing;
therefore

quasi, *adv.*, as if

quatiō, -ere, quassī, quassum,
to shake violently

-que, *conj.*, and

quemadmodum, *adv.*, how;
introducing simile, just as

queō, -ēre, -īuī, -itum, to be
able (to) + *infinitive*

queror, -ī, questus sum, to
complain; lament

quī, quae, quod, *pron./adj.*,
who, what; which

quia, *conj.*, because

**quīcumque, quaecumque,
quodcumque,** *pron./adj.*,
whoever, whatever

quid, *adv.*, why?

quīdam, quaedam, quoddam,
pron./adj., a certain (one,
thing)

quidem, *adv.*, certainly, indeed;
nē . . . quidem, not even

quiēs, quiētis, *f.*, rest; peace,
quiet; quiet life

quiescō, -ere, quiēuī, quiētum,
to be at rest

quiētus, -a, -um, *adj.*, peaceful,
quiet

quīlibet, quaelibet, quodlibet,
pron./adj., whichever it
pleases, whatever,

quis, quid, *pron.* who? what?;
quid ergō?, what, then?,
well?; **quid rēfert,** what does
it matter?; *after* **sī,** someone,
anyone, etc. *See also* **quid**

**quisquam, quaequam,
quicquam,** *pron./adj. after
negative*, anyone, anything

quisque, quaeque, quidque,
pron./adj., each (one, thing)

quisquis, quidquid, *pron./adj.*,
whoever, whatever

quō, *adv.*, to where; to where?;
quōnam, to where on earth?

quod, *conj.*, that; the fact that;
because; **nōn est quod,** it
isn't the case that

quōmodo, *adv.*, how

quōnam = *intensive form of* **quō**

quondam, *adv.*, once, formerly

quoniam, *conj.*, since, because

quoque, *adv.*, also; even

quotiens, *adv.*, as often (as),
whenever

rapax, -ācis, *adj.*, voracious

rapiō, -ere, rapuī, raptum, to
seize, snatch away

rārus, -a, -um, *adj.*, rare,
uncommon

ratiō, -ōnis, *f.*, account; reason,
rationality

ratis, -is, *m.*, raft, ship
recens, -entis, *adj.*, fresh, recent
recidō, -ere, recidī, —, to fall
back, revert
recipiō, -ere, -cēpī, -ceptum, to
take back, receive
reclīnō (1) to recline, rest
recordor, -ārī, -atus sum, to
remember
rectē, *adv.*, rightly
recurrō, -ere, -currī, -cursum,
to race back, return
recursus, -ūs, *m.*, course back,
return
reddō, -ere, -didī, -ditum, to
give back; *followed by direct
object and acc. predicate adj.*,
render
redūcō, -ere, -dūxī, -ductum,
to lead back, restore
referō, -ferre, rettulī, relātum,
to bring back, give back
rēfert, rēferre, rettulit, —,
impers., it matters; quid
rēfert, what does it matter?
rēgālis, -e, *adj.*, royal, of a king
regiō, -ōnis, *f.*, region, territory
rēgius, -a, -um, *adj.*, royal
regnum, -ī, *n.*, kingdom
relegō (1) to send out of the way,
remove
relinquō, -ere, -līquī, -lictum,
to leave, abandon
relūceō, -ēre, -lūxī, —, to shine
out, shine back
remaneō, -ēre, -mansī, —, to
remain, stay behind
remedium, -iī, *n.*, remedy,
therapy

rēmus, -ī, *m.*, oar
renouō (1) to renew
renuntiō (1) to report; revoke
an order
repetō, -ere, -petīuī, -petītum,
to seek back; repeat
repōnō, -ere, -posuī, -positum,
to place back; lay aside, store
up
rēs, reī, *f.*, thing; situation; rēs
pūblica, the state, republic
rescindō, -ere, -scidī, -scissum,
to cut open again
resistō, -ere, -stitī, —, to resist,
stand up to, + *dat.*
respiciō, -ere, -spexī,
-spectum, to look back at,
look to
responsum, -ī, *n.*, response,
reply
reuertor, -ī, reuersus sum, to
turn back, return
reuocō (1) to call back
reus, reī, *m.*, the accused,
defendant, party to an
action
rex, rēgis, *m.*, king
Rhēnus, -ī, *m.*, the Rhine
(river dividing Gaul and
Germany)
rigeō, -ēre, —, —, to be stiff;
rigens, *pple.*, stiff
rigor, -ōris, *m.*, stiffness,
inflexibility, firmness
rogō (1) to ask; summon
Rōmānus, -a, -um, *adj.*, Roman
rubeō, -ēre, —, —, to be red;
rubens, *pple.*, red
rubor, -ōris, *m.*, redness

rudis, -e, *adj.,* rough, unschooled

ruīna, -ae, *f.,* ruin, devastation

rumpō, -ere, rūpī, ruptum, to break, break through

ruō, -ere, ruī, rutum, to crash down, fall to ruin

rursus, *adv.,* again, again in turn

sacer, sacra, sacrum, *adj.,* sacred, holy

sacrum, -ī, *n.,* rite, ritual

saeculum, -ī, *n.,* race; generation, lifetime; age

saepe, *adv.,* often

saeuitia, -ae, *f.,* ferocity, cruelty

saeuus, -a, -um, *adj.,* ferocious, cruel

salūs, -ūtis, *f.,* health, safety

saluus, -a, -um, *adj.,* safe

sanguis, -inis, *m.,* blood

sānitās, -tātis, *f.,* health, wellness

sānō (1) to heal

sānus, -a, -um, *adj.,* healthy, sane

sapiens, -entis, *adj.,* wise; *m.,* the wise person, the sage

sapienter, *adv.,* wisely

sapientia, -ae, *f.,* wisdom

satiō (1) satisfy, content

satis, *adv.,* enough, sufficiently

satis *or* **sat,** *n. indecl.,* enough; **satis est,** it is enough (to) + *infinitive*

saucius, -a, -um, *adj.,* wounded

scelus, -eris, *n.,* crime, evil deed

sciō, -īre, -īuī, -ītum, to know; know (how to) + *infinitive*

scrībō, -ere, -psī, -ptum, to write

scrūtor, -ārī, -atus sum, to examine thoroughly, rifle through

sē, *gen.* **suī,** *pron.* himself, herself, itself, themselves

secō, -āre, secuī, sectum, to cut

secrētus, -a, -um, *adj.,* secret, separated, mysterious

sēcūritās, -tātis, *f.,* freedom from care

sēcūrus, -a, -um, *adj.,* free from care, without a care

sed, *conj.,* but

sedeō, -ēre, sēdī, sessum, to sit

sēdes, -is, *f.,* seat, position

sēditiōsus, -a, -um, *adj.,* factious, turbulent

sēdūcō, -ere, -duxī, -ductum, to separate off

sēmet = *intensive form of* **sē**

semper, *adv.,* always, constantly

senex, senis, *m.,* old man

sententia, -ae, *f.,* opinion; maxim

sentiō, -īre, sensī, sensum, to feel, perceive; think, believe

sequor, -ī, secutus sum, to follow

sermō, -ōnis, *m.,* speech, discourse

serpens, -entis, *f.,* a creeping thing, serpent

seruīlis, -e, *adj.,* of a slave

Seruīlius, -iī, *m.,* Servilius

seruiō, -īre, -īuī *or* **-iī, -ītum,** to serve + *dat.*

seruō (1) to save, preserve

sērus, -a, -um, *adj.*, late, too
late; later

seruulus, -ī, *m.*, *diminutive*,
(dear little) slave

sēsē = *intensive form of* **sē**

seuēritās, -tātis, *f.*, strictness

sī, *conj.*, if

sīc, *adv.*, thus, in the same way

sīcut, *adv.*, just like, just as

silentium, -iī, *n.*, silence

similis, -e, *adj.*, similar (to) +
dat.

simulacrum, -ī, *n.*, image,
representation

sine, *prep.* + *abl.*, without

singulāris, -e, *adj.*, unique

singulus, -a, -um, *adj.*, single,
individual

sinus, -ūs, *m.*, breast, lap;
embrace

sistō, -ere, stitī, —, to stop;
cause to stand still

situs, -a, -um, *adj.*, located,
lying

situs, -ūs, *m.*, position; neglect,
inactivity

sīue *or* **seu,** *conj.*, or if; **sīue . . .
sīue** whether . . . or

socer, soceri, *m.*, father-in-law

socius, -iī, *m.*, accomplice, ally

sōlācium, -iī, *n.*, comfort

sōlāmen, -minis, *n.*, comfort

soleō, -ēre, —, solitus, to be
accustomed (to), to always, +
infinitive

solidum, -ī, *n.*, a firm
foundation, solid ground

solidus, -a, -um, *adj.*, firm,
solid

sōlitūdō, -dinis, *f.*, solitariness;
desolate place

sollicitūdō, -dinis, *f.*, worry,
anxiety

sollicitus, -a, -um, *adj.*,
worried, anxious

sōlus, -a, -um, *adj.*, alone, only

solūtus, -a, -um, *adj.*, loose,
undone; *pf. pass. pple. of*
soluō

somnus, -ī, *m.*, sleep

sordēs, -dis, *m.*, filth; *pl.*,
mourning garment(s)

sors, sortis, *f.*, lot, fate

Sōtiō, -ōnis, *m.*, Sotion (teacher
of philosophy)

spatium, -iī, *n.*, space, stretch,
extent

spectāculum, -ī, *n.*, spectacle,
show

speculum, -ī, *n.*, mirror

spērō (1) to hope

spēs, speī, *f.*, hope

spīritus, -ūs, *m.*, breath,
breathing

spoliō (1) to despoil, deprive
(of) + *abl.*

squālidus, -a, -um, *adj.*, filthy

squāmifer, -fera, -ferum, *adj.*,
scaly

squāmōsus, -a, -um, *adj.*,
scaly

statim, *adv.*, immediately

status, -ūs, *m.*, standing,
position; condition

stirps, -pis, *f.*, stock, lineage

stō, stare, stetī, statum, to
stand; cost (a certain price)
+ *gen.*

stolidus, -a, -um, *adj.,* coarse, stupid, dull

stomachus, -ī, *m.,* stomach; taste

stringō, -ere, strinxī, strictum, to draw tight; touch lightly upon; *of swords,* to unsheath

struō, -ere, struxī, structum, to pile up, lay, organize

studeō, -ēre, -uī, —, to study

studium, -iī, *n.,* enthusiasm; pursuit; *pl.,* studies, learning

stupeō, -ēre, -uī, —, to be stunned, struck senseless

sub, *prep.* + *abl.,* under, beneath

subdūcō, -ere, -dūxī, -ductum, to draw away, remove (from) + *dat.*

subiciō, -ere, -iēcī, -ectum, to throw down; throw beneath + *dat.*

subigō, -ere, -ēgī, -actum, to put down, suppress

subinde, *adv.,* immediately after; from time to time

sublīme *adv.* aloft

subsum, -esse, -fuī, -futūrus, to be beneath + *dat.*

succurrō, -ere, -currī, -cursum, to run to the aid (of) + *dat.*

sum, esse, fuī, futūrus, to be

summittō, -ere, -mīsī, -missum, to put down, lower, yield

summus, -a, -um, *adj.,* top, uppermost; utmost

sūmō, -ere, sumpsī, sumptum, to take up, assume; consume

super, supera, superum, *adj.,* above; **superī,** *m. pl.,* the ones (gods, people) above

superbus, -a, -um, *adj.,* proud, arrogant, insolent

superō (1) to overcome, defeat

supersum, -esse, -fuī, -futūrus, to be left over, remain, (for) + *dat.*

superuacuus, -a, -um, *adj.,* redundant, superfluous

supīnus, -a, -um, *adj.,* lying on one's back, supine; thoughtless, careless

suppleō, -ēre, -plēuī, -plētum, to fill up; make up for, repair

supplicium, -iī, *n.,* punishment

surgō, -ere, surrexī, surrectum, to rise; stand up

suus, -a, -um, *adj.,* his or her own

taceō, -ēre, -uī, -itum, to be silent

tacitus, -a, -um, *adj.,* silent

tam, *adv.,* so; **tam . . . quam** as . . . as

tamen, *adv.,* nevertheless

tamquam, *conj.,* as though, + *subjunctive;* as if, like

tandem, *adv.,* at length, finally

tantum, *adv.,* only

tantus, -a, -um, *adj.,* so great, so much

Taurus, -ī, *m.,* Taurus (mountain in Asia Minor)

tellus, -ūris, *n.,* the earth

tēlum, -ī, *n.,* weapon, spear

temeritās, -tātis, *f.*, rashness, recklessness
temptō (1) to try, test out
tempus, -oris, *n.*, time; occasion; **ad tempus,** to suit the moment
tenebrae, -ārum, *f. pl.*, darkness
teneō, -ēre, -uī, tentum, to hold
tenuis, -is, *adj.*, thin
tergum, -ī, *n.*, back
terminus, -ī, *m.*, boundary
terra, -ae, *f.*, earth
terror, -ōris, *m.*, fear, terror
testis, -is, *m.*, witness
testor, -ārī, -atus sum, to testify, bear witness
Tēthys, -yos, *f.*, Tethys (sea-goddess)
thalamus, -ī, *m.*, marriage chamber; wedding
Thulē, -ēs, *f.*, Thule (island to the north of Europe)
Ti. = **Tiberius, -iī,** *m.*, Tiberius
tigris, -is, *f.*, tigress
timeō, -ēre, -uī, —, to fear
timidē, *adv.*, fearfully, tentatively
timidus, -a, -um, *adj.*, fearful, tentative
Tiphys, *gen.* **Tiphyos,** *acc.* **Tiphyn,** *m.*, Tiphys, the helmsman of the Argo
tīrō, -ōnis, *m.*, newly recruited soldier
Tītan, -ānis, *m.*, Titan, the Sun
tonitrus, -ūs, *m.*, thunder
torpescō, -ere, torpuī, —, to grow stiff, numb
torus, -ī, *m.*, bed, couch

tot, *adj. indecl.*, so many
tōtus, -a, -um, *adj.*, whole
tractātus, -ūs, *m.*, touching, handling
trahō, -ere, traxī, tractum, to draw, drag
tranquillitās, -tātis, *f.*, tranquillity
tranquillus, -a, -um, *adj.*, calm, tranquil
transeō, -īre, -iī *or* **-īui, -itum,** to pass
transferō, -ferre, transtulī, tra(ns)lātum, to carry around from one place to another; transplant
transfuga, -ae, *f.*, deserter
transitus, -ūs, *m.*, transition, passing
transmittō, -ere, -mīsī, -missum, to pass by, pass over
transportō (1) to transport, remove
tremō, -ere, -uī, —, to shake; quake at, fear
trēs, *gen.* **trium,** *numeral*, three
tricēsimus, -a, -um, *adj.*, thirtieth
trifidus, -a, -um, *adj.*, split into three parts
triformis, -e, *adj.*, three-formed
tristis, -e, *adj.*, sad, bleak
tristitia, -ae, *f.*, sadness
tū, *gen.* **tuī,** *pron.*, you (*sing.*)
tueor, -ērī, tūtus sum, to protect, watch over
tum, *adv.*, then, next
tumidus, -a, -um, *adj.*, swollen

tumultuor, -ārī, -atus sum, to make a disturbance

tumultuōsus, -a, -um, *adj.*, disturbed, restless

tunc, *adv.*, then; at that time

turba, -ae, *f.*, crowd, multitude

turpis, -e, *adj.*, disgraceful

tūtēla, -ae, *f.*, protection

tūtus, -a, -um, safe

tuus, -a, -um, *adj.*, your

uacātiō, -ōnis, *f.* freedom, time off; *as military term*, exemption

uacō (1) to be free, available, (for) + *dat.*

uadō, -ere, uādī, —, to go, walk, stride, go

uagor (1) to wander, roam, be unstable

uagus, -a, -um, *adj.*, wandering, dispersed

ualeō, -ēre, -uī, ualitum, to be strong, well; **ualē,** goodbye

uārius, -a, -um, *adj.*, diverse, different, varying

Vātia, -ae, *m.*, Vatia

ubi, *adv.*, where; when

ubique, *adv.*, everywhere

uehor, -ī, uectus sum, to be carried, ride, (on) + *abl.*

uel, *adv.*, or; certainly, even

uēlōcitās, -tātis, *f.*, speed, swiftness

uelut, *adv.*, just like

uēnālis, -e, *adj.*, for sale

uenēnum, -ī, *n.*, poison

uenerābilis, -e, *adj.*, deserving of reverence

ueniō, -īre, uēnī, uentum, to come

uenter, -tris, *m.*, belly

uentum, -ī, *n.*, wind

uerbum, -ī, *n.*, word

uereor, -ērī, ueritus sum, to fear, be afraid

uēritās, -tātis, *f.*, truth

uērō, *adv.*, truly, indeed

uersor, -ārī, -atus sum, to turn oneself; dwell, spend time

uērus, -a, -um, *adj.*, true

uestīgium, -iī, *n.*, footstep; trace, sign

uestis, -is, *f.*, clothing

ueterānus, -ī, *m.*, seasoned soldier, veteran

uetō, -āre, -uī, -itum, to forbid (to) + *infinitive*

uexātiō, -ōnis, *f.*, harassment, barrage, stress

uexō (1) to harrass, batter

uia, -ae, *f.*, path, road

(uicēs), uicis, *f.*, turn, alternation; position, role

uicēsimus, -a, -um, *adj.*, twentieth

uictor, -ōris, *m.*, conqueror

uideō, -ēre, uīdī, uīsum, to see; **uideor,** to be seen

uigor, -ōris, *n.*, force, liveliness

uīlis, -e, *adj.*, cheap, worthless

uilla, -ae, *f.*, villa

uincō, -ere, uīcī, uictum, to defeat

uinculum, -ī, *n.*, bond, restraint

uindex, -dicis, *m.*, avenger

uindicō (1) to liberate; avenge

uir, uirī, *m.*, man; husband

uirgō, -ginis, *f.,* unmarried girl, virgin

uiritim, *adv.,* man by man, individually

uirtūs, -tūtis, *f.,* manliness; excellence; virtue

uīs, uis, *f.,* power, strength; force, violence; *pl.* **uīrēs, uīrium,** (physical) strength

uiscera, -erum, *n. pl.,* inner parts of the body, flesh, internal organs

uīta, -ae, *f.,* life; **uītam agere,** to live (a) life; **uītam exigere,** to spend one's life

uīuō, -ere, uīxī, uictum, to live

uīuus, -a, -um, *adj.,* alive, living

uix, *adv.,* scarcely, hardly

ulciscor, -ī, ultus sum, to get revenge

ullus, -a, -um, *adj.,* any

ultimus, -a, -um, *adj.,* furthest, most distant; final

ultrix, -trīcis, *f. adj.,* avenging

ultrō, *adv.,* spontaneously, unasked; wantonly

umquam, *adv.,* ever

ūnā, *adv.,* together

ūniuersum, -ī, *n.,* the whole world, universe

ūnus, -a, -um, *numeral,* one; only, alone

uōciferor, -ārī, -atus sum, to cry out

uocō (1) call; summon

uolō, uelle, uoluī, —, to wish, be willing, (to) + *infinitive*

uolūmen, -minis, *n.,* bookroll, volume

uoluptās, -tātis, *f.,* pleasure

uōs, *gen.* **uestrī** *or* **uestrum,** *pron.,* you (*pl.*)

uox, uōcis, *f.,* voice; word, utterance

urbs, urbis, *f.,* city

ūsitātus, -a, -um, *adj.,* much used, conventional

usquam, *adv.,* anywhere

usque, *adv.,* all the way

ūsus, -ūs, *m.,* use

ut, *conj., with subjunctive,* that; *with indicative,* when, as

utcumque, *adv.,* in whatever way; nevertheless, in any event

uterque, utraque, utrumque, *pron./adj.,* each (of two), both

ūtilis, -e, *adj.,* useful

utinam, *adv. + subjunctive introducing wish,* if only

ūtor, -ī, ūsus sum, to use + *abl.*

utrum, *adv. introducing alternative question,* whether

uulgāris, -e, *adj.,* common, vulgar

uulnus, -neris, *n.,* wound

uultus, -ūs, *m.,* face, expression

uxor, -ōris, *f.,* wife

ℬℭ LATIN Readers

Series Editor: RONNIE ANCONA, HUNTER COLLEGE
AND CUNY GRADUATE CENTER

Other Readers Also Now Available

A Livy Reader
Selections from
AB URBE CONDITA
MARY JAEGER
(2010) ISBN 978-0-86515-680-6

A Lucan Reader
Selections from
CIVIL WAR
SUSANNA BRAUND
(2009) ISBN 978-0-86516-661-5

A Plautus Reader
Selections from
Eleven Plays
JOHN HENDERSON
(2009) ISBN 978-0-86516-694-3

A Sallust Reader
Selections from
BELLUM CATILINAE,
BELLUM IUGURTHINUM,
and HISTORIAE
VICTORIA E. PAGÁN
(2009) ISBN 978-0-86515-687-5

A Suetonius Reader
Selections from the
LIVES OF THE CAESARS
and the
LIFE OF HORACE
JOSIAH OSGOOD
(2010) ISBN 978-0-86515-716-2

A Martial Reader
Selections from Epigrams
CRAIG WILLIAMS
(2009) ISBN 978-0-86516-704-9

A Terence Reader
Selections from
Six Plays
WILLIAM S. ANDERSON
(2009) ISBN 978-0-86515-678-3

A Roman Verse Satire Reader
Selections from
Lucilius, Horace,
Persius, and Juvenal
CATHERINE C. KEANE
(2010) ISBN 978-0-86515-685-1

Forthcoming in 2011 and Beyond

An Apuleius Reader
ELLEN D. FINKELPEARL
ISBN 978-0-86515-714-8

A Caesar Reader
W. JEFFREY TATUM
ISBN 978-0-86515-696-7

A Cicero Reader
JAMES M. MAY
ISBN 978-0-86515-713-1

A Latin Epic Reader
ALISON KEITH
ISBN 978-0-86515-686-8

An Ovid Reader
CAROLE E. NEWLANDS
ISBN 978-0-86515-722-3

A Propertius Reader
P. LOWELL BOWDITCH
ISBN 978-0-86515-723-0

A Roman Army Reader
DEXTER HOYOS
ISBN 978-0-86515-715-5

A Roman Women Reader
SHEILA K. DICKISON
and JUDITH P. HALLETT
ISBN 978-0-86515-662-2

A Tacitus Reader
STEVEN H. RUTLEDGE
ISBN 978-0-86515-697-4

A Tibullus Reader
PAUL ALLEN MILLER
ISBN 978-0-86515-724-7

VISIT THE SERIES WEBSITE FOR UPDATES
ON AVAILABLE VOLUMES:
www.bolchazy.com/readers